D1096072

Praise for *Just Wa*

"I have all of Rosemarie Aquilina's crime dramas and love every one of them for many different reasons. Like birthing a child, each book she writes is clearly Rosemarie's baby. That said, she is a fierce mama bear who writes with discipline, nurturing, a wicked sense of humor, galvanized truth, and unabashed dressing down of bad behavior. While the crime dramas she has written are remarkable, insightful, addicting, and criminally entertaining, I have found that I love Rosemarie's memoir *Just Watch Me* most of all. Her memoir is intrinsically, and undeniably Rosemarie. No holds barred as she bares her soul so authentically that I am inspired to dig deep within myself for the gold nuggets that surely must be there. Rosemarie has an uncanny gift for making people want to be a better version of themselves."

—Kate Romero, actress

"*Just Watch Me* is an inspiring and gripping read for anyone who has struggled in their life. Judge Rosemarie Aquilina is compassionate to the victims and defendants who appear before her in court for a reason: she's been through it all. From a difficult childhood to military dedication to single motherhood, to an abusive relationship, she is grateful for all her experiences because they made her who she is today: a fierce survivor who is a dynamic leader for young and older women everywhere. In *Just Watch Me*, Aquilina proves it's never too late to go after your dreams."

—Hayley Krischer, author of *The Falling Girls* and *Something Happened to Ali Greenleaf*

just watch me

a memoir

Just Watch Me, a Memoir by Rosemarie Aquilina.

First produced as an Audible Original by Hello Sunshine in partnership with Audible (release date December 10, 2020). Written and performed by author Rosemarie Aquilina.

First print edition published by Sabieha Press
Copyright © 2021 by Rosemarie Aquilina. All rights reserved. Printed in the United States of America, international by permission. No part of this book may be reproduced in any manner whatsoever without permission except in the case of brief quotations used in critical articles, in reviews, or for teaching purposes. For information, contact AuthorAquilina@gmail.com.

Original cover art by Joshua Lerman.
Cover and interior layout by Melissa Williams Design.
Proofreading by Abby Forrest of Render | Editing Services.

Ordering Information:

Print:
IngramSpark at www.ingramspark.com,
Amazon-Books at www.amazon.com, or
Request through your local bookstore.

Audio:
Audible at www.audible.com or
Amazon at www.amazon.com

Author Aquilina virtually attends book clubs upon request based on availability (in-person attendance depends on location). Make your request through AuthorAquilina@gmail.com.

Requests for reproduction or other permission should be addressed to Sabieha Press, AuthorAquilina@gmail.com.

Direct requests for speaking, talent, or other opportunities, should be made through Creative Artists Agency at caa.com.

Just Watch Me is available in Audible, regular print, large print, and eBook.

ISBNs
979-8-9855134-0-0 (paperback)
979-8-9855134-1-7 (hardcover)
979-8-9855134-2-4 (large print)
979-8-9855134-3-1 (eBook)

ALL RIGHTS RESERVED

just watch me

a memoir

Rosemarie Aquilina

Sabieha PRESS

Just Watch Me is dedicated to everyone without a voice.

I See You.

I Hear You.

I Stand with You.

You Matter.

Judge Aquilina Quotes

Don't just take a seat at the table.
Be the chandelier and *shine a light*
on everyone around you.

Go out and do your
magnificent things!

PMS = *P*romote, *M*entor, and *S*upport Women

Inaction is an *Action.*
Silence is *Indifference.*
Justice requires *Action* and a *Voice.*

From *Wounds & Wisdom,*
Warriors are *Born, &*
Wars are *Won.*

Talk.

Take Action.

Treat Yourself with Kindness.

God put *N & O* in the alphabet for a *reason.*
Use it. *Follow your gut,*
not someone else's bad behavior.

The *power* we have within us is
unshakeable when we stay
true to ourselves.

Author's Note

I am grateful to Reese Witherspoon, Hello Sunshine, and Audible for believing in me and taking a chance on me. It was Reese who motivated me and convinced me to write my memoir. She gives her heart to the issues and people she believes in. The time she has given me and so many others in hope of righting the wrongs in this world inspires me to do better and to continue my lifelong journey of being a troublemaker for meaningful change in more public, outspoken ways.

The events and experiences that I reveal are all true. In some places, I have changed names and identities and other details for the protection, privacy, and integrity of those discussed. As is always true, there are two sides to every story, and their story is not mine to tell. My intent is not to hurt anyone, rather to hopefully help and inspire others who, like me, have felt confused, alone, abused, and abandoned, despite being loved. I have told the story of my life from my point of view, recollection, and feelings.

I have learned a lot of lessons, and I still have many more to learn. I find joy in both success and failure because, in moving forward, I always find a new adventure and a new reason to smile at the doubters, finger-pointers, and naysayers and say: *Just Watch Me.*

foreword

Over three years ago, the world witnessed over two hundred young women speaking their truths in the trial of Dr. Larry Nassar. For the first time in history, the public watched the downfall of an esteemed and respected doctor for athletes competing on the collegiate and Olympic level. After months of investigations and depositions, hundreds of young women had their day in court. In 2017, Nassar was sentenced by a female federal judge to 60 years in federal prison on child pornography charges. He was also sentenced in 2018 up to 175 years in the Michigan Department of Corrections state prison after pleading guilty to seven counts of first degree criminal sexual conduct, all life offenses. During the seven days of sentencing, the world had the opportunity to watch Judge Rosemarie Aquilina change the course of sexual assault survivors around the world and escalate the #MeToo movement.

From the onset of the case and then the sentencing, sexual abuse survivors and advocates were struck by Judge Aquilina's ability to convey empathy and understanding on a topic that has been misunderstood and pushed under the rug for centuries. Several of my patients and colleagues commented on Judge Aquilina's sentencing and ultimate ruling, struck by the judge allowing all Nassar victims to read their impact statements to him, directly, in a very public courtroom. She responded personally and distinctly to each of the 169 people (156 Sister Survivors and 13 others) who chose to speak their truth. Judge Aquilina let each one know they were heard, valued, and mattered.

Millions of men and women who have been abused by coaches, doctors, teachers, and even family members never had their day in court. Of those who have been sexually assaulted, only a small percentage of victims will speak up and get the help they need from qualified therapists and trauma specialists. *Just Watch Me* is not a book about the Larry Nassar trial. Judge Aquilina takes the reader on a journey to show readers where her passion began to allow others to be seen and heard. By overtly broadening the term *victim* to *anyone affected by the crime, not just the actual victim*, Judge Aquilina has enlightened people that the trauma experienced by a victim extends to all those connected to the victim.

This is not a book about "woe is me." This is a book about grit and determination. One of the themes interwoven throughout the memoir is how Judge Aquilina remained focused in her fight to have the life she wanted, even when others tried to bring her down. Readers may be surprised that she did not share more about the Larry Nassar trial and the aftermath of making a controversial decision to allow all victims the chance to give a victim impact statement, something she has always allowed while serving on the bench. During that sentencing, the world was unaware of where her passion and dedication to help victims and offenders came from. It is clear throughout the book that Judge Aquilina wants readers to be a witness to her backstory, versus focusing on a piece of her life covered worldwide by the media.

Judge Aquilina begins the book by taking the reader back to her very early childhood when she lived with her grandparents. Aquilina's voice shutters as she describes the confusion and helplessness she felt after being ripped away from her grandparents without being informed that she was to return living with her parents. Her resiliency pours through her storytelling with the description of her life from this early trauma and through many other events.

Throughout the book, Judge Aquilina speaks about a variety of experiences that left her feeling disempowered and unheard. One of the most uplifting parts of this book was when Judge Aquilina speaks about her mantra, "Just watch me." Throughout the book she describes how that statement kept her focused and moving forward since she was a young child, no matter how belittled or beaten down she felt by others.

Judge Aquilina bears her soul throughout this book. She speaks about countless occasions both in her marriage and early in her career when male colleagues tried to usurp and disempower her. Her vulnerability and honesty emanate through the pages when she talks about living in an emotionally abusive and toxic long-term relationship after her marriage ended. She shares details about her relationships with men in her personal and professional life when she felt misunderstood and disconnected. Throughout the book, Judge Aquilina tells the reader what she thought and how she felt when life wasn't going the way she wanted it to. She empowers the reader when she speaks about what she wanted to feel in her relationships with her partners, her family, her children, and her colleagues. Her vulnerability is an inspiration to many trauma survivors who relate to the intimate details she provides, especially when she speaks of the disapproval from friends and family when she made big decisions in her life.

There are moments of heartbreak, followed by moments of triumph in every chapter. *Just Watch Me* is a must read for anyone struggling with shame, fear, or grief. For instance, she reveals a rare medical illness she developed while preparing to take the bar exam in her mid-twenties. One of the most poignant moments was when Judge Aquilina describes the brutal childbirth of her oldest son. Her voice was full of anger and disbelief when relaying her experience of giving birth under awful circumstances. Throughout the last couple of years, people have been searching for stories that will leave them feeling hopeful. Judge Aquilina offers many examples of how she coped with feelings that could have left her paralyzed. At one point, she shares her passion for fiction writing and crafting. She speaks to the reader about how she kept her head held high when she wanted to call it quits. Her examples of self-care and self-compassion are needed now more than ever.

This book causes the reader to laugh and cry and leaves the reader wanting to jump up and scream with hope and joy. Every story she shares ends with a victory. Her mantra, "Just watch me," which she developed as a young child, proves to be the key to her success. No one is going to stop her from living her life her way. No one was going to tell her to give up her dreams, be quiet, or go away. *Just Watch Me* is an extraordinary example of how people can use their earlier traumas and battles to empower others.

—Shari Botwin, LCSW

introduction

Welcome to the Judge's Chambers

In many ways, that morning was just like any other day. I did what I always do, which was to get the kids up for school and make them breakfast. I have five children: David, thirty-eight; Jennifer, thirty-seven; Johanna nineteen; and Marissa and Michael, ten. That day was two years ago, so Johanna was seventeen and Marissa and Michael were eight. Let me first say that I am *not* a morning person. I'll stay up all night reading cases, writing, and browsing the internet until all hours. My sanity in the morning is a combination of coffee and hairspray. They are the life-and-death ingredients that glue me together.

That morning I needed as much caffeine as I could get my hands on because it would be the first day of testimony where I would hear scores of young women, many of them gymnasts, who were sexually abused by their once beloved, once revered doctor, Larry Nassar. Nassar wasn't just an average doctor for USA Gymnastics—he was a man who all the young women said was their confidant; their best friend; the man they could turn to during long, brutal training camps when they felt isolated and alone. He was also the man who manipulated, abused, and assaulted these young women. He was the man who groomed everyone, including the parents, into thinking that his "treatments" were crucial to the athletes' healing. I expected eighty young women to speak when the hearing first began, but the number would top one-hundred and fifty.

I had about a half an hour to get the kids packed and ready for school before I got to court. If I were a more organized person, I would have their lunches packed the night before. I'd have their clothes picked out. Their backpacks together. When I didn't have small kids in the house, I could roll out of bed and get to work in thirty minutes. But when you're racing around the house with two fighting kids—because the twins are *always fighting*—trying to make some semblance of a lunch and some semblance of a breakfast, mornings are a battle. This is every morning. I mean, every morning. If you stood outside my house and if you were law enforcement, you'd ring the bell to say, "Uh, is everything okay?" But we're Maltese. Maltese are fiery, and we're loud. The good news is that my kids are old enough to tie their shoes, but I still have to make them lunch. If I had them make their own lunch, we'd end up with no sandwich and five Fruit Roll-Ups.

Winter added a whole other complication because my kids are always trying to negotiate out of wearing winter gear. They slip on a flimsy T-shirt when it's twenty degrees out. Or walk out of the house with one glove, or *no gloves*, or tennis shoes when there's three feet of snow. And I'm the mom who walks into the school and says, "Here's their boots; otherwise, don't let them outside." One time they refused to go to school with mittens on, so I called the school. "Can you pull some out of the lost and found so they learn a lesson?"

As much as they love to argue with each other, my twins love to argue with me *even more*. I've raised two lawyers. These two are going to go to much higher offices than me because, at seven years old, they were already fantastic negotiators. I've raised them to say *no* when they mean *no*. But I didn't intend for it to be directed against me!

Johanna, my middle daughter, who was seventeen at the time, didn't need help getting out the door—she just needed to get out of bed. Literally. Every morning I would say the same thing, sounding like a broken record: "Johanna, get out of bed you're going to be late for school."

And like clockwork, Johanna would come up with a reason not to go to school on time. "I don't have class," she would say, or "I don't like the teacher, so I'm just going to show up late. You need to call me in."

"I'm not going to call you in! This is *not* acceptable," I'd say.

Johanna's response: "Well, I'm getting all As. So, what does it matter to you, *Judge*?"

It's safe to say Johanna and I were going through a rough time. Sure, mother-daughter relationships can be especially tense. Sure, the teenage years are difficult. But when my daughter was about fourteen, she stopped calling me Mom and started calling me Judge. That's right. Not Ma. Not *Omm* (the Maltese word for mother.) Not Mom. Judge.

Ouch.

My daughter deemed herself Rapunzel and me "Judge" because she argued I wouldn't let her out of the house. (Sidebar: I did let her out of the house!) She thought I was too strict and too harsh. And *I thought* she needed to follow my very reasonable rules.

Growing up, I had a strict Maltese father who I had to battle. I often felt like an outsider because of my different cultural background. I've dealt with controlling men. I've had to fight for everything I have and fight to be heard. But I'm not sure I've dealt with any force as willful as my middle daughter. I felt lucky that morning that we were talking at all.

Did I mention that my eighty-five-year-old parents also live with me? Just as I'm running out the door, my parents are always asking me for something: "Rosie, can you fix the phone?" "Rosie, can you mail this?" "Rosie, can you pick up my prescription?" And because my life wasn't chaotic enough, I also had two eight-month-old puppies, Lily and Ollie.

Johanna was a junior in high school at the time, so she knew the Nassar case was going to begin. But what she didn't realize was that girls who went to her school, girls who were her friends, girls just like her would be testifying as his victims. At this point, she was pretty in the dark. She did know something was going on enough to ask me about the case as she was heading out the door. My response was the same as it always is: "I can't talk about it." I never talk about my cases until they're over. My kids know this. My family knows this. My parents know this. I don't look at the news. Not one single newspaper. Nothing.

I finally arrived home after driving the twins to school. Time to get dressed. I put on my typical court day outfit: jeans, a comfortable shirt, and my cowboy boots, which I always wear. On my left ankle, I clasped a spur or a boot bracelet, a ritual I began when I was seventeen. I got my first pair of boots at a little store I worked at called Town and Country. Cowboy boots are not cheap, so when I was able to buy my own pair, they became a real symbol of independence for me. (And I have an amazing collection of boots now, by the way.) They're a reminder that I'm always going to do my own thing. And I always have. I'm going to wear one boot bracelet, not two. I'm going to streak my hair red if I want to. Four colors of eyeshadow? My decision.

Anyway, that day it was January in Michigan—the dead of winter. It was cold and a trace of snow lingered on the ground. Trees shot up frozen branches to the sky.

My transformation from mom to judge begins on that ride to work. After I crank up the seat heaters, I usually listen to an audiobook or music. I like uplifting and fun artists like Charlie Puth, Chris Isaak, Phil Collins, Diana Ross, Cher, or Adele—something I can blast on the Bluetooth and sing my way to a different mind frame. It clears out the noise from the morning. Yes, I sing horribly, but I don't care. That's when I can fully unwind before I get to a long day as the judge.

When I finally arrive at the office, I greet my staff and grab my second or third serving of caffeine for the day. I can down three espressos before noon without even a single twitch. And it's my sole source of nourishment until my mid-morning break. That's when I'll have something more substantial like a protein bar, or a protein shake.

Now comes the time for the true metamorphous: my robe. My *magical robe*. It's the shield over my inner gut that gives me the ability to block out the thousands of things that attack me every day. I turn into a different person. It's my brain's signal that I'm ready to listen, to look at files, to make tough decisions, to shut out the rest of the world except for the case in front of me. (The only downside of my robe is that it's heavy and hot. When I look back at photos of myself that day, it appears that I'm wearing a large amount of blush, but really, with the courtroom at full capacity, I was just overheated. I was flushed!) When I'm in the robe, I'm not Mom, I'm not Daughter, I'm not Rosie. I'm *Judge*.

For example, just the other day, my daughter Marissa's school called to say she had caught the stomach flu and I needed to pick her up. I was still in my robe, far from Mom mode, and so I took about five minutes to finish up. Marissa was in good hands with the nurse, but she didn't like waiting. No kid does. But when I'm in that robe, sometimes that's a decision I must make, because once it's off, my focus is gone. It's an ongoing conflict with myself.

I know you working moms across the country are nodding your heads with great compassion and understanding. It's a never-ending balancing act, isn't it? Of course, my children always come first, but my career is also everything to me and I'm not going to make any apologies for it. People say to me all the time, "How do you do all that you do?" I get it done because it's on my list. I get it done because that's my life. I've always done the best I can do. That's really the truth. That's all we *can* do.

With my robe on, head cleared, and coffee in hand, the final touch was my lace collar, a tradition I've had since the day I was first elected as a judge in 2004.

As I mentioned earlier, eighty-eight victims were scheduled to speak when the hearing began. That's a lot, but ultimately even more, one hundred and fifty-six Sister-Survivors, a total of one hundred and sixty-nine victims, spoke over the course of those seven days. I have *always* let everyone speak in my courtroom—victims *and* defendants. "Leave your pain here," I say, "and go out and do your magnificent things." Look, I was a trial attorney, I built my own family law practice, I was a military judge for twenty years, I was a district court judge, and now I'm a circuit court judge. Throughout every step of my career, giving people a voice has been my guiding principle.

While the Nassar case was the worst case by numbers, it was hardly the first or even the most physically shocking sexual assault case I've adjudicated. Let me be clear. It's impossible to compare cases, especially sexual assault cases, because you can't say one person's trauma is worse than another person's trauma. You just can't do that. Yet I've had cases where women have been thrown down the stairs, where they've been running out in the street naked with burns, women with bloodied faces. I have locked eyes with hundreds, maybe thousands, of predators in my courtroom. Larry Nassar was not the first and, sadly, he will not be the last. I share all this to say that so much of that day was like every other day.

But in many other ways, it was like nothing I had experienced.

The second I opened my judicial door and walked into the courtroom, I saw the crowd. People standing shoulder to shoulder, people sitting everywhere, the press packed against the jury box like sardines. We couldn't even see the carpet. My courtroom was so full it was a bit stunning to me. My law clerk said, "All rise." I looked up and said, "You may be seated." And then it hit me again. Stunned. Every spot was filled. Every seat taken.

I've been in full courtrooms before. I've had other high-profile cases. Before I walked in, I knew therapists and therapy dogs were right outside ready to support the victims if they needed it. I was aware of the tremendous news coverage, not just in Michigan, but all over the country. My office had been swarmed with media requests for weeks. But until I physically entered that space, I really hadn't grasped the full magnitude of this case. Yet in that moment I thought, *Wow.* It almost took my breath away.

In my gut I felt extreme tension, almost like a riot was going to happen. Not an *actual* riot. Because a riot would *never* happen in my courtroom. You must understand. I have military training and so I prepared that courtroom the way I would in a military operation. I met with the Lansing Police Department. I met with our sheriff's office. I met with the state police.

They said to me: "What do you want, Judge?"

I told them I needed strategically placed uniforms. I needed extra security. I needed plainclothes police officers. Law enforcement with full jurisdiction coverage who could instantly subdue any threat, inside the courtroom, the building, and the outside. I could not jeopardize the well-being of families and children and victims who were in the courtroom that day. And I figured someone would lunge at Nassar.

It's also why I put Nassar in the witness box. I did this for multiple reasons. Nassar, if you remember, complained in his letter that I placed him in the witness box because I wanted the cameras on me. Because I wanted to make it more painful for him. *Neither* are true. I did it so that we could have an exit strategy for him. To protect him. If something happened, if someone had charged at him, or rushed at him, law enforcement could take him through the door into the judge's corridor and then take him into a safe space. (I wanted to prevent what happened in Judge Janice Cunningham's courtroom when Randall Margraves, the father of three of Nassar's victims, asked for "five minutes in a locked room with this demon" and then ran at him.)

I also wanted the victims to be placed in the safest, yet most direct, location to allow them to confront him without turning back around toward him. I wanted them to focus and shed their nervousness. They didn't need to see people in the back watching them; they did need to speak clearly into the microphone for the ease of the court reporter, Jean Ann Hamlin, who prepares the written record. With fourteen years of allowing victims to speak and anticipating safety issues, my military training did not disappoint me and worked as beautifully as it always had. Any kind of ruckus, riot, or attack on anyone was out of the question; however, that morning was charged. You could feel it in your chest. Adrenaline rushed through my body. But I *thrive* on adrenaline. When I arrived at my judge's bench that morning, my heart was beating hard. I was doing what a professional athlete might do before getting ready for an event or a game. *I got in the zone.* When you're playing sports, if you're in little league or high school football, you don't see Mom screaming on the bleachers. You don't see your coach. You don't see if there are 5 people or 1,000 people or 10,000 people watching you. You see that ball in front of you.

That's me. When I'm in the courtroom, I'm in the zone. Everything else, everybody else is wallpaper. They're background noise. The only thing that I'm focused on is that case in front of me.

And for seven days in a row, I focused on the sentencing in that case. I focused on all those victims. I heard their pain. I encouraged them. I complimented them. I was empathetic to their stories. I became their advocate. I *listened* to them. Girls who had been holding in their pain and their trauma for decades. Girls like Larissa Boyce who, after she spoke out at sixteen years old, was told by a Michigan State University coach that this didn't happen to her. Girls like Trinea Gonczar who said that she was assaulted by Nassar approximately 856 times. These girls were not heard. They were not valued. I knew the magical power of the robe would change them, help them begin to shed those years of pain.

Every night in those seven days I had people texting me and calling me. Therapists, friends, asking me if I needed help. "No, I feel fine," I'd tell them. "I can't talk about it," I'd remind them. Was it upsetting? Yes. Of course. But I compartmentalized it like I do in any disturbing case. I went home. I made dinner. I didn't listen to the news. I tuned in reruns of *Gilmore Girls*. My family had the papers stacked up for me at the end of the kitchen counter. I couldn't read any of them.

And then one night at dinner, Johanna brought it up. Like I said, Johanna *knew* some of those girls. She was around the age of many of those girls when they were abused.

"I know these people, Mom. How does something like this happen? I know you can't talk about the case, but I want to be there."

She wanted to come to my courtroom. So on the fourth day of the victim impact statements, my daughter came to the sentencing. She watched, completely engaged, until the very last day. To have her in my courtroom for the last three days of the sentencing meant the *world* to me. Because if there's one reason why I am doing *any* of this, it's because of her. Because of all of my kids. Because I'm a mom. And, for all the moms out there.

I ask every single person who enters my courtroom: "What would you like me to know?" And I listen to their stories.

Now it's *my* turn to tell mine.

Here is what I want you to know.

chapter one

Two Sets of Parents

My earliest memories are with my grandparents. Everything that a parent would do, my grandparents did. In my mind, I *was* their child. I don't mean that I loved them like they were my parents. I mean, I actually thought *they were* my parents. And I deeply loved them.

My grandfather and I had a morning ritual along with my younger brother Joe. We were living in Detroit, and I was about two years old, Joe a year old. My grandfather would get up for work around zero-dark-thirty. That's military speak for *very early morning* . . . before dawn. He had soft brown eyes and a chiseled cleft jaw. He always had rosy cheeks. He wore white sleeveless undershirts that looked like a tank top and had white hair from a pretty young age.

Every single morning my grandfather shaved his thick stubble. And every single morning I would watch him. I was fascinated by my grandfather. The way he moved, his careful approach to everything he did. When he shaved, he'd use a traditional shaving mug and brush. He'd lather the foam in the cup, spread it evenly across his face and then shave with a straight razor. He sharpened and cleaned that razor on a leather belt. He always did that. Every morning.

After he shaved, we'd go into the kitchen where he'd prop me up on the counter. I'd watch him carefully as he sliced the thick, fresh bread, lightly toast it over the open flame, then spread it with butter—real butter—thick and yellow.

My grandmother made the coffee in a glass percolator. It's an old-fashioned thing. She'd fill the center with coffee grounds, pour water in, and put it on the stove until it boiled. It was absolutely perfect. The best coffee ever. Yes, we'd all drink it, even me as a little preschooler. There's no coffee that could match my grandmother's. Nanna was a little bit plump—not fat, but a little plumper, with a round face and smiling chocolate eyes. She always had her hair done. She always had it curled, always had a perm. She always wore lipstick.

I would sit on my grandfather's lap, and he would take the toast, dip it in the coffee, and hand it to me, then another piece to Joe. And I have always done it that way. To this day, I will take buttered toast and dip it in my coffee. There is nothing better in the world to me than that. It was a daily ritual when I was a child, weekdays and weekends too. In the evenings, our treat was tomato paste spread on fresh bread and drizzled with olive oil. Another treat I still enjoy.

My grandparents are from Malta, an island country just below Sicily, with gorgeous cliffs and blue seas, medieval structures as well as Neolithic temples from the Stone Age. Aquilina is a popular last name in Malta. It means *small eagle*.

My grandfather did what many other families did from Malta after World War II: he moved his family to Detroit, Michigan. My father was only seventeen years old when they first arrived. After only a few months in this country, he joined the US Army and served during the Korean War. After serving, he went to medical school in Germany on the G.I. Bill, and that's when he met my mother, a young beautiful German girl on a train. They were married a year later.

In nine months, I was born, and then eleven months and two days later, my brother Joe came along. As you can imagine, having two children under two years old was a lot of work! On top of that, my father was in medical school full time. They were young, had two small children in diapers, and were so poor that when they were first married, they would buy napkins and cut them in half. That poor, okay? My mother still talks about that to this day.

They decided that me, my mother, and my brother would live with my grandparents in Detroit and my father would stay in medical school in Germany. Once he graduated, he would join us.

Now my father had already become a citizen when he came over with his parents. But at that time, Americans who'd been naturalized had to wait ten years to pass on their citizenship to their children. My mother, who was German, couldn't pass her citizenship to us either. Why? Because at the time, the German laws only recognized the citizenship of the *father*. Not the *mother.*

If you look at my passport from when I was a child, it doesn't say citizen of Malta. It doesn't say citizen of Germany. It says "stateless." That's right, *stateless*. So, there we were, my brother and I, with our little *stateless* baby passports.

This *infuriated* my father. He's still angry about it to this day.

In fact, early in the '90s, my father filed a case over this that made it to the US Supreme Court. He felt cheated. He felt that we were *all* cheated because he couldn't pass on his citizenship to his children.

The US Supreme Court felt differently. They ultimately said he didn't have standing to bring the suit because it didn't affect *him*. This wasn't *his* problem, they said. This was *our* problem. His argument has always been that it *did* affect him because not being able to pass on his citizenship to his children made him a second-class citizen. The wisdom of the US Supreme Court was this: no, your children need to bring it to us on their own to show how it affected them.

Could I have taken it up with the court? Sure. But I've never felt the need to do it. I've never felt like I was going to run for president, and that would be the only reason to do it. Also, it would take a tremendous amount of time. I'll admit, part of me likes my stateless passport. Truly. The stateless passport is evidence that I have a rich cultural heritage that I'm proud of. I'm an American, yes. I'm also Maltese and German. For me it's another connection to those places, to my heritage.

Anyway, the result of living in my grandparents' house with my father overseas was a little girl who thought her grandparents were her parents. In Maltese, we use the words *Nannu* for grandfather and *Nanna* for grandmother. I thought Nannu meant Dad. I thought Nanna meant Mom. Some of this had to do with my uncle Ben, who was the youngest of five and was still in high school. He called my grandparents Ma and Pa because they were his parents. I think I thought Nanna and Nannu meant Ma and Pa. I was so young, so attached to them. Looking back, it's hard to understand my logic, but it's absolutely what I was thinking.

Yes, of course, I had my mother. She was employed at the Aetna Life Insurance Company, calculating premiums. When she came home from work, I thought of her more as an older sister. She played with us. She bathed us. She slept in the next room with my brother. I slept with my grandparents. I watched my mother change Joe's diapers. But the daily tasks, the cleaning up messes, serving us meals, going to the playground, *all of that* I did with my grandparents. My grandparents' habits became my habits. My grandparents' rituals became my rituals. Their routines became my routines. I looked up to them. I admired them. I cherished everything they did, every lesson they taught me, every saying they said. One lesson causes me, even at my age now, to hear Nanna's voice. I was about four and I walked by a piece of paper on the floor. Nanna told me turn around and pick it up, and she said: "When you walk by that piece of paper without picking it up, you make me your maid." To this day, I can't walk by something on the floor without picking it up and whispering a thank-you to her.

One of the many things I admired about Nanna and Nannu was their passion for tailoring and sewing. It wasn't just a trade for my grandparents, it was a way of life, an art form. They made clothing that lasted. They put their heart into every stitch. Occasionally, they would treat themselves to buy something, but generally, they made all our clothes. My grandfather even made his own suits. I have a memory of being in Malta with him when I was about twelve years old. We were walking through the streets of his old neighborhood in the small village Qrendi in the Southern part of Malta. People were greeting him, telling him how glad they were to see him. How glad they were that he was back. He was in one of his suits that he made, and someone commented on what a nice suit it was. Right there, right in that very moment, he took off his jacket and said to the man, "It is now yours. I will deliver the pants." He didn't even think twice about it. That's the kind of heart that I hope to have and to show to the world and to show my children. He was never selfish, always giving, always made a difference in everybody's life.

Detroit experienced its heyday during the years my grandparents lived there. They lived in the old Maltese neighborhood in Detroit, along with thousands of nationals who came to the booming Motor City after the war, looking for work at the Big Three auto companies: Ford, General Motors, and Chrysler.

Nannu's first job in Detroit was working for the Ford Motor Company repairing fabrics. It was the mid-1950s, and during that time, Ford was gold, designing and turning out iconic cars like the Thunderbird, the Fairlane, and the Victoria. One way or another, my grandfather learned that the Ford factory wasted *a lot* of fabric and materials because when defective seats rolled off the line, they would be thrown away. The story goes like this: being a tailor and needing a job, my grandfather walked into the office of Henry Ford II and explained that he was a tailor and that he could save the company money by fixing imperfect seats with his skills. And that was that. He was given a job on the spot. In this way, his sewing skills and frugal Maltese nature came together. It's hard to believe nowadays that there was a time when you could walk into an office building and talk to someone like Henry Ford directly, but I guess that's the beauty of the '50s.

One of the great downfalls of Detroit in the '50s was that the city relied too heavily on the success of the auto industry. So when the auto industry started shedding jobs in the '60s, middle-class, white suburban folks began to move away, and it gutted the city. Racial inequality became an enormous problem. When the Detroit riots erupted in the summer of 1967, they became some of the most destructive riots in American history. I was only nine years old, and though I don't remember much, I do remember my parents and grandparents talking about it. I remember it being on the news every night. I remember the fear.

While Detroit changed dramatically during my late childhood, those early years with my grandparents were sheltered and innocent. We didn't have anything—really, we were very poor. I still remember going to Goodwill to get the tricycle that my brother and I shared. Then later, a bicycle that we also shared. This might sound cliché, but we didn't know what we were missing because we had love. We grew up very poor but very happy.

When you don't have many toys, you use your imagination. I used to tell my brother stories, and his face would light up. I was less than a year older than him, but he looked up to me then. (That changed when we got a little older. His demeanor was always so calm, so steady, that sometimes I felt he was the older brother and I was the younger sister.) He would bring me anything with writing—a newspaper, a cereal box, the *TV Guide*, *anything*—and he'd say, "Read this to me. Read me a story." Now, I probably wasn't even three years old. I couldn't read. But I wasn't going to admit this to him! I'd make up the stories with my imagination, and he wasn't the wiser.

Once we were in the hospital. He was about four and I was five, both of us getting our tonsils out, and he was crying because the popsicle the nurse gave him wasn't soothing his throat. I remember him begging me to read to him. So, I "read" him the sugar packets, and it made him feel better. He loved hearing my stories, and I loved telling them. I was five years old when I realized that telling stories would somehow, some way, be in my future—that one day I would be a writer.

* * *

When I was about five years old, my father came back from Germany. He'd graduated medical school, and there was a celebration. Everyone was thrilled because of course. It was a happy occasion. This was a man that everyone loved. This was their son who had been living in Germany just to go to medical school. And now he was home. But it didn't occur to me that my father's return meant leaving the safety of my grandparent's house. No one ever said directly to me, "Rosemarie, this is your father. Now that he's done with medical school, you must live with him."

Of course, this should have been obvious, but I was very young, and I thought my grandparents *were* my parents, and my father, on the other hand, was a stranger to me. A sweet stranger, but nevertheless, a stranger. Yes, I had seen him a couple of times that I remember, but he was more like Santa Claus. He brought presents. He stayed a while. He played with us, and then he left.

My entire life changed in that one afternoon. They piled us in the car. They didn't explain that we were leaving my grandparents' home forever, and it only dawned on me as we were leaving. Yes, I saw the bags packed. Yes, goodbyes were said. Hugs and kisses. Tears from my grandparents. And that's when I realized it. Wait a minute, he's not just visiting. *He's staying.* And wait a minute, I'm not leaving for a short trip with these people. (These people being my mother and my father.) I'm going *with them*. This was permanent.

Why didn't my parents sit down and explain this to me? I'm not sure. Maybe they didn't realize how connected I was. Maybe they didn't realize that I was confused. And why would they . . . they are my parents, after all. Maybe they were thrilled to finally be getting on with their lives after it being on hold for so many years. No one said a thing. No one told us we would be moving 105 miles away. The adults' decision ruled. Our opinion as the children was not part of the equation. In fact, how we felt about leaving wasn't explored at all. I didn't cry in the car that afternoon. I think children cry when they feel safe, and I didn't feel safe. I felt scared. I felt apprehensive. I knew to keep my feelings in. I knew crying wouldn't be appreciated. I've done a lot of silent crying in my life, and it started on that day.

I felt kidnapped. Kidnapped from Nanna and

Nannu who I thought were my real parents, the primary go-to-people in my life, and from my uncle who I thought of as a brother. It was a very confusing, traumatic experience, and it's the primary reason that I want to hear people's stories when they enter my courtroom.

It's why I ask: *What would you like me to know?*

Because when I left my grandparents' house that day, I didn't have a voice. No one asked me how I felt. No one told me when I'd see them again. No one considered my feelings. And I never want that to happen to anyone else ever again.

That little girl in me still feels kidnapped at times. When I lose my voice, when I don't feel heard, I go right to that place in that car where we're driving away and I'm watching the house get smaller and smaller through the rear window.

chapter two

School Days

I missed my grandparents tremendously. There was a gaping hole in my heart. The transition wasn't easy. But the reality was that I wasn't their daughter. I had to accept that my parents were my *parents* and that *I* was *their* daughter. I had no other choice. But leaving my grandparents' house would kick off a succession of moving from state to state. My father was going through medical training in different cities and states across the country, and like military kids, we went where he went. We moved all over. From Detroit to Saginaw, Michigan to Buffalo, New York, to Iowa City, Iowa, to Des Moines, Iowa, to Mankato, Minnesota, which was the longest place we stayed, which was about two years. We never had much money, but we were happy.

When we finally returned to Saginaw after Mankato, we were a bigger family. A family of six. When I was about six years old, my brother Tom was born in Saginaw. One year later, when I was about seven, my sister Helen was born in Buffalo, New York.

It seemed that we had the perfect American family. The four kids. The father who was a doctor. The suburban house. The stay-at-home mom. But on the inside, we were a little different. For one thing, I didn't live a life with closets of clothes and multiple games and toys.

I had about a week's worth of clothes and outfits I really liked in my closet. Going to Catholic schools, I'd had uniforms and didn't have the need for many extra clothes, nor could we afford extras. I didn't mind. I didn't know any different. But now in Saginaw, for the first time in my education, I attended public school. I was in the sixth grade, and we'd moved midyear. I didn't know anyone, and being the new girl, no one spoke to me. I wore the clothes I liked. During that first week of school, I wore the same outfit twice. I know, *a travesty*. Unfortunately, children can be mean, especially in middle school. You don't wear the same clothes on a Monday and on a Thursday. That was just not done.

The kids called me out for it. "You're wearing the same thing," they jeered. From that first week, I got picked on for everything. "Don't you know that you don't wear a white purse before Memorial Day?" someone said. "Don't you have anything decent to wear?" They were constantly making fun of me for my clothing choices—or my lack of clothing choices. Not one student was kind to me. Not one teacher recognized the difficulties I was having. No one inquired if I needed help. I never told my parents what was happening at school. They had other children to care for. They had other issues to deal with. I could handle this myself. And I was grateful my parents moved us all to Catholic school when the new year began and it was back to wearing uniforms.

It made an impact on me. To this day, if I find something on sale that I really like, I'll buy one in every color. I never want to run out of clothes or have to wear the same thing at an event. (I assure you I love to wear the same clothes at home.) My family makes fun of me, including all five of my children, because I'll buy extra clothes for them as well. Sometimes too much! It's such a small thing, but that little sixth grader who was made fun of and bullied because she wore the same thing *two times* in the same week—that little girl—never got over that hurt. I am proud that I can give my kids something I desperately wanted and that they don't have to ask for. I am proud that now I can say, "I can take care of that all by myself."

Recently, I spoke to my mother about it. She was very upset. "Why didn't you tell me?" she asked. "We would have bought you more clothes, whatever you needed." But at the time, I didn't know how to ask. It's just not what we did in our family. We weren't selfish, we didn't spend money on things we didn't need, and we made do with what we had. We were proud to have each other. And I knew I could take it and do without. Even in sixth grade, I knew my clothes didn't define who I was on the inside. I knew the bullies who made fun of me didn't know just how strong I was and just how little I thought of them. But, still, it hurt. The strength of my family and the self-worth that my grandparents instilled in me allowed me to triumph over those who hurt me. That holds true today.

Okay, I didn't have a closet full of clothes. And, okay, we were a little different than everyone else, culturally. But there was one big thing I still didn't have: statehood. I still had my little baby passport that read, to my father's dismay, "stateless." All that changed when I was eleven years old. That's when I became naturalized in Minneapolis, Minnesota, before we moved to Saginaw. That's when my brother Joe and I *finally* became American citizens.

Even though I was proud of being stateless, it felt incredible to finally become an American citizen. Not a person with permission to live here, but a person who had a right to be here. Here's the reality: being an American comes along with a prideful status that people who are born here take for granted. Yes, I've been here almost all my life, but even at eleven years old I understood this was one of the most important things I would do. I took the oath and signed that I was an American. America is a shining beacon for so many immigrants, including myself and my family. I still have the paper. I stare at my youthful cursive writing and know that, on that day, I proudly affixed my name in the best possible handwriting I could produce.

It wasn't easy during my formative years. And it wasn't just about being the new kid over and over again. It wasn't just about not having enough. I came from a very different cultural background, and while all the other parents were socializing and all the other children were having playdates, we would stay as a family very close, very guarded, and very sheltered.

Despite the arrival of the 1970s and the beginning of the women's movement, I was raised in a German-Maltese patriarchal home. That meant *everything* revolved around the father. The father was the focus of the family, and we were to never question his rules. There are certain behaviors that we simply accept about my father: We know my father does not clear the dishes. He does not make his bed. My mother does. It's just the way it is. When we eat on paper plates, we set my father a porcelain plate. If he has fish, he has two forks; if he has pasta, he has and a fork and a spoon. There's always going to be a napkin and water on the table for him. Whether he drinks the water or not, it's there next to him.

He sits at the head of the table. That's his seat and that's just where he sits, where he has always sat. We all have our places at the table. It's just the way it is. It's just what we do.

My mother had her place too. She stopped working outside of the home after my father returned. She cooked. She sewed. She crocheted. She knitted. She saved money couponing and all those things. She wore a dress every day. She went once a week to have her hair done and did what she was expected to do as a housewife. When I was in high school, she went to work in my father's office, helping run everything and ensuring that the billing was done properly. My mother, brilliant in math and logic, never achieved her dream of becoming an architect because her needs always took a backseat to my father and her four children. She says she doesn't regret a thing. But I've often wondered what she would have built. I believe she would have made architectural history, but sadly, we will never know. It's another reason I push through the naysayers and the haters. I want to know the possibilities and embrace them, not fear them—not have someone else limit them.

To this day, my father will always have certain things he wants, when he wants, the way he wants. When my father's friends visit, they get the same treatment as my father. And we all abide by this. I love my father and have accepted that this is just who he is and what he expects. He's worked incredibly hard and given us what he could. He's from the old world. And if it works for my mother, then it works for me.

My children accept my father the way he is too. It's not as if every man who comes into my house gets treated like the king, okay? When my brothers, my oldest son, my son-in-law, or brother-in-law comes over, they do not receive special plates while everyone else is eating on paper plates. Okay? Okay.

It is true however that my brothers, Joe and Tom, were taught certain things, like how to invest in stocks and how to be assertive, things my dad felt would prepare them to be successful in the world. They were also given opportunities to experience living in a foreign country for their education and to learn a language. My sister Helen and I were left out of these lessons. When I asked about it later (because I asked about *absolutely* everything), they told me, "Oh, you were never interested." Well, I would disagree with that. I would say that I was never put in the *position* to learn those kinds of things, to have the opportunities that would have broadened my skills and my worldly knowledge.

It was expected that my brothers would go to medical school, and they both did. Joe is a urologist. Tom is an anesthesiologist. Both are brilliant. Both are great doctors. Joe was in practice with my father, also a urologist, for about a decade. However, both Joe and Tom now work for different pharmaceutical companies. I would never fault either of my brothers. They have each worked very hard. But what I'm saying is that I don't know what choice Joe and Tom would have made on their own—without the pressure of "be a doctor." I do not think either one regrets going to medical school. My dad was a doctor, therefore my brothers were not going to be less. They were going to medical school.

For me, it was more complicated. I was expected to attend college and graduate school—but I was also expected to learn how to be a good wife. To be an obedient woman in society. My mother served my father. And to this day, she still serves him. I saw my grandmother serving my grandfather. But with my grandparents, I also saw them as more of a team, helping each other out in every way possible. Outside of those cultural differences, we were all ultimately treated the same. If my parents were handing out ten dollars, then we each received ten dollars. So, technically, we were treated equal, but we were *not* equal.

It's interesting, because when I was young, my mother didn't expect me or my sister to do housework or chores at all. I wasn't expected to do the laundry, help change the beds, sweep the floor, or clean the bathroom. Being a child of war in Germany, mother wanted us to have a real childhood, so she didn't ask us to take on some of the bigger chores, not even gradually. She also had such an old school sort of mentality that she didn't want to make her children responsible for any of those tasks. My mother liked to have order around her. She liked to do it her way. She was one of eight children and didn't have control of many things that happened to her and her family. She wanted us to have a better childhood in every way than she had, so her happiness always took a backseat to my father and to her children.

You must understand that my mother grew up during World War II. They lost everything in the war. She grew up with very little. She didn't have a childhood. When she was a teenager, because of lack of money, she sold her thick, long, mane of hair. She left for Spain at seventeen to be a governess for the children of a wealthy family for two years. She got married when she was barely twenty-two, so very young, and my father was twenty-one. She really wanted her children not just to have a childhood but to also fully enjoy being a child without worries and responsibility. But more than that, both of my parents wanted us—above everything else—to focus on our education. That was the *most* important thing. This is a real immigrant mentality. Education. Education. Education. Education equals succeeding in America. We were to be Americans who went to college and graduated from school. We were to focus on getting good grades. We were to have a childhood.

Without warning, when I reached puberty, entered junior high school, and spent more time out of the house, my parents suddenly had a lot of things they wanted me to do on their time frame. Now it was, "You have to do this," and "you have to do that," and "do it before you enjoy any of that."

By the time I entered high school as a freshman, my father was doing well in his career. He had a private practice; worked at three hospitals, in addition to the

Aleda E. Lutz VA Medical Center; and worked on-call in the ER at St. Luke's Hospital to make extra money. We'd been living in Saginaw for just over two years. My parents were ready to move again from our three-bedroom colonial to a bigger house. We were all getting older, and we needed more space. Except I was fourteen, and my entire world was encompassed by my best friend Patti Riffel. And she and her family were like a second family to me. If I wasn't at my house, I was at her house.

This time I put my foot down. I didn't want to move again, not out of the neighborhood, not out of Saginaw. I needed to be near Patti. My brother Joe also wanted to be near his friends, but I was adamant about it.

"I'm not moving away from Patti," I told my parents. It was a deal breaker for me. I didn't know where I was going to live, but I was sure that I wasn't going to live far from Patti. She was a bike ride away, a few short streets and a corner away. I wasn't giving that up. I had moved too many times to agree to that. I had never had a long-term friendship or a best friend, and I finally had both with Patti. Surprisingly, my parents honored my wish! They looked at bigger homes in different neighborhoods but found one a few blocks away from Patti, on the other side of the neighborhood. They finally seemed to understand how important my relationship to her, having her as my best friend, was. It was one time I really remember being heard.

My parents bought a bigger house in Saginaw Township in the kind of neighborhood you'd see on television. Located at the end of a dead end, it was a four-bedroom, two story house. My brothers shared a bedroom until my parents remodeled the basement and my brother Joe moved downstairs. My sister and I each had our own bedrooms. My parents had their room. We had a large basement with a pool table that was eventually finished. A more spacious kitchen. A solarium.

A study. Marble floors in the foyer. A round winding staircase leading upstairs with a white banister and red carpet, where I always pictured Scarlett O'Hara stepping down to meet Rhett Butler. The house wasn't by any means a mansion, but to us, where we came from, it was special. It was a very big deal. We were really living the American dream my grandparents always spoke about.

So, we had this bigger house. And suddenly, my parents wanted me to take on responsibility. *Substantial things*. And I had to do them on time. When my father asked. Not a minute later. Not an hour later. *In that moment*. I knew what was expected, but I couldn't or wouldn't always comply. For example, at this new house, we had a rose garden that went all the way down the right side of the driveway. The plants were all rose bushes, all sizes, many up to your chest. They were beautiful roses, all different colors like yellow, pink, peach, and white. There were about forty in all.

My father loves his roses. I mean, *loves* them. My father would come in from work and snip a few roses when they were blooming and place them in crystal vases around the house. He's always loved a rose on the dinner table. To this day, we have roses in the house for every occasion. We have roses planted around our house in every spot they will grow. His favorite rose is the Peace Rose, a large golden-yellow rose with some light pink shading on the edges. My parents were married with my mother holding an enormous bouquet of yellow roses. My father always gives my mother yellow roses. It's sentimental to them.

Roses aren't exactly easy to take care of. They need to be regularly pruned, and you can't just behead them or chop them down. They must be pruned on an angle above a five-leaf shoot. You don't want to cut them too low. You need to remove the dead leaves, especially those with black spot and mildew. Roses can be feisty. They can be picky. You can't over water them; you must water them at their roots, and you cannot get any water on their leaves. I took a class on the care of roses at the Saginaw Rose Society. My parents ensured I would know how to tend to my father's roses. Very quickly, watering and pruning these prized roses became *my* responsibility. It seems crazy now that I think about it. Why would he put me in charge of the roses that he loved so much? In a way, it might have been a gesture of trust. He *trusted* me to trim his beloved roses. Or maybe it was more of a question. A test: *can* I trust her with the roses?

Either way, it was my job to trim them.

The first summer I worked while in high school was at age fifteen; I worked at the movie theatre at Green Acres Plaza. Then, during the school year, I started working at Howard Johnson's as a waitress. I made sure I found work close to home. My parents said, "If you're getting a job, we're not going to drive you back and forth. You will have to walk." That was fine with me. Green Acres Plaza and the then Howard Johnson's were on State Street, several blocks away from our house. I walked to work. Rain or shine. No matter the weather. No matter the time. Because the restaurant was open twenty-four hours, I sometimes walked home at two o'clock in the morning, which I would never let my children do now!

My parents hated, and I mean *hated*, that I worked. Their mantra was, "If you want to work, then you work at home." This wasn't just because I was a young woman. They wanted all of us home. That's just how they were. My brother Joe was very different than I was. He followed their rules, and instead of working outside of the house, he worked around the house, and he took extra classes. Yes, I got good grades. But Joe got *phenomenal* grades. While I was taking macramé and drawing classes, Joe was fighting to be valedictorian. My parents didn't have to tell these things to Joe. But I was always bouncing around. My parents would say, "Focus on your schoolwork." "You need to make your bed." "You need to trim the roses." "You need to help your mother."

"Okay," I said, "I can do it all. I can work, I can do my chores, I can be a pompom girl, and I can do my schoolwork."

I was in the top ten percent of my class and always on the honor roll, so I didn't see the problem with taking on other activities. I was receiving academic accolades and making great tips at Howard Johnson's! There were things I wanted, like the clothes I mentioned earlier, and like extra paperback books that I devoured because writing fiction was the career I wanted. I didn't want to have to ask them for anything extra. They worked so hard. Had to put four kids through college. No, you shouldn't have to pay for my extras, I would think. I wanted to handle it all. And so, I did.

Yes, we were American. But my parents were very old school—very Maltese, very German. They didn't get that even if they were going to pay for college, I wanted to stockpile my own spending money. They absolutely *did not* understand extracurricular activities. Ultimately, they just didn't comprehend a life separate and outside of the family, nor did they discuss the issues with me.

My parents were so conflicted. They desperately wanted us to have an American education. They desperately wanted us to be American and have an American way of life. But they saw the American school, our American education, and our integration into the American culture as a threat to their dreams for their children . . . for me. They didn't see any way but their way. And I wanted to fit in—in a way they didn't or couldn't understand. So I was going to do it my way no matter what.

On one hand, I often felt like an outsider because my family's culture was so different from everyone else's. On the other hand, I was a very busy, very driven American teenager. I had a lot of energy and a ton of goals. When I was a freshman, I joined the basketball team. I was more of a benchwarmer who earned a lot of splinters, not baskets, but I loved being part of a team. At the end of my freshman year, my best friend Patti and I tried out and made the Crusader Pompom Squad. Being a Crusader Pompom girl for my school, Saints Peter and Paul Area High School, was the most American thing I could have done. I was exhilarated to participate, support, cheer on American sports—football and basketball and hockey—and be part of a squad of girls who always supported each other.

There was an element of belonging that I really responded to. When I was in my pompom uniform, I didn't feel different. Same when I joined the military. I wasn't an outsider anymore. I wasn't that strange foreign girl whose mother said *garach* instead of *garage* and *droy-yer* for *drawer*. I wasn't the new kid who always had to make a new friend, trying to fit in. Here, I was part of an army of sixteen girls, and we were friends with the cheerleaders because we had a common goal. These girls are still some of my closest friends to this day. But it was so much more than that. I poured everything into the Crusader Pompom Squad. There were intricate routines, and we had practice every single day. In the summers, we practiced routines at six in the morning because that's when it's cooler. We all worked so hard and became an award-winning team that I was so proud to be part of. I loved it with all my heart. It was an important part of my life. But my father . . . he didn't get it. My mother, always supporting my father, often being the peacemaker, didn't get it either. The way they saw it, it was always family first. I had no say.

As important as the Crusader Pompom Squad was to me, it was equally unimportant to my parents. As far as they were concerned, the Crusader Pompom Squad was just another thing I was doing to waste my time outside of the house and defy them. The more time I spent outside of the house, the more my father began to obsess over what I wasn't doing *in* the house. Particularly, he started to hyperfocus on how I wasn't making my bed. I wasn't taking care of the roses. The rose bush trimming wasn't around my schedule. It was around *his*.

My brother Joe always did the right thing. If he was told to take out the garbage, he would immediately take out the garbage. If he was told to mow the lawn, he immediately mowed the lawn. Whatever he was asked, he dropped what he was doing and did it. Maybe because of that, my parents never gave us a hard time when we went bowling after Sunday morning church service.

But when it was time to trim the roses, it was a different story. One day, I had a football game to go to. In the morning before school, my mother said, "Please, for your father, before you leave, just do the roses!"

My response? "I'll get to them this weekend. Tonight after school is the game. I can't do them today. What is the big deal with waiting one day to do the roses?"

My father's version of the story was this: "*You* are always a problem. *You* are a troublemaker. *You* always shirk your responsibilities and what little we ask of you." Because if you were supposed to do it *that day*, then that was the day you were supposed to do it. There was no negotiation. Even to this day, I think, *What was the big deal?* I had so much going on during the week. I was doing my homework. I was getting all As. I was going to practice. I was going to work. I was never home. But you can see—that was part of the problem. I was *never* home.

Of course, my father's controlling behavior and obsession over me doing the roses had nothing to do with the roses. I do believe my father doubled down on his controlling behavior because he feared losing his little girl again. He'd first lost me to his parents, and now I was growing up. Over time, I came to the realization that since I was the oldest of their four children and I was the first child to experience the "growing up and leaving the house phase," I was a bit like their private experiment. My leaving was something my mother accepted and my father had latent issues with. I was confident. I was independent. I needed to explore the world without them. Upon reflection, I think my parents learned what to do and what not with me. My independence and constant defiance scared them. They wanted to hold onto me for dear life, afraid of what could happen to me in the world. It's unfortunate that my father couldn't communicate this to me, but it's not an uncommon thing for a parent to hold on tighter just as their child is letting go. I have always said, and wholeheartedly feel, that I was raised by completely different parents than my three siblings—and not just because of my relationship and bond with Nannu and Nanna but also because my parents had an incredibly soft, understanding approach with them.

So, I was about to go to the football game, and I hadn't done the roses yet. I figured the roses could wait. Of course, this was a *terrible* idea. Don't ever make the roses wait. The day before, I had picked up my pompom uniform from the dry cleaners. It was a little red and white wool uniform with a pleated skirt. After school, I looked all over the house and couldn't find my uniform anywhere. Here I was frantic, in a panic. Where was my uniform? Someone had to know something. I began to ask questions.

I'm not sure who broke the news to me first—my mother or one of my siblings. But my father had taken the uniform. He buried it. Buried it *where*? Look in the rose garden; you'll find it buried.

In a frenzy, I sprinted to the rose garden to search for my little white and red uniform. It was in a badly dug hole, deeply buried, and covered in dirt. It was not in the dry-cleaning bag that might have protected it. It was blackened with dirt in every crevice. I shook it and watched the dirt fly. I tried to brush the dirt off. I desperately attempted to smack the dirt out of it, but I couldn't. It was mashed into the fabric. Filthy. Ruined. An absolute mess. I was distraught. We paid for our own uniforms. I paid for mine by earning the money through fundraisers with the other pompom girls. I only had the one uniform. There were no extra uniforms owned by me or by the team. Even if there had been one, it wouldn't have been tailored like this one was for me. There was literally nothing I could do. So I went to the game to support my squad, to support our football players, to honor my high school. I sat on the bleacher, head held high and, at the same time, humiliated. I sat and watched the other girls perform. That day, I told my best friend what had happened. She consoled me. Acknowledging this to anyone outside of my reflection in the bathroom mirror, even her, was a big deal for me.

Sometimes it wasn't the roses. Sometimes, it was my bedroom. It was hardly a mess but was rarely in an organized, put-away condition. And my bed was never made. This drove my father crazy. He felt that I should make the bed before school in the morning and then became hyper-focused on me when I didn't do it. It was part of his power play; part of his annoyance that I wasn't listening to him. His feeling: *Can't she just make the bed?*

My father expected beds made and really thought it was an insult if I didn't do that. I figured: *My* space, *my* room, *my* choice. I was okay getting into a bed that was not made. If I wanted to make it, I certainly could do that before I got into it. Again, this was a small power struggle. Normal teenage stuff. He'd scream and yell. I'd threaten to leave.

My father saw my refusal to make the bed as

disrespectful. As the ultimate rebellion. I know, I know. Some kids were skipping school. Some kids were doing drugs. Some kids were running around drinking and constantly partying. But me, I was an A student who wouldn't make my bed.

Some days, he would just take the sheets off the bed and the mattresses off the platform; other days, it included dumping out all the contents of my drawers and closet. My jewelry box. Everything. Several times that happened. Everything I owned would be sitting in chaos in the center of the room. So, "No, you didn't make your bed, so now you have to clean everything." I took the punishment. I was tough about it. I would just silently put it away. After I reorganized everything and put it away, I'd lock myself in the bathroom. Then, I'd relax into tears, leaning over the bathroom counter while my eyes filled and dripped and refilled. I stared at myself in the mirror. I tried not to blink. I stayed stoic. You can do this, I'd tell myself. You are strong. Talking back to him wouldn't accomplish anything. It would just get me punished. And I was punished enough. I just wanted it to be over.

I'm not complaining—I've had a good life. I think my parents did their best. They gave me everything they could. And the things they didn't know, they couldn't give. At some point in your life you come to understand that not everybody has a perfect parent. Not everyone has a parent who can remain neutral, who doesn't have a temper. We all know that kids don't come with rule books. And luckily for me, I had my grandparents. They reassured me and were empathetic to what I was going through with my father. They thought I was great. I would call my grandparents after my father's explosions, and my grandfather would always respond the same way: with great compassion. With his voice soft and warm, he would say, "He's just a kid. He's just a kid."

My grandmother used to say: "You're the best one." And it wasn't that I was the favorite one, although I always like to believe that my brother and I were her favorite because they raised us when we were little. Because we were more like her kids, and she treated us like her kids. But telling me I was the best one meant "you can take this. You're better for it."

I always felt that my grandparents had my back. And because I felt so very protected by them in every way, I thought, *Okay, I really can take it*. They always reminded me that they were always there for me. But more, they also reminded me that my parents were good people. That they were stressed. That they work hard. That parents aren't perfect. I truly have learned that to go forward, you must forgive the people who hurt you, but you also must forgive yourself.

Because I forgave my father and maybe understood where his rage was coming from didn't mean that his outbursts just suddenly stopped. My father was very much about control. Here was the problem with that: He had raised me to be *my own person*! He raised me to be independent. To fight for what I believed in. Except, I guess, when it came to him.

One day, my father was particularly enraged at me. I had a balcony off my bedroom, and so he threw all my belongings over the balcony onto a large sheet. He was so angry at me for not making the bed that I came home to watch all my stuff going over the balcony. Then he began dragging my entire room, now on the large sheet, into the backyard. He didn't do anything halfway. He was going to show me who was boss. To him, my independence was a sign that I didn't want to be part of the family. He gave me everything, so he could take everything away from me. He screamed that the least I could do was make the bed. Again, *it wasn't about the bed*. Nevertheless, he took all of it. I don't mean just the sheets. I mean *everything* that hung in my closet, the jewelry in my jewelry box, hairbrushes, hair clips, books. Everything I had in my room was in that large sheet.

It had been a clear night. But in that moment, I recall it like it was something biblical, like you could open a page in the ancient text and this story was there. My father was screaming at me while he was pulling at and dragging all my belongings, which ended up strewn across the front lawn into the back lawn. My mother trying to calm him. My siblings silently watching. I stood stoic, and the sky suddenly darkened, turning into a heavily cloudy sky, an angry sky that perfectly matched his rage. And this was all over my unmade bed.

And my mother was shouting, "Don't do this. Don't do this!" My brother—everybody—was saying, "Are you kidding? What are you doing?" But my father was incensed, not listening, totally focused on teaching me a lesson.

Then the worst happened. He began to set all my things on fire. Because the fire would teach me a lesson. I couldn't put my things away. I didn't own anything. Everything I had was because of his hard work. That would show me how important my family was and his rules were. Fire would teach me to obey. Fire would get me to make my bed. And he tried. He really tried to set my things on fire. I watched him try. That's when God intervened.

It rained. Torrential rain. I'm not an overly religious person, but I really do feel that the rain was a blessing, a biblical-size miracle for me. God didn't let him do anything more. He couldn't set my things on fire because it rained. God stepped in and said, *Enough*.

In my head, I said, *Thank you, God*. My mother and my siblings carried everything back into the house. He just stalked away. He'd made his point to me. I was happy that God made His point to him. I walked to my best friend's house and spent the night there. I didn't ask for my parents' permission. I wasn't going in the house, at least not that night.

What was his point? To this day I'm not sure. I know it wasn't about the bed. I knew it wasn't going to stop me from moving forward in my life and from speaking out and doing things my own way and in my own time. It didn't change my goal to be independent. I knew I was a good kid. I knew I was a good person. I knew in my gut that I was doing the right thing and making the right choices for myself—despite not caring if I slept in a made bed! I was a good student. I was working. I had nice friends. I didn't break any laws. I was on an award-winning pompom team. Again, it wasn't about the bed. It was about me. About me growing up. It was about me asserting my independence. He saw it as a threat to our family, to our whole way of life, to him as a father.

Even after that day, I still didn't make the bed. I was that stubborn of a child. Do I make my bed now? Did it teach me a lesson? Hell no. I never made my bed after that day, and I still don't!

Here's the thing: I love my parents. When they retired, we built a house so that we could live together and to ensure that, as they aged, they will not go into a nursing home. I will manage their care at home. We've lived under the same roof for the past seventeen years. We live together—my parents, my three children, and my two puppies—to *this day*. Family is the absolute most important thing to me. Growing up, my parents saw me as a rebellious kid. I know this is almost impossible to believe since I was a good kid. I mean a seriously really good kid. A responsible kid. A hard-working kid. Here were the real problems: First, I was using my voice and speaking up when I was expected to be silent, be compliant, and conform. There was no complaining in my house. I was to follow the rules. I was not allowed to question the rules. I was to make the bed. I was to cut the roses when he said to cut the roses. I was to dedicate my time, any extra free time I had outside of studying, to the family. Second, because I didn't do that; because I had other interests; because I didn't make the bed when I was supposed to; because I questioned my parents' authority over me, my parents' roles in my life choices, and the rules, I was deemed rebellious. I was deemed a troublemaker. My father would say, "What is it I haven't done for you? What? Why are you doing this to me? Why?"

I saw him as a bully. He saw himself as a victim of my rebelliousness. And the two could not coexist.

If my father had said to me, "What would you like me to know? What's going on with you, Rosie? How can I help? Why aren't you making your bed? Why aren't you taking care of the roses? Why are you always running around all over the place?" I could have told him. I could have said, "Pa, I'm sorry about the bed, but I was up late studying, I was tired and running late in the morning. I'll do it later. I promise." Or, "Pa, can you give me some more time? I'm sorry I can't do the roses today because I have a game and that's important to me. Can I do them tomorrow?" Or, "Pa, I know you feel that I'm separating from the family because I have friends and because I've gotten a job, but it's not about that. I want to be independent. You've taught me to be a hard worker, and I saw you being a hard worker. I want to do the same. I love the family, but I have a life too." I wish I could have said, "Pa, recognize me for who I am and the good things I have accomplished and can accomplish."

I am not a puppet. If you want a puppet, go to the store and buy one. It's not me.

To this day, I honor that rebellious, troublemaking, misfit girl inside of me because that rebellious girl gave me the woman's voice that I have now. That rebellious girl would not be who she is now without that rebellion.

Without standing up for myself. Without that childhood, without experiencing that heavy-handed upbringing, I would *never* have been able to stand up for so many people in the courtroom, as a lawyer, with clients, for my children, and in everything I do.

People are going to hear my voice whether they like it or not.

My father's behavior also left me in a unique position. I've always felt inspired to stand up and speak out for children. I've always felt inspired to do what's right for women, for men, and for anyone who can't stand up for themselves. I don't see it as a choice. It is just what I do. It is who I am. I also need to acknowledge that my father saved lives. He was an exceptional doctor who helped thousands and never looked at the ability of his patient to pay. I also recognize that very positive influence on me as well. His example also taught me to do good and to make a positive difference in people's lives.

Once, when I was an adult with kids of my own, my Uncle Mike and I were going to Florida together. Uncle Mike, my mother's youngest brother, has been part of my life for as long as I can remember. We have a family condo, through the foresight and hard work of my parents, in Florida that they bought when they finally began having a little extra money. And sometimes we would go there for vacation as a family, or with different members of our family, for a few weeks. So, Uncle Mike and I were at the Tampa airport in Florida, waiting for our flight home. Now, this was over spring break. You know what the airport is like during spring break. It's chaos. Standing room only. A thousand people all around, surrounding the gate, surrounding adjacent gates, everyone anxious with their bags, on edge to get on their flights.

Suddenly, I hear a man yelling. He's drunker than you can imagine and with a girl about ten or eleven who is clearly his daughter. He's fighting with the gate agent. "I'm dropping her off," he's yelling, slurring. And the gate agent is arguing with this drunk, angry man, saying, "No, it's too early, sir. You can't drop her off."

This guy did not care. "Well, I paid my fifty bucks, and you need to take her now." There's a huge scene going on, and this poor little girl is stuck in the middle of the whole thing. She's acting like she's twenty and trying to calm her father down. A ten-year-old. This child is saying, "Dad, it's okay. You can just go. Dad, it's okay." My heart broke for her. She was so embarrassed, so scared. You can see that this kid is just trying to placate him so he would leave.

I'm watching this in front of me, and no one is doing a thing. Everyone's staring at this man screaming, and he's getting louder, bigger. The gate agent continues to argue. He's not calling security. He's not calling the cops. He's just standing there fighting with this utterly irrational man.

"Take care of my bag, will you?" I said to my uncle, and I dropped my bag next to him. Because I don't just stand around watching kids get treated like property.

I knew this child had been going through something very serious. She was acting like the adult in this situation with the way she was trying to calm him down. The way she was telling him it was okay to leave. The way she was saying it would be okay. Obviously, none of it was okay. It was very wrong, and to top it off, not one person, or the gate agent, was doing anything about it.

"What do you think you're going to do?" my uncle said.

"I'm going to fix this."

"How? What can you do to fix this?"

I turned to my uncle and said: "Watch me."

I pushed through the crowd, walked over to the man, and quickly put my hand out to shake his.

"Sir, I'm an attorney. My name is Rose Aquilina." I just treated him like he was the sanest person. Not drunk at all. Like he was my best friend. "Sir, here's my business card. Aquilina Law Firm. I practice family law. If you would allow me, I'm going to Detroit. And so is your daughter. I will be happy to take guardianship of her. If you give me power of attorney, I will make sure she gets there. I'll wait with her. I'll sit with her on the plane. I'll make sure she gets to the right people in Detroit. I'll take care of this. And then you can leave." I smile and stare him in the eyes. He's following everything I say. "Would you give me power of attorney, sir?"

Now this guy is thrilled. He's got this big lawyer on his side, right? And here's the gate agent saying to me, "Ma'am, you can't interfere in this. Ma'am!" But I ignore him because my focus is this child. I must get this child into safe hands. And so I said to the irritated gate agent, "Sir, I need a piece of paper. Can we go over there and get one?" I turned to the father. "Sir, would you just sit with your daughter quietly and I'll make sure that the power of attorney is completed. I just have to draft a few lines and then you can sign it and leave." I pointed him to a place he could sit down with his daughter. Then, I pointed the agent away from the crowd. "Let's find that paper." And we walked away.

Now, I wasn't actually looking for paper to draft the power of attorney. And I didn't practice law in Florida, but I didn't care. The idea was to protect the child. So, we walked over to a quiet place and the gate agent is still yelling at me. "You can't interfere. You can't do this." But I've calmed down the man. I can still see him behind the irate gate agent, and he's grinning at me. And still, all through this, the gate agent is still yelling, "You can't do this!"

But when you don't feel protected as a child, as I

sometimes did not, you know how urgent it is to help children whenever they are in need.

This gate agent was clearly not looking at the bigger picture. He was not looking at it from the experience of the child. He wasn't thinking about protecting the child, about being the voice for the child. So, I had a little talk with him.

"Sir, remember your job," I said. "I need a piece of paper. And, while you get me that piece of paper, you need to call law enforcement for drunken and disorderly in public and for child abuse. I want protective services called, and they need to be advised to call protective services in Detroit. I don't know what's happening to this child, but this cannot happen. So, we need to be the voice for this child who doesn't have one. Think about your job. What are you doing?"

He looked at me without a word, with shock. Then his eyes grew wide as it finally sunk in what was happening. It wasn't about asking for this man to wait. It was about protecting this little kid.

"I see," he said. "Thank you."

He scurried behind a desk and got me a piece of paper and a pen. I began to write. He got on the phone.

I looked around at everyone watching. And there was not one other adult, not one person in the whole place, getting help for this child. There were hundreds of people there.

The gate agent, once it hit him, did make phone calls to law enforcement. Which they *have* in the airport in an *instant.* And they made a report. We all made a report. Then we returned to the child. Dad gave his daughter the thumbs up, even in his drunken state. She hugged him goodbye, and he told her that we were going to finish the paperwork and that she can go. She looked at me with grateful eyes and a sheepish smile and took my hand.

"Are we good?" I asked her. She nodded. "Yes, we're good."

The girl and I walked toward the gate and a stewardess took the daughter into the plane as dad and daughter waved a final goodbye.

"Honey, I'm going to see you on the plane," I said. The girl nodded.

They escorted her onto the plane in that moment so that she didn't have to watch her father get arrested. That would have been even more traumatic.

By now, the crowds had lost interest because there was no more show. Everything had calmed down. After the girl was on the plane, her father out of her sight, law enforcement arrived and arrested him. CPS came. We made a report, and I asked them to call Detroit CPS because these child protective services would need to work together. The airline, by the way, came over to my uncle and I and asked us to stand in an area to the side.

"Did you just get us in trouble?" he asked.

"I have no idea," I said. Not that it mattered. I will always step in to help a child in need.

A few minutes later, the same gate agent came over to us. "Thank you," he said, then handed us two first-class tickets.

My uncle picked up our bags and grinned. "You can do this any time."

"Well, hopefully I won't have to do it again!" I said.

I didn't think, *Oh, I could be arrested.* I just didn't give a shit. Someone was going to talk to this kid and handle things, and it was going to be me. Because, look, if you do something at the airport that can be considered threatening or interfering, it's very easy to get arrested! But I'm not going to worry about crossing a boundary when it's to help someone. I'm not worried about the consequence I might have to face. I'm just not going to do it. I don't care. I'm going to do what I need to do and then figure the rest of it out later.

Soon enough, I learned a lot about that little girl. Her mother had died, and her father was taking care of her and a few other siblings. She was sent on the plane by herself to visit her extended family in Detroit. She wasn't withdrawn; she was sweet natured and cheerful. But she was tired. You notice that with abused children—how tired they are.

CPS was waiting for us when we touched down in Detroit along with the family members. They had guessed that something was wrong with the living situation of the girl and her siblings, but they didn't know *what* was wrong. The family was simply too far away to know what was happening. And one thing that people must understand is this: abused children love their parents. This little girl wasn't about to call up her grandmother and say, "Daddy is in trouble. Daddy needs help. I need help. My sisters need help." That's very hard to do. Especially since her mother had died and their father was all they had. That child understood her father was grieving too. I'm certain that little girl felt very alone and had felt very alone since her mother passed away.

When I spoke to the family, they immediately wanted me to be their lawyer. I can't be your lawyer, I told them, I'm a witness. But I can refer you to a lawyer. Eventually, they went to court, and ultimately, an aunt in Texas took custody of the children. They were protected.

There have been many, many instances in my life where I've done things like that because it's the right thing to do. And I truly believe that this started when I was in high school and in those intense battles and power struggles with my parents. I never did it to benefit myself. I didn't help that little girl in the airport because I thought it would benefit me. I didn't make sure every single girl in the Nassar case was heard because I thought it would benefit me. I allowed the girls to speak in the Nassar case and talked to each one of them because I believed them and wanted them to know that they didn't do anything wrong and that they matter.

The day I was to leave for college, I went into my father's medical office because he hadn't said goodbye to me at home. In fact, he'd said nothing. I wasn't sure if he even remembered I was leaving. When I arrived, he refused to acknowledge the significance of the day and simply said something like, "Good luck." That was it. I felt horrible going to college without any real goodbye, without any acknowledgment I would be gone, but I was happy I made the gesture. Reflecting on it later, I realize how hard that day must have been for my father. He didn't want to let us go; my leaving was the signifier that, eventually, all four of his children would leave. It stemmed from love, yes, but it was also controlling. I think he was like so many loving parents—he wanted to hold us *too* close.

My parents are from the Old World. I know I always say this, but it's true. They didn't believe in the pomp of graduation. They didn't believe in the circumstance of the ceremony. They believed in success. They'd congratulate me once I ultimately made it.

When I graduated from high school, my present wasn't a car, it wasn't a party, now was it even a dollar. My father said to me, "You've graduated. You're eighteen. What you do in the world now is for you, not for me. You make a mistake, it's yours. If you do something great, it's yours. It's your life. You do what you want to do. It is not mine." That was the present. That was my gift. And you know what? I've done okay for myself. I'm proud of myself.

I've thought about his words over my whole life and recognized that whatever I accomplish in the world is mine. I own it. It's *my* name. It's *my* success. It's *my* accomplishment. It's who I am. I now represent that little girl who never had a voice. I now represent other little girls; other people like me. I always wanted to make my mark in the world to show my children that they can be anything, and now I hope I have. But there is much more work for me to do.

I truly didn't think about becoming a lawyer. It never crossed my mind, never made the list of career possibilities. I had decided, from the time I was a young girl sitting there with my brother on the front porch stoop, telling my brother stories at my grandparent's home, and which was solidified for me in the hospital room after we had our tonsils out, that I would be a writer. Also, when I was in high school attending career day, I was always drawn to the military speakers. I was fascinated by the army, the navy, the air force. I knew I wanted to join the military. My friends would laugh at me. "Oh, that's you Aquilina. You've always got to be different." They never believed I would go into any military job. Not one person in my life ever believed that I would ever join. My response? "Whatever." Again, I didn't listen. I just laughed it off. I attended only the military career speakers. I didn't care what anyone said.

My major at Michigan State was English. I had a journalism minor. I was convinced I would be a writer. (Which is a goal I have achieved, but more on that later.) My father, of course, didn't like this. He didn't see it as a *practical* major. He didn't see it as the kind of major that would get me a job.

"And what are you going to do with this English degree?" my father kept asking. "How are you going to support yourself?"

These questions went on through my senior year. Near graduation, when I was home for school break, my father was once again barraging me with questions about what I was going to do with my life.

"I'm going to be a lawyer," I said, looking him straight in the eyes.

You might think that this was the kind of answer that my father was looking for. Most other parents in the world would be happy with this answer. But that's not why I said lawyer.

I said lawyer because I knew he would hate it.

For one, doctors hate lawyers. But also, I knew that I needed to choose a path so that I could support myself independently. If I was going to defy my father and not be a doctor, it had to be for good reason. What if he doesn't pay for anything else? Could I survive? I knew that with my English major I could always be a teacher. I added classes to attain my teaching degree to ensure I could work and pay for school if he refused, since, again, I was once again defying him. And as part of my degree I also became a reading specialist. I wanted a job that I could always fall back on no matter what.

When I announced my plan to be a lawyer, I connected with the angry little girl in me. The one who was in trouble for not making her bed. The one who got punished for being on the pompom squad. It was the angry little girl in me saying, "I know you hate lawyers. Therefore, *that's* what I'm going to become." And what's more, one day I was going to be a judge.

"Oh? How are you going to do that?" my father asked.

"Watch me."

chapter three

Rules of the Heart

Despite our differences, I was my father's daughter. My goals as a teenager were college and my career. Still, I dated *a lot.* At first, I thought my parents would insist on meeting whomever I was going out with, shaking his hand, interrogating him, and insisting he'd have me home at a certain time.

Nope. None of that.

"Don't you want to meet my date?" I would ask.

"No," my father would say. "I only want to meet the man you're going to marry." That became his rule.

Nevertheless, I still went out on dates. Lots of dates. Maybe I was testing my parents. Maybe I wanted to see how far they'd go with this.

You don't want to meet my boyfriend, I thought. Not even if he comes to the door to meet you and shake your hand? Okay, fine, I'll sit outside in his car with him. Maybe we will talk. Maybe we'll be making out. Maybe both. You want to meet him? Come out and meet him. *I dare you.*

It should come as no surprise that my growing up, my independence, my dating, drove my father crazy.

He retaliated by relentlessly opening and closing the garage door. My father would stand in that garage, pressing the button, watching the door crawl up, then down. He would be outraged, fuming with each lift of the garage door. It just kept opening and closing; up went the garage door, down went the garage door, up and down, up and down, five times, ten times . . . sometimes it felt like fifty times. Oh, he came out, but he wouldn't go past the garage door button. This went on until I got married. Me torturing *my father* by dating, and my father torturing *me* by opening and closing the garage door.

None of my boyfriends were serious. I was in a bowling league with my brother, and we bowled together on Sunday mornings. Sometimes I met guys that way. Sometimes I'd date someone from another school. I never actually dated anyone from my own high school. Once there was a summer romance. But I never thought about getting married.

That was until I met Dave. They say you never meet the man you're going to marry at a bar, but that's what happened. He was a good friend of a guy I had briefly dated. I met that guy and group of friends because he was the cousin of one of my best girlfriends. Dave was a hunk. A towering, oozing, sexy hunk. I had never seen such a hunk except on television. Tall; bright blue eyes; black hair; the warmest, friendliest smile. And somewhere around six feet tall, maybe taller. It was the '70s, and *Saturday Night Fever* disco dancing was in style. Dave wore blue "high-heeled" shoes the first time I met him. He was larger than life, cuter than John Travolta.

That first night, Dave and I danced. We fit together like matched gloves. There was a lot of chemistry between Dave and me. We're both hot-blooded. He's Italian. I'm Maltese. When I was with him at the bar that night, I forgot about everything and danced. I met up with Dave a few more times—we kept it casual, just dancing, until he eventually asked me out, but that was nearly a year later. Dave and I attended different universities. He went to Western Michigan. I went to Michigan State. So that was that. I remembered how great of a dancer he was, how good looking he was, how truly decent he was, but I never thought about tracking him down.

Instead, I threw myself into college life at Michigan State. I was busy with my English major and journalism minor. I made new friends and was working hard and enjoying freshman year. Dave was the last thing on my mind. Instead, I was more excited about joining in on the football season that was in full swing at Michigan State. One cold day, after a game, I was back at the dorm hanging out with friends when suddenly, Dave appeared. He had come to MSU with a few friends to watch the football game and decided to track me down. It was a wonderful and totally unexpected surprise.

Remember, this was before cell phones. He couldn't just text me. He had to physically find out where I lived and ask people where I was! Finding me took genuine effort. And I thought, *Wow. This is a really nice thing to look me up.* There was no pressure. He wasn't there to spend the night. He just wanted to say, *Hi, I'm here.* It was very spontaneous, very fun, and very different than my past experiences with boys. I've always been more of a free spirit. I'm not a planner at all, so I loved it. It was like the cosmos were telling me not to let this guy go: that this one was special. More important, that finally someone thought I, too, was special.

From that moment, Dave and I started dating regularly. We were both still in college, but we wanted to spend free time together, and that summer, we fell in love. Of course, he didn't know my family—remember my parents wouldn't meet anyone until I was ready to get married—yet Dave felt so familiar, like family. He came from a very traditional Italian background like mine. His father owned a popular meat market, one of those old-fashioned butchers with prime cuts and an enticing meat showcase that was very well known in the Saginaw community. His grandmother was very much like mine: loving; always cooking traditional Italian cookies, cakes, and meals; always doing whatever she can for you. His father was also traditional, a lot like my father.

Dave treated me with respect. He wasn't a rule-breaker. Education was important to him. Hard work was important to him. He had a great group of friends. He took great pride in his relationship with his two sisters. He held chairs out for me. He made sure other people acted the right way around me. Once we were at a hockey game in Saginaw to see the Saginaw Gears. There were some men behind us swearing, drinking, and just being overtly obnoxious. Dave turned around and said, "There's a woman present. You do not swear." Those guys clammed up. I thought Dave was a knight in shining armor. He was the guy who would going to speak up for me when I needed it, protect me when I needed it, be there whenever I needed it. I never had a man stand up for me like that before, and as much as I know that I was perfectly capable of standing up for myself, it felt nice. More importantly, it felt right. I had always been me against the world, and now I felt like I had an ally.

Dave and I had a lot of laughs. We spent weekends up north canoeing. We had great plans. I was going to go to law school. He was going to finish his business degree then open a business. We had a lot of common goals, but more, we were in love. I was raised Catholic, and though I had dated many guys, sex was for the man that I was going to marry. Dave, on the other hand, had been with other people. He was the first person I had sex with—well into the relationship, of course. But we were together. That was it for me. I just thought, *Okay, this is the guy.*

There was a lot of passion between Dave and me,

and our relationship had reached a tipping point. We were either going to get married or break up. It wasn't so much that he popped the question. It was more *Where are we going to go from here?* And so together, we decided that we were going to get married. We even went shopping for rings. Getting married was like checking items off a checklist. Went to college, check. Apply to law school, check. Getting married, check. It wasn't exactly romantic. It's certainly not the way to start a lifelong marriage. Plus, he was waiting to meet my father so that he could do it the old-fashioned way and ask my father for my hand in marriage. That's right: he had *still* not met my father.

Not long after we became serious, things took a sharp turn. I got a call from Dave. His father just had a heart attack. His stepmother called 911, but they couldn't save him. Dave was distraught but stoic. He had been very close with his father. His grief was so raw, so palpable, and I empathized with him. At that point in my life, I was still grieving over the loss of my grandfather who had died when I was a senior in high school, only a few years earlier. I understood what it's like when the center of your life is gone. Dave's father was the glue that held his family together. Dave's mother had been out of the picture for a long time, and really, his father raised Dave and his two sisters. Dave's grandmother filled that maternal role in many ways—but when it came down to it, Dave had been missing that traditional mother role in his life. Many years after we were married, and especially today, I see that he saw me as a "mother" replacement. I was too young to have seen that, and there wasn't anyone who'd met him or who knew him who could point that out to me.

Almost immediately, Dave's grief changed him. He suddenly went from this very happy-go-lucky guy to an I-make-the-decisions-around-here guy. And he was terrified—terrified he was going to die, terrified he was going to have a heart attack, terrified to be the man of the family. He bought life insurance, a lot of life insurance, because he was convinced he was next. He started working out obsessively. He was working at the meat market and helping manage it with his stepmother. I graduated from college in three years instead of four because I went year-round. I attended MSU for three trimesters, then took classes in Saginaw at Delta and Saginaw Valley every summer. I was destined for law school. I used the time I had between graduation of MSU and beginning law school to plan our wedding.

Dave had wanted to keep working at the meat market, but unfortunately, his stepmother had decided to sell it. There had been no will. There was little he could do. He was happy, though, to get a good-paying job at Rainbo Bread and decided to quit college. The plan was for him to go back once things were stable again, but things were happening at such a fast pace. He and his siblings were way too young to have lost a parent, and my heart went out to them. I completely understood why all these changes were happening, but there was a disconnect. Dave and I were supposed to be planning our lives together. Instead, he was taking control, planning his life, and our life, on his own.

It worried me. *Of course*, it worried me. If Dave was able to make these big decisions without even talking to me, did he expect me just to go along? I was concerned that this new life of ours wouldn't include me going to law school. I'm not entirely sure if Dave ever said to me, "You're not going"; nevertheless, because of the way I grew up with such a dominating father, and because of Dave's traditional values, I was worried that he would want me to give up on my dream.

Look, we were very young: I was barely twenty-one, he was twenty-three. I didn't want another man coming into my life to control all my decisions. I wanted to emotionally support Dave, yes, but my plan to go to law school wasn't going to change. And he needed to know this.

"I am going to law school," I forcefully told him one night. "It doesn't matter if you stay here. It doesn't matter if you go back to Western. But I am going to law school. I can't marry you if I can't go to law school."

He agreed and said he wanted me to go to law school and do anything else I wanted to do. But I was still uncertain. My truth was that I worried that Dave couldn't handle me going to law school in Lansing. He said the right words, but I remained doubtful of the contents of his heart. And there was one other thing. We'd gotten our rings. We were engaged. Or so I thought. But he didn't want to tell anyone—for a while. His older sister had been silently engaged for a few months before they told anyone, and he wanted to do the same thing. I wanted to do our thing, not hers. I wanted to move forward with everything.

But I also had a nagging feeling in my gut. Dave had been going through so much. His father had just died a few months earlier. He had taken a leave from college. What if these were all signs we were not meant to be?

I needed a break—some space to think.

So I gave Dave the ring back. There was a lot I was willing to compromise on, but not law school and not being open about an engagement. I didn't want to feel like I had to ask his permission to follow my career. I didn't want to keep secrets from my family. Surprisingly, Dave understood. We broke off the engagement, but we didn't break up. We were still together, just without the intention of marriage. To me, it felt like our relationship was back in limbo—my life was on hold. I was uncomfortable about the direction of my life and my choices for the first time since I'd entered college and decided to go to law school.

A few months later, Dave asked me again to marry him. At this point, I had gotten accepted into Thomas M. Cooley Law School (now known as Western Michigan Thomas M. Cooley Law School). I didn't want to say yes to him until it was clear we had the same goals for our future.

I had two conditions. First, if you're going to marry me, we must make this public. He wanted to speak to my father before we did that. Agreed.

Second, I was going to law school. No matter what happens with you, no matter what you do with college or your family business, no matter if we have to live apart. No matter what it takes. I'm going to law school. I needed him to promise me that he wouldn't fight me on this.

Dave wanted to make it work. He supported me even though it meant I was going to school just a bit over an hour away from him. He promised he would finish his degree once we were both in Lansing. He applied to the MSU Business College. We had the same traditional values and backgrounds, and now we had the same goals. And now finally—*finally*—Dave went to my father and asked him for my hand in marriage. It felt like we had the recipe for a forever marriage.

Though to be honest, the whole thing was underwhelming. My older self now says, *How dare you get married when it's underwhelming?* I don't even recall his proposal. It wasn't special. It wasn't memorable. Marriage, from dating, to proposal, to wedding, should be the biggest thing! At that point, I was only focused on the prize. On graduating college. On going to law school. On planning a wedding. Instead, I should have been focused on my life and what was going to make me happy as a person for the rest of that life. Like most women, I wasn't taught to focus on myself. I saw my life as a series of checkboxes that I had to mark off. If I had to live my life again, would I use a checkbox for everything? No. I would learn to enjoy the moment. To walk away or shift directions when things didn't feel right. I'd be more reflective. I would try to understand myself more. But that's not what I did. I plowed ahead with blinders to everything, including my gut, my intuition, and my growing number of questions.

Dave went to my father and asked for my hand in marriage. For the first time I was bringing home a man, the man I was going to marry. I thought they would be thrilled. Dave had a job. He was Italian, which is similar to Maltese. We had the same values. We lived in the same neighborhood.

My father said yes, but my family wasn't happy. Not at all. I didn't hear comments one way or the other at this point from my father because my father and I have never had, not then, not now, any heart-to-heart conversations. If my father was unhappy about something, he'd make quips. His favorite one for Dave was "well, I didn't pick him for you." Mostly, he'd complain through my mother. My mother is pretty easy going, but she's German. She is very direct and honest, but often what she says sounds harsh because it is always brutally honest. She's the one who broke it to me.

"What do you two have in common?" she asked. "How is he going to provide for you while working at his father's butcher shop or selling bread?" and "Is he going back to college?" and the question that still haunts me today, "What do you even talk about?"

I was furious. Defensive. I couldn't believe I was hearing this now after all this time. After all those boys sitting in cars outside of the house. After all those boys who were not allowed in my house, to meet the family. All those hours of listening to him torment me by opening and closing the garage door. Now they wanted to give their opinion? *Now*? Dave was not only the hardest working guy I knew, but he promised me that he would be there with me and that together we would raise our children, which was not my experience growing up. My father was always jumping up from the table to run to the phone or to the hospital for a patient or an emergency. While I understood my father's work and appreciated what he did for us, his absence was not conducive to meaningful conversation with him as a family at the dinner table, or any other time. Dave said he would be home with us, like his father was with him. That we'd have a stable family. I concluded that the problem was my parents didn't know him. Not at all.

"You've never gotten to know him," I cried. "You never wanted to get to know him. I don't care what you say now because you have nothing to base your comments on."

It was too late. I had my heart set on marrying Dave. I didn't need my parents' approval. Nor did I need or want their input. Not anymore.

Everything was running smoothly, like clockwork. The caterer. The menu. The guests. That was until it was finally the day of the wedding and Dave's older sister turned to me in the church parking lot as I'm about to enter the church to put on my wedding dress. "Rosie, are you sure you want to go through with this?"

While she may have been joking, and while it may have been kind of funny, it made me pause . . . did I really want to go through with this? You know, here you are, the rest of your life. *This is it.* I started getting butterflies in my stomach. My mind went wild with anxiety. *Oh my God, I've only had sex with one person my entire life. Is that what I want? What if I live to be 100? Can I live with this person for 80 years? Do I even want to be married to one person for 80 years?* But at that point, so much money had been spent on the flowers, the cake, my dress, his tux, the dinner. I thought, *Okay, it's just nerves. Everything is fine.* To this day, I can't understand why I didn't return to my car, dress in hand, and drive away. Without knowing it, his own sister had given me a sort of permission to do that. Instead, I told myself to calm down. If it doesn't work out, you can get a divorce. That's not the way anyone should *ever* enter a marriage.

The music started. Time for my father to walk me down the aisle. My father must have seen my stricken face or maybe he was just being himself. "You can't back out now," he said. "Let's go." It was shocking to me—like for once he'd read my mind. I looked at the Cathedral door behind us and almost turned out the door. But hearing his voice, his words in that second, made me determined to follow through. I reached up, grabbed his arm, and we turned toward the alter. I was smiling, but in my mind, the mantra was "you'll be fine. Follow through. It's just nerves. Tomorrow everything will be fine."

I walked down the aisle with my father toward Dave. He was very handsome in his white tux, and I suddenly felt okay, reassured with each step forward. My father released his arm and took his seat. I stood next to my fiancé and saw his smile. I knew everything would be okay.

In retrospect, I think Dave would have been okay if I would have said, "I can't do this today. Let's think about this much later down the road. Let's live together instead." In fact, at one point, I did ask my parents how they would feel if we lived together. The exact question was "would you pay for law school if I decided not to marry Dave and just live with him?" I think they were so shocked at the *idea* of it that they didn't even respond. I still feel the chill of that silence. Sure, it was the early 1980s and we had just gotten out of the sex, drugs, and rock 'n' roll 1970s, but my parents were old-school pre-1950s, maybe further back than that! They were of Old Country village mentality! There was no way I could have lived with a man before marriage. Based on their response, or lack thereof, to me, I figured my living with a man would have *broken* them.

Nevertheless, we had a fabulous wedding thanks to my parents. Family came from all over: Germany, Canada, Malta. There were a couple hundred people there. We had fountains of champagne and chocolate. There were three choices of food: beef, chicken, and a vegetarian option. We had an enormous wedding cake, with heart cakes around it, that had stairs leading to the higher tiers. There were four flavors of cake: white, chocolate, banana, and cherry. For favors, we gave out the traditional Italian white candy-coated almonds in netting with a little thank-you note. My best friends from high school were my bridesmaids; my sister, who was about thirteen, was my junior bridesmaid. My grandmother (Oma) from Germany came, which was very special. My Maltese grandmother (Nanna) from Detroit was there. It was an incredible family event and a truly romantic day. We had a wonderful, wonderful wedding. And my parents helped pay for our Hawaii honeymoon.

When we boarded the plane and the cabin crew learned we were newlyweds, they moved us into first class. We were so happy. I was so relieved. But then everything changed after we arrived at our hotel to really begin our honeymoon. Dave made an entire itinerary without talking to me. He booked tours. He rented a car. He made reservations. I didn't want to go on any tours, especially not the first day we were there. It was a long flight, and I was exhausted from the wedding. I wanted to sit on the beach, plus I was worried about money. But more importantly, it's not that I wouldn't have wanted to do those things, it's that I didn't want to be *told* I was doing them. I had enough of that growing up. For me, that was game over. I thought I'd married not just my friend but an equal partner.

Dave thought because he was the husband, that he was *the king*, and that all the decisions were up to him. "You go on whatever tour you arranged," I stated. "I'm going to the beach."

He was furious. I was furious. He went on his tour, and I went to the beach. I was so angry that I decided to stay out in the sun until I was burned. It made no sense to punish myself because I was mad at Dave, but that's what I did. After I burned to a crisp, I stormed up to the hotel room and sat in a freezing cold bath. What a *great* honeymoon.

I never once thought, *Oh, this is sweet.* Or *How nice that he's making all the plans.* Not once. Before we were married, we made all the decisions together. What movie to go to. What restaurant to go to. I didn't realize that *the minute* I said, "I do" I became property. *His* property.

When I searched my soul, *really searched* for red flags, there were none. Really, there was no neon sign that lit up, no message from the heavens that said, "This man is going to want to *own* you, to put himself and his plans before yours." We never had a deep discussion about gender roles, about my place in the family, or about his place in the family. In his mind, he was starting a traditional family. In my mind—well the only thing on my mind was law school. I couldn't see that Dave seemed to want me in the role of a submissive '50s housewife and was ultra conservative when it came to family roles. I couldn't foresee that Dave wanted traditional roles in our home and that I would lose my voice and have to take a backseat in everything we did. That he was going to want to call all the shots. That I had been demoted. That I lost my voice and my choice and my independence. That I was now a second-class citizen without a voice, and my choices were limited. That once I said "I do," he didn't.

And, over the years I've chastised myself for getting married and not seeing all this. But here's what I've realized: we're all prone to choosing not necessarily who is *best* for us, but someone *familiar*. Dave's controlling nature was a lot like my father's. I was probably attracted to that side of him without realizing it.

"This is *our* honeymoon," I said to Dave when he got back to the room. "It's not *your* honeymoon." He apologized, explaining that he had never been anywhere before and he was just excited about traveling. Instead of taking the opportunity to have a deep discussion about what we expected from each other, we just patched it up by compromising. We agreed to spend the rest of the trip together, and I just tried to get over it. What else could I have done?

Though divorce occurred to me, the truth is that my parents had been married for over twenty years. My grandparents stayed together for life. On my wedding day, Nanna said to me, "Now you work with hands, and feet, and teeth." In my family, once you get married, you stayed together and worked it out. *This is what you do*. I kept making excuses and telling myself that everything would be okay. I kept repeating Nanna's words to myself in my head, trying to honor and understand what she said and what she meant. I would not give up. I thought about marriage counseling early on but didn't think Dave would have understood why we needed it. At that time, people just didn't talk about even the idea of counseling—especially not men—especially not to open communication to prevent divorce.

Now, when I talk to young people in college and law school about marriage, I always tell them the same thing: do not get married until after twenty-five, because your brain is still developing until then. You want to make sure you have finished your education and training because that changes you. You want to be a fully actualized person when you're married. You want to make informed decisions that are going to affect the rest of your life. It's also incredibly important to follow your gut. If an alarm bell is blaring in your mind—listen to it! It's probably for a reason. Don't shrug it off. Don't talk yourself out of it. Walking out on a wedding is awful—but what's worse? Walking out on a wedding or being married to a person who isn't right for you?

* * *

Back from the honeymoon, Dave was busy working for the Rainbow Bread Company and earning a very good income. It was April. It was springtime. We were newlyweds. I was working at Town and Country at Fashion Square Mall in the shoe department and began selling Tupperware for extra money. We had a new apartment together. He'd moved into it a few months before we were married. I moved into it after the wedding. We were having a brand-new start living together in Saginaw. I was unpacking, organizing, writing thank-you notes, and making sure dinner was on the table when he got home. I wasn't set to go to law school until January, which was about nine months away. And for someone like me, who is always busy, always on the go, waiting nine months felt like an eternity.

"You shouldn't wait," my father said to me one day. "Let's drive to Lansing and meet with the dean and ask if they can move you into the September class."

I don't know why he decided to help me, except that he believed in education. Maybe because I got married. Or maybe he saw me as an adult now. Anyone who has had a turbulent relationship with a parent knows that all you want is love and acceptance.

"Really?" I said. "You don't know anything about law school."

"It doesn't matter," he said. "This is the way things get done. You're going to get into the early class."

Finally, after all these years of fighting me, my father was supporting me. He might have had an ulterior motive, maybe he was concerned about my marriage, maybe he was concerned that I would drop the idea of law school after settling in with Dave, but either way, it was a meaningful journey for us. Anyone who has had a turbulent relationship with a parent knows that all you want is love and acceptance. When we got there, my father and I talked to the dean and my father said, "I'd like to see her in the September class. Is there anything we can do?"

The good news was there are always people who defer and or change their minds. The dean put me on the waiting list for September. Sure enough, mid-summer, I received a congratulations letter that I'd been accepted into the September Blair class.

I was thrilled. Dave was not. He didn't want to live apart at all and definitely wanted to stick to the January plan.

But that's not how I saw it. I liked the spontaneity. I loved being able to pick up and go. An unnecessary delay wasn't in the spirit of what Dave had promised: I could attend law school and do whatever I needed to do. I didn't have his support. I tried to convince Dave it was going to be fine. After all, my parents lived apart for practically the first five years of my life: my father in Germany and my mother in Detroit with her in-laws. And they had two kids. We didn't even have any kids! We could do this. Finally, begrudgingly, he agreed.

A friend of mine from high school, Kathy McGraw, was also starting law school. Her parents had bought her this cute little house, and after learning we would be in the same class, she asked me if I wanted to rent a bedroom from her. It was perfect. I had my own space to study with no distractions, which was great because going to law school is like being thrown into a different country and having to learn a whole new language. A *legal* language. But I loved it. I went from being someone who was chastised for arguing to someone who was *encouraged* to argue!

Living apart from Dave, on the other hand, wasn't perfect. I saw him every month or sometimes every couple weeks—as often as my studies allowed. There is a lot of homework in law school, and the first term is especially hard. Dave didn't understand how tough law school was. He wanted me to be his wife. I wanted to be a law school student. I kept moving forward with my goal. My father's graduation words never left me: "From now on, what you do is for you." It's become my life's mantra. People always ask me, "How can you do so many things?" I say to them, "How *can't* you? If you have one thing to do in a day, that is all you do; if you have five things to do, you get them all finished." From a very young age, I knew I had to be self-sufficient. I knew I'd always have to tread water otherwise I'd go under. And I needed to swim.

In my law practice, I saw the ugly things people do to each other. On the bench, I see so much pain in the victims, often in defendants too. I have to remind people that it takes emotional intelligence to recognize you need help and it's a sign of strength to ask for it. It's never wrong to ask for help, and you should keep asking until you get what you need. That is a sign of independence. A sign of success.

When something is wrong, you have to *recognize* it's wrong. You can't pretend that everything is okay when it's not. I think that's what happened in my marriage. I didn't know that I should be asking for help. I didn't know I wasn't being supported in the proper way, and more, I thought it was a sign of weakness to admit to anyone that we were having trouble right from the start.

I was so young, married thirteen days before my twenty-second birthday. I simply didn't know I could say, *We're having problems. We need help. Let's find someone to help us work these things out.* I thought it was my job as "the wife" to clean up the mess—physically and emotionally. I wanted everyone to think that everything in my life, that everything I was doing, was perfect, just as it appeared from the outside. Even though it was all falling apart

chapter four

Legally Mom

By my second term in law school, Dave had moved to Lansing, and we were living together. He was working, and I was busy studying. We were so busy, not really spending much time together, which was probably good for us. It's hard to think about problems with your marriage when you spend so much time apart. Suddenly, I started feeling strange. My stomach was getting hard, and I was worried. I'd suffered from ovarian cysts since I was fourteen. Did I have an enormous cyst? Did I have stomach cancer? What was wrong with me? I was on birth control pills, and I had my period, so being pregnant was not on my radar. I went to the doctor to find out what was going on.

The doctor looked at me strangely. "You're at least four months pregnant."

What? His answer did not compute. How could it be with the birth control pill and two periods? And I was so thin. I hadn't gained an ounce. I was actually underweight. Pregnant?

"I can't be four months pregnant."

"Well, you are," he assured me as he measured my uterus. "I'd guess about eighteen weeks pregnant. Due the last week of August."

Well. The baby would be born during break, so it

wouldn't affect law school. But I knew life was about to change. I knew I'd better hurry and tell my husband, Nanna, and the rest of my family.

I called Dave immediately to make sure he'd be home for dinner. Over his favorite meal, I made the announcement, and he was thrilled. I also informed him that the family, beginning with Nanna first, needed to be told, personally by us, so we had some driving to do. Dave and I made the ninety-mile trek from Lansing to Detroit to tell Nanna. She was thrilled, immediately pulling out her crochet books and insisting I select colors for a baby blanket. Next stop, on the weekend, was my parents, not quite seventy miles away in Saginaw. My parents were floored and not exactly in a good way. My mother took it better than my father, immediately excited for her first grandchild. She was already deciding what baby clothes and blankets to crochet and wanted me to buy a cradle that she would pay for.

My father, on the other hand, drilled me with questions. "How are you going to finish school? How are you going to take care of your child and study? What makes you think you can do this? Why did you decide to get pregnant now, before you finished law school?" These questions sounded like I was at fault for something wrong, that what I did would take me way off course, that my goals were now far behind the rainbow. I was bombarded with the kind of judgmental questions I tell people to not ask because "why" blames and shames. I hadn't done anything wrong. Sometimes life happens. I didn't plan to get pregnant. Yet here I was, already out of my first trimester. Once I realized it was real, I was proud of being pregnant. I was married. I didn't do anything wrong.

I was proud of being in law school. I was proud to continue with all of my plans. There was nothing about this circumstance that would cause me to change my goals or back down. I would make the best of the situation, control the outcome, and not let the situation control me. It's not in my nature to give in or to allow anyone to naysay me into defeat. I rose to the challenge with more fortitude than ever. I would accomplish all I set out to do and much more. *Just watch me.*

"I'm going to finish law school, that's how," I told them. I was as adamant about my future as I always had been. "Besides, you had two babies while you were in medical school," I said to my father. "What's the big deal here?"

He made it clear that it wasn't the same. My mother worked, placed us in daycare, and cared for him, my brother, and me in Germany. Then, when it became too much, it was my grandparents who helped raise us until I was five years old. It didn't occur to him that my husband should pick up the slack, that Dave would be able to help with the baby while I was studying. No, because although my father helped my mother a bit and played with my brother and me, his focus was medical school, and helping with babies was not a husband's role.

"Well, I'm going to do it," I said. It wasn't an issue. It wasn't a question. It was my choice. I would do it all.

And eventually my father calmed down, and he and my mother jointly said, "Every baby is a blessing."

It wasn't just my father asking how I would finish school and be a mother. Dave was asking the same question. While Dave's grandmother was a stable female figure in his life, he mostly grew up without his mother, so having a connected family with a committed mother was important to him. He was worried I couldn't play that role and continue to pursue my career goals. Being a good mother was important to me too, but I also wanted a career, and I certainly didn't see the two as mutually exclusive.

I had a very easy pregnancy. I was busy with law

school while Dave continued to build his career. Despite being only a few credits away from his business degree, Dave never returned to college after David was born. He focused on his real estate license and additional training, and he quit working for Rainbo Bread Company. He was supporting our growing family, and I was really proud of him for it. His goal was to own numerous rental properties. He purchased his first one shortly after he was licensed. He was doing really well—well enough for us to afford a small fixer-upper Cape Cod house with a large backyard. It was severely in disrepair—which included leaky plumbing everywhere and buckets under every sink, holes in the walls, dirty cupboards, and falling plaster—every room needed paint, and there was so much more that we discovered was wrong. I was shocked it passed inspection. Dave said, "Either we buy this house, or we stay in the apartment. This is what we can afford, and I want to learn how to fix it up." I agreed. I had been given no choice but to agree. And I understood the lack of money and sacrifice. It was how I grew up. The baby was coming in a few months, and I needed to stay focused on school.

Despite our unresolved differences and decisions, we were happy. I was certain Dave had no clue I had any doubts. And anyway, I convinced myself to move past my concerns for the good of the baby and for the good of my career goals. I didn't want to rock the boat. Overall, it was a good time for us. With some luck, the house would be ready enough for the arrival of the baby and I would get the things for the baby after my exams. The timing couldn't have been more perfect.

Except August wasn't going as planned.

Our perfect starter house was taking much longer to fix up than we thought. Plaster dust became a permanent study companion. Then, when I removed the contact paper to paint the linen closet, the ceiling inside it caved in. And half of our sinks still had buckets. The house was an absolute money pit. The heat that summer became so extreme it was deadly. There were warnings to stay inside and to stay hydrated. So, except to go to attend class, I stayed indoors in air conditioning with something cold to drink and a daily slush or ice cream. My feet had gotten so swollen that I could only wear the Doctor Scholl's slide sandals on the widest possible buckle, and even those left deep indentations in my feet.

My brother Joe, despite his busy study schedule at MSU's medical school stopped over to check on me daily because of my swelling. My father, learning about my swelling, especially in my legs and feet said, "This baby is coming soon and will be here within a week." My brother agreed and tried to prepare me for this reality.

"No, no, the baby's not due for two more weeks, after my exams," I insisted. The baby couldn't *possibly* come early. Everything was perfectly timed so he or she would arrive neatly after my last exam. Plus, I didn't have any baby stuff at home. I mean *nothing*. No shirts, no diapers, none of the basics. All I had was the crib and sheets that my mother bought me and a cradle, plus a few outfits and blankets she and Nanna had crocheted.

And my outlines in preparation for my nearing exams weren't completed. (A law school outline is basically a detailed review of what you've learned in that course.) I stayed up late working on the outlines every night, fearful they wouldn't get finished.

Two weeks prior to my due date, pain erupted in my morning classes. I placed my hand over my stomach and tried to get through it. *This is just Braxton Hicks*, I told myself. It has to be. But something inside of me clicked. A rush of adrenalin. *What if it was the real thing?*

My first thought was that I had to go to Kmart. I didn't even have diapers! I drove from class to Kmart, praying the baby would wait just another ten days. I entered Kmart with a list of what I needed that I'd made in class. By now the pain was so bad that I was tossing things into the cart and hanging onto the shelving every time a contraction barreled through me. When the contraction subsided, I convinced myself it was fine, that it wasn't really labor. I focused on my list and continued throwing things like bottles, diapers, baby butt cream, and a baby bath into my cart. If it was baby related, I grabbed it.

Home, finally, in agonizing pain, I called my sister-in-law because she's a nurse. "Diane, I'm having severe contractions. I don't know if it's Braxton Hicks. I just can't be in labor. Besides," I rationalized, "Denise (their youngest sibling) was due two weeks ago. She has to have her baby first."

Diane laughed. She was excited. "Sounds like you are in active labor. Call Dave and tell him to come home."

Dave was out with customers showing houses. It was early afternoon. I left messages at his office, and eventually, I got hold of him. I explained that I was having contractions and that Diane thought I was in labor. "Come home now," I begged. I thought he understood what that meant. That now meant now. Clearly that wasn't the case.

I truly didn't know how I would get through the pain. Contractions shot through my abdomen and my lower back. I was an absolute mess. I called my parents. I called other family members. The clock was ticking, and my pain was getting worse. I tried to concentrate on my nearly finished outlines. Studying would get me through the pain. Meanwhile, Dave still wasn't home. I sat on the couch. Focused and diligent, I finished my outlines, read them, and studied them over and over. I had three exams to take. I kept praying that I wasn't in labor, and praying that, if I was, Dave would arrive before the baby did. How could he be showing houses while I was dying on the couch? Should I have called 911? Or my ob-gyn? Maybe my brother? Yes. I probably should have. But none of that occurred to me. I was used to doing things myself, taking care of myself in every way. I wasn't used to asking people for help. Asking for help wasn't in my vocabulary. I would learn soon enough that when you have children, you *have* to ask for help. You're left with no choice.

Plus, I was still in denial that this was the real deal. I tried to convince my body not to have this baby yet. *I'm finishing these damn exams, not having a baby,* I told myself between every contraction. Eventually, I was in so much pain the words on the pages blurred.

As women throughout centuries have learned, when a baby is coming, a baby is coming. You can be in a field, you can be in an apartment lobby, or you can be in the middle of first year law school exams. You have no control whatsoever.

The contractions were getting closer together and more intense. Dave still wasn't home. Soon it was four o'clock. Then five o'clock. Then six. I watched the shadows of the day turning into early evening and the shadows of darkness were beginning to emerge. Dave came home—finally—at dusk. "Where have you been?" I demanded. "We need to go to the hospital, now."

Dave was stunned. When I talked to him earlier in the day, I thought "Come home now" truly meant come home now. Apparently because I didn't say, "Get your ass home now," or because I didn't say, "Dial 911!" Dave didn't see it the same way. Once again, we were clearly not communicating.

Dave gingerly loaded me in the car, clearly overwhelmed by how much pain I was in. And though the hospital wasn't far away, the contractions were excruciating. Every bump in the road was torture. The hospital was like a scene from an old movie. There was paperwork, and I was admitted. The maternity ward was almost empty when I got there.

The birth plan was to have a natural childbirth because that's what they were promoting at the time and we had taken all the classes. But by the time we arrived, the pain was excruciating, and I immediately begged the nurses for medicine.

"No medicine," Dave told them. "No drugs. I don't want you to take anything that will hurt the baby."

I was arguing, "Hell yes, give me medicine! Give me what you got!"

Dave told them no. By the time we agreed that I could take medicine, the doctor told me it was too late for me to be given any. It was horrid. Absolutely horrid. After that experience, I believed in drugs and took them for my other labors.

After several hours, in what felt like endless labor, Dave turned to me and said, "I'm going to get something to eat." I didn't blame him for wanting to eat. But what he decided to eat was a peanut butter sandwich. I didn't see him eat it, so how did I know? Well, because when he returned, he tried to help me with some Lamaze breathing. Yes, Mr. Peanut Butter Breath was breathing on me, at me, telling me, "You're doing it wrong; you're not breathing the right way." This is not what you tell a woman in labor, and you definitely do not breathe peanut butter food fumes on her. Especially after you made her wait several hours in labor alone before you bothered to show up.

You're telling me you know *better than I do* about breathing Mr. I-Get-To-Sit-And-Watch? I didn't want to be anywhere near him. "He has to leave," I told the nurses. "Get him out of here!" That's right. I kicked Dave out of the delivery room. I begged the nurse to stay, took hold of her arm, and held her hostage. "You have to stay!" I pleaded with the nurse, wrapping my arm around hers, "You are with me. He is not. Get him out. Get him out now." The nurse quietly explained that what had been a quiet maternity ward when I entered was now jam packed and they were beyond room capacity. She couldn't stay—she needed to do her share to help tend to all the women in labor. When they finally wheeled me to the actual delivery room, I saw pregnant women lined up in beds on both sides of the long hallway and was grateful I'd had a room.

Dave eventually returned from banishment because my labor was going on so long, and at some point, the doctor asked if he could bring residents in to check me. It was a teaching moment, and I was fine with it. Dave was not. "No one is going to touch you down there except for the doctor." Again, it was just another instance of Dave acting as if he had control over me and my body. "My dad is a doctor, my brother is training to be a doctor, it's okay with me," I said. I gave permission to the doctor and residents to check me. Dave was upset. He didn't seem to understand that there was nothing sexual or sexy about me heaving in pain while I was in labor. This was about him exerting control over me.

Fourteen hours had gone by, and the baby was still not coming. They placed a monitor inside me to ensure the baby was not in distress. They finally discovered after all this time that the baby was posterior, which means his head was down but he was facing the wrong way. He was face up instead of face down. The doctor inserted his hand and flipped the baby into the right position. "Is he going to come out now?" I screamed through the pain. I was told there were still more hours to come.

After six more hours of excruciating labor, the doctor finally said, "You can push now." I will never, ever forget this because I pushed as hard as I could—and peed all over the doctor! Urine dripped from his glasses and the wall behind him, and he yelled at the snickering nurses,

"Did you at least give her an enema?" That did it. The nurses and I all openly laughed our asses off. I didn't feel badly or embarrassed. It actually felt good that someone else was suffering too. The nurses laughed louder. They were the ones who had been sitting with me doing all the hard work—not just with me but with *all* the other women in labor on the floor! My husband and the doctor were horrified. I thought it was brilliant.

My perfect baby David was born, twenty hours after I'd gone into labor. In a single instant, I was completely focused on David, my beautiful, healthy six-pound seven ounce baby. Holding him was an incredible moment. I instantly forgot the torturous labor as soon as he landed in my arms. He was all mine.

The doctor proceeded to the next phase of his job, which was to repair the episiotomy that he'd given me during the birth process. He grabbed a long needle and the attention of my husband. I heard the men talk. It seemed I was no longer in the room. "I'll sew her up as good as new," my male ob-gyn reassured my husband without addressing me at all. The men smiled and nodded in conspiracy.

I could not believe what I was hearing. This was more embarrassing than me peeing on the doctor. Only men could ignore the cut-wide-open naked woman in the room and discuss the tightness and renewal of my vagina. How this could be discussed as if I were invisible, without feelings, and without inclusion, was beyond me. How my body wasn't discussed with me was beyond me. It was a completely male-bonding, selfish moment between my doctor and my husband that invisibly scarred me. It remains something I have remembered and will feel embarrassed about for the rest of my life. There I am, twenty-three years old, just coming off a very long tough labor and delivery with all my body parts showing, thrilled to be holding my beautiful boy, and the men were concerned about what they deemed important to them. I didn't matter. The mantra in my head? *Marriage, an undivided whole, with the woman as property and the man as owner.* I'd felt this before, and here it was again invading the most important milestone of my life. Ugh. Male bonding over an episiotomy says it all.

Male culture has a general lack of sensitivity about trauma and understanding that words hurt. I am not a piece of property. I am human being. Not just a baby maker. I am first and foremost a woman and a human. In that moment, I felt more like a cow that just gave birth, that you put out to pasture to make sure she produces good milk and does what she's supposed to do.

I wasn't a woman; I was a commodity. I've never forgotten that feeling.

At some point later, I spoke to my mother about it. She was equally disgusted but not surprised. I don't remember talking to Dave about it because it was so humiliating. I didn't trust he'd understand and didn't want to hear that it was my problem, that it didn't matter because it was something important to him. It was more evidence I had to depend on me. Dave was my husband, yes, but not my partner.

I was completely overwhelmed with all the responsibilities of being a law school student and a new mom. My parents were an hour away—too far away to help on a regular basis with the baby. They paid for two months of a diaper service. My younger brother, Tom, and sister, Helen, were still in high school; my father was still working long hours; and my mother was managing his office. With the little money I had, I hired an older woman in the neighborhood to take care of David for three hours a day while I had class. I'd wake up early in the morning, make his bottles, pack a diaper bag, and drop him off at childcare. After class, I'd pick David up and take care of him, preparing dinner, doing laundry, then studying while he slept. Even when Dave was home, he rarely changed diapers or helped with David because he said his hands were too big to change a diaper or give him a bath. He'd never taken care of such a tiny infant. After dinner, I'd put David to bed, have a shower, then study all night and get up early and do it all again.

It all worked until I got the flu, had a high fever, and was practically debilitated in bed, unable to take care of myself, let alone a baby. "Dave, you can't go to work, don't leave me," I said. But Dave thought the baby and I could sleep together all day. The cradle was next to the bed. It would be fine, he told me. He had some fantastical notion of what it was like to care for an infant—none of it based in reality! He went to work. I was left incapacitated in the bed. Too weak to lift the baby—*his baby*. I shouldn't have even been around the baby. But he left. I called Nanna. I asked for help. Thankfully, my grandmother took the next bus in from Detroit and saved the day. She stayed with us for a few days, taking care of me. Taking care of the baby.

Yes, it was clear my husband was not part of the taking-care-of-the-baby-and-house equation. Occasionally I made him help fold the laundry or pick up something at the grocery store. When he was home, he enjoyed playing with David, but for the most part, expected me to do it all—woman's work. Before David was born, I'd filled the freezer full of homemade bread, pies, cookies, chili, and other meals so I could defrost them when I got home from the hospital. I bought into this idea that I was *supposed* to do it all. It was exhausting.

One night Dave came home close to midnight. It had been another long day for me. I watched him take off his coat, then I announced, "I'm leaving." I put my jacket on and started walking out the door. "Where are you going at this hour?" he said.

"I'm going out," I told him.

He looked at the counter and inside the refrigerator and said, "There's no formula. Are you going to make it?"

"Read a label," I said, and I slammed the door.

Oh, it was a party. I went bar hopping all night long. Okay, that's not what happened *at all*. I went to Kmart until it closed and then I went to an all-night supermarket, Meijer, and walked through the aisles until three o'clock in the morning. This was my way of having some adult time to myself. Quite the party.

I didn't know how to ask for help. I didn't want to be seen as a complainer. I complain about other things, like injustices in the world, but not when it's about me. The burdens were my own. I refused to ask for help. I didn't know how. And I didn't want anyone to say, "I told you so. You did this to yourself. You didn't listen."

In the 1980s, women were independent; we were working full-time jobs, we were working toward our careers. Yet, we were still responsible for all the other domestic responsibilities we had always been responsible for. Studies at the time showed that working mothers spent an extra month each year laboring around the house more than their husbands. And things haven't changed much since the '80s. Why? Researchers say that we women don't feel entitled to put our own needs ahead of our husband's. Stanford-based researchers Phil and Carolyn Cowan call this "unentitlement." What's interesting to me is that I always put my ambitions first. Always. Yet, everything else took a backseat: My health. My needs. It was a concept I'd have to learn to change—but it wouldn't occur to me until much later in my life.

In retrospect, the hardest thing to see was how alone I was in all of this. I changed diapers. I made the formula.

I shopped, cooked, cleaned, *and* passed my exams. And through all of this, my resentment for Dave grew. The more I accomplished, the more I pondered, *Why am I in this marriage? I'm doing it all by myself. What do I need him for?* Except I never saw myself as a divorced woman. Culturally, I believed until death do us part. As tattered as our relationship was, we were still together. He was a faithful husband and a good father.

And we still had sex.

My second pregnancy came as a complete and total surprise just as the first one did. My mother had given me $100 for my birthday and I decided to use the money to plant a garden. I thought Dave and I would be able to spend time together and bond over it, and our son could play in the yard while we worked in the garden. Gardening was a hobby that took me outside into the sunshine and away from my studies. But gardening is also a lot of physical labor. I was busy bending over, dragging big bags of soil, digging, and planting.

Suddenly, I started having fainting spells. I thought I was sick, or maybe it was just my low blood pressure. "Surprise," the doctor said, "you're pregnant." Another child conceived on birth control! The failure rate of birth control is pretty small, but I fell into that percentage. My two oldest kids were just meant to be here—that's the way I see it.

"Take it easy," the doctor told me. "Start taking care of yourself," he said. "And, no more lifting heavy things. No more bending over gardening."

I left the doctor's office in a daze. Absolutely shocked, I drove home, thinking about my life. *How am I having another baby? Do I have to stay married? How am I going to finish school?* All of this and I wasn't even twenty-four years old. Everyone's doubts about my future in law school and having a family felt real. How *was* I going to do all of this?

That's when I heard the police siren. I was speeding and didn't even realize it. I've gotten other tickets in my life, but this was my wake-up call. Could I do this? *Of course* I could. Plus, my brother and I were eleven months apart and look how close we were. My children would only be a year and a half apart and they'll be close like Joe and I are. I wanted to have a second child. So, what's another baby? Now was as good a time as any.

My father always said that with every child comes a blessing. While my father can be brash, he has some good rules to live by. And truly, Jennifer, my daughter, was a *great* baby. I thought David was a great baby. Never fussed. Jennifer, I could not believe, was an even *better* baby.

With two babies, I decided to take one semester off. I needed to get used to being a mom to two infants. No one believed I would go back to law school. No one. Yet, to me, it wasn't a question. I was going back. Why hadn't everyone figured out that once I said I would do something, it would get done? After I returned to school, I was busier, but my schedule didn't change much. But I was more worn down than ever. So, before my final semester started, I met with the dean. A typical law school semester at that time was about ten credits. To finish in one more semester, rather than two, I needed to take twenty credits.

Desperate, I pleaded my situation with the dean: I've got two kids. My marriage is probably going to fall apart. I missed the exams for one semester classes because I was in the delivery room with my first child. I've already done the work and my outlines are already prepared for the exams I missed; I just need to retake the classes. I begged him. He felt my determination and said he'd never allowed it before, but for me, he would allow me to take a double load.

While I'm proud that I pushed myself then, I look

back now and wish I had slowed down. I graduated college in three years. Graduated law school only one term late because I took the one term off when I had Jennifer. With a husband, a house, and two babies, I wish I'd taken more time to mature, not been in such a hurry, and not been so hard on myself. There was always that fear of failure ringing like a bell inside me. And because of it, I was always beating myself up, always wanting to prove the naysayers wrong—from my husband to my friends to my parents. *The hell with you,* I wanted to say. *You don't believe in me? I believe in me. And here's what I've done. And I did it. I did it all.* But now I ask myself: *At what cost to me? At what cost to my children?*

I've counseled other lawyers, other women, and my own kids. I've told them that it's okay to take the five-year plan. It's okay to give yourself permission to fail or to take time off, to spend time reflecting, to change course if you need to. I lived in such fear that if I didn't continue to move forward, to juggle as many balls as I could, that I wouldn't be accomplished and that I couldn't achieve my dreams—that I couldn't live my life. Or worse, that I would be stuck living someone else's dreams. That fear-factor kept me in overdrive. There is something to be said when you are growing, developing, and learning, about taking time to absorb it, taking time to figure out who you are, and to make sure that you're doing what you want to do. That took me a long time to learn. You have to give yourself permission to slow down. Permission to fail. Permission to walk away. Permission to change course. Permission to be the person you want to be, instead of the person you are expected to be. Most importantly, permission to be happy.

chapter five

Listening to My Body

Not long after I had my baby girl, I woke up in the morning and I could not feel my arms. It wasn't the first time. Ever since Jennifer was born, I had been feeling a creeping numbness in my arms and it seemed like my body was taking a long time to wake up and start fully functioning. I wrote it off—the numbness, the inability to move properly. I kept thinking that I was just tired from all I was doing, convincing myself I'd slept wrong and my arms had just fallen asleep. But as time went on, it was getting worse. Thankfully I had taken the semester off from law school. But tasks like changing the baby's diapers, including lifting the tape up to open and remove the diaper or put a fresh one on, was not only challenging, but it was also exhausting. Gripping the grocery cart handle to push the cart up and down aisles was not only difficult, it was daunting. My hands couldn't grip the cart, my fingers couldn't place heavier items like flour and detergent into the basket. I couldn't lift filled shopping bags into my car. I had no strength and very little power to maneuver anything. I was fearful of lifting the children.

There was a pattern. If my arms were hanging down, I felt fine. If I held my hands partially up, I felt weak. If my hands were held all the way up, I lost feeling and my arms became dead weight. They would drop, and I had absolutely no feeling. The only way I could feel my hands again was to leave them straight down for a while, no higher than my heart. And even that didn't always immediately help, and returning feeling to my hands was taking longer as days went on. But I kept writing it off, thinking it would go away, thinking I was doing too much. Then I went back to law school, and it just got worse. After all, the babies were growing and my law books were thick and heavy. *I just need to break up my load and alternate what I am doing*, I told myself. In short, I blamed my busy, overscheduled life. As mothers and as women, we often put everyone else ahead of ourselves. This is especially true for new mothers, and it was true for me. I simply rerouted what I was doing, but I didn't slow down, didn't stop, didn't ask for help. My best friend in law school, who remains like a sister to me today, Suzanne Dugas, a married mother of two, recognized I was struggling. With a smile on her face, she helped me carry my books with each pregnancy. When she was still helping me after I returned, she expressed concern. I saw the worry on her face every time she shouldered her books, then grabbed mine.

It wasn't that I thought it was normal that I couldn't feel my arms, but I just didn't have the time or the energy to make a doctor's appointment. I didn't have the mindset that there could be something medically wrong, only that I was at fault and that I could fix myself. The last thing I had time to do was think about myself and my needs. All I could focus on was making sure my children were cared for and I was doing well in school, keeping on task to graduate.

When I was young, I thought that taking care of others *was* taking care of myself. Now the media is all about self-care, but it simply wasn't something people talked about or valued at that time. It was not in my vocabulary or on my radar. Even the popular advertisement for the bubble bath where the woman exclaimed, "Calgon, take me away," meant that you could relax *after* all your expected work was accomplished. Calgon was the reward for completion. As for me, I was hell-bent on making sure everything around me was handled, working, and in place to achieve my goals, when in fact I was in serious trouble.

One morning, about six months after this all began, the alarm bells blared, and this time I couldn't turn them off. I literally couldn't lift my arms, couldn't move my fingers. I couldn't use my hands to even push a shopping cart. I couldn't feel fabric. And worst of all, I knew I couldn't hold a pencil long enough to finish the bar exam that was looming ahead. It wasn't just that my arms were asleep, I actually couldn't feel them, even when hot oil splashed on my hands when I was frying food. When I saw the look on my ob-gyn who saw the burns, it left an impression when he said, "You need to be there for your children." I don't recall the rest of his words. My heart simply agreed.

I was getting scared. And I finally had to admit the numbness in my arms and fingers was not because I was busy, and waiting for it to go away or fix itself was not okay. Since my father was a doctor and my first contact when I had any medical issue, I called him.

"Something's wrong with me," I told him when he answered the phone. Then I explained what had been going on. "I'm starting to think this is more than my arms just falling asleep," I concluded fearfully.

My father was immediately concerned. He advised me it needed to be investigated right away, that it could be anything from MS to severe carpal tunnel. I needed to see a specialist immediately, and he began making me appointments with doctors in Saginaw who he trusted.

I saw about a half dozen specialists. At least four

of them made me undergo a conduction study to check for carpal tunnel. In this test, they placed small electric shocks on my hands and wrists and measured how fast my muscles reacted. This is a terrible test. I felt like I'd been placed in the electric chair, like I was more experiment than girl. The doctors didn't confer with each other, nor did they trust the tests ordered by the previous doctor. So, four times this horrid test invaded my body. The four tests I had proved nothing except that it wasn't carpal tunnel. One doctor from Detroit, where I was eventually referred, made me wear a body brace that made my arms hang away from my body. Almost immediately the symptoms were more acute, but I gave it a few weeks to work. I got much worse. I was given a hand brace. I got worse. I was given exercises. I got worse. This trial and error went on for almost a year, and the numbness not only persisted but also got increasingly worse. By now I couldn't hold a pencil and I couldn't write long enough to take down a phone message or complete my exams. Peeling the tape of disposable diapers had gone from difficult to impossible.

Worried, my father continued to research my symptoms and became convinced he knew what I had. However, he could find no doctor he trusted who agreed with his diagnosis. I knew about the Mayo Clinic, a world-renowned medical facility, because we had lived in Minnesota and asked my father to send me there. He promptly not only agreed but also made me an appointment through a doctor friend he had at the Mayo Clinic. A week later, I arrived in Rochester, Minnesota, and was immediately scheduled for multiple tests—the first of which involved placing two cuffs on each arm, one on each forearm and one on each upper arm. The cuffs were hooked up to a machine that looked a lot like a heart monitor. I was asked to place my hands in different positions. They discovered that if my arms were in any other position except down next to my body, there was no blood flow.

Within an hour after my appointment at the Mayo Clinic, the chief vascular surgeon, Dr. Kenneth J. Cherry Jr., diagnosed me with thoracic outlet syndrome, also known as first rib syndrome. The doctor explained that the condition I had was not usually seen in people as young as me, but it was often seen as a result of car accidents or from a repetitive job or sports injuries. In my situation, he believed that with two pregnancies close in time, along with all the heavy lifting, the blood vessels in the space between my collarbone and first rib became compressed and caused numbness. The first rib on each side of my body was pressing against the main nerve, cutting off the blood supply to my hands.

"We usually see this in line workers and with people who do the same actions over and over. We're not quite sure what happened to you, but you need surgery."

Except I was graduating from law school. I didn't have time for surgery. I needed to take the bar exam.

The doctor looked me straight in the eye and said, "If you delay any longer, you will lose both your arms in four to six weeks."

"Seriously," I said, "I need to take the bar exam."

"Seriously," he said, "you are not taking it. If you try, you won't have any arms to do it with."

My mind went blank. I'd graduated. I'd overcome everything. Now I faced the loss of my arms. There was no room for compromise or making a deal. It was shattering.

What could I do? I had to accept that it would be another setback. The bar would have to wait. The doctor had a hunting trip planned, and I had to go back to Michigan to arrange childcare for my kids. I would need to undergo two separate eight-hour surgeries: one for my left rib and the other for my right rib. They would do the first surgery, let me recover, then a week later, perform the second. I'd be hospitalized for about two weeks. Before I traveled back to Minnesota, Dave and I drove the kids to stay with my parents in Saginaw; they'd stay there while I was at the Mayo Clinic. Lansing was only an hour away from my parents' home, so it was easy for Dave to hop in the car and visit the kids when he could. Once everyone was settled, I was on my own: I packed a light bag with pajamas, hair rollers, and a few bar exam books and got on the plane to Minnesota.

Staying in the hospital for two weeks is not fun. Between those surgeries, I was bored out of my mind. When I awoke from the surgery in my hospital room, I found that they'd not only attached me to an IV for fluids but also attached me to the wall where there was a bottle collecting drainage from around the surgical area. For the first four days after surgery, I didn't leave, hadn't been out of my room, and was only out of my bed to use the restroom. But when you're like me and you have a tremendous amount of energy, you start going stir-crazy. I wanted something to do besides read and watch television, both of which were difficult because of the pain medicines. I couldn't stay in bed anymore. I needed a change of scenery. And, on the fourth day, the drainage bottle was removed, and I felt well enough to decline some of the medications.

I told the nurse that I wanted to get dressed so I could go to the gift shop. She agreed that was fine. I did make it through the hospital gift shop door and walked around the entire shop. But it became clear this was simply not going to be enough. So, holding my healing arms close to my body, I looked straight ahead and not only walked out of the gift shop but also walked right out the damn front door of the hospital and went downtown to do some shopping. I wasn't nervous at all. I felt free and exhilarated.

I found this cute little shop just a few blocks away that had needlepoint. It was something creative, and it was about all I could do with my hands at that point. I bought all I could carry—enough to all that would occupy me for a few weeks—then headed back to the hospital. Back from my little excursion with a bag full of scissors, needlepoint, and colorful threads, I returned to the hospital exhausted but as happy as could be.

I soon discovered that while I'd been enjoying hospital jailbreak, the nurses and doctors had been looking for me. They pounced on me when I entered my room.

"Where the hell were you?" the doctor demanded with a glint in his eyes.

"I was bored!" I told him. "I know the liability for leaving is on me, but I couldn't stay hostage any longer."

"I've never had a patient escape," he chuckled, no longer angry now that he knew I was okay. "Look, I can write you a prescription so you can go out, but you have to tell us that you're going!"

Fair enough.

Unfortunately, the second surgery wasn't as easy as the first one. Once the surgery was over, I had trouble breathing. There was a tightness in my chest, a horrid unbearable pain, and I struggled to breathe. They discovered I had a tear in my lung. When you can't breathe, it really does feel like the end of the world. I had been through so much in the past three years: two pregnancies, law school, a rocky marriage, having to miss taking the bar. Look, when you can't breathe and you've just gotten out of surgery, it's easy to convince yourself you're going to die. Anything is possible, and I thought maybe this was really it. Maybe this was my fate.

Convinced I was going to die, I told the nurses to turn off the phone because I didn't want any calls. I didn't want anyone to worry about me. I didn't let any of my family know what was happening. I had learned to do that in any crisis—shut down and take care of myself. So that's what I did. I didn't reach out to Dave, to my siblings, or to my parents because I told myself I didn't want to worry them. I didn't want anybody to rush over to Minnesota. I didn't want anybody to talk to the doctors. I didn't want any interference. I didn't give my family permission to talk to the doctors either. My thinking was that I had excellent doctors. I was in an excellent hospital. What else could my family have done? I always took care of myself in all sorts of situations. Nothing was different now.

Alone in my hospital bed, I assured myself that my kids were in good hands with my parents. If it was my time, it was my time.

I knew my parents loved me. I knew my grandparents loved me. I knew my siblings loved me. I knew all of that. But there is a huge difference in knowing that you're loved and being able to tell someone you're hurt and that you need help. At that time in my life, I didn't know how to do that. And because I was so sick, and because my breathing was so labored, I was ready to die alone in that hospital. I was ready to come to terms with my very short life. And I was okay with that.

The *good news* was that they were able to make me more comfortable, and my lungs improved. But I learned a lot from that moment. It was yet another time in my life I needed support but didn't ask for it. This is not just an issue that I faced; it is one that I still face. This is an issue that I think all women face. We are so used to feeling that the weight of the world is on our shoulders and that we must take on the burden for everyone else. But of course, this isn't the case. I also know that the way I was raised, to be independent and self-sufficient, just sealed that mindset.

As a judge now, I make sure that people in front of me know that there is strength in asking for help, not from *not* asking for help. This is something I struggle with even now. It's still really difficult for me to ask for help. Luckily, I have a few people I can trust, and I am able to say, "I need help with this" or "This is what happened to me." I've learned to pick and choose who to be vulnerable with, who to trust, who to ask for help. I'm not great at it, but I'm better at it now than I was forty years ago.

After two long weeks in the hospital, I was able to go home. Thankfully, I'd packed light. I had to be very careful. I was not able to lift anything, and my arms needed to stay by my sides. When my plane arrived in Lansing, my husband picked me up from the airport and took me home to my kids and mother. Thankfully, she saved us, essentially acting as my nurse and caretaker for that first month. Really, I could not have recovered without her. I could use my hands slightly, but I had to retrain my muscles and my brain how to use my arms. I had been given very specific exercises to do to slowly learn to rebuild the muscles and allow them to reconnect and repair from the surgery. My skin turned very warm and tingly as the healing occurred. My hand movements were still limited to needlepoint. For the first weeks, I couldn't lift anything heavier than a needle. All my nerves needed time to recover and grow back. I couldn't cook. I couldn't pick up the babies. I couldn't do laundry or change a diaper. I couldn't drive. I couldn't write. Dr. Cherry would call me to check in with me and make sure I was following his orders—after my escape he wasn't sure he could trust me.

My mother helped me dress and bathe, cooked, cleaned, and took care of the kids. She did everything. Eventually, I got to the point where I could do small things like fold laundry, then cook, slowly lift things, write, and finally, after a month, pick up my babies again—but slowly and carefully. It was a long recovery.

It took a full year to regain everything, but the exercises that the doctor had given me helped me to not only retrain my arms but also undo some of the atrophy that had occurred. While my muscles were getting stronger, recovery was slow and painful, and I still hadn't learned to ask for help. As the nerves came back, there was a terrible burning sensation that I couldn't avoid. There was a loss of strength that would never return, But I had my arms and my life.

There are still parts of my muscles that atrophied because of that lost year I went undiagnosed. I can [illegible] in parts of my hands and arms. That damage couldn't be reversed. I'm never going [illegible] one hundred percent. I'm not going to win the strongest woman contest. I thank my fabulous doctor, Dr. Cherry (who I am still friends with), and the Mayo Clinic every day. I have my hands, and I'm stronger than Dr. Cherry and my father thought I'd be, and that's the most important thing.

About three months after my surgery, I took the bar exam. I passed. It was one of the happiest moments of my life other than the births of my children. I was now officially licensed to be a lawyer. Because I graduated a term late apart from the class I began with, and because we are not a family who celebrates every achievement, I decided not to go to the graduation ceremony.

"It's just a formality," I told my friend Suzanne. And I really did feel that way.

Suzanne refused to take no for an answer. "Not only are you going to go, but we're going to have a celebratory luncheon for you."

The group of female girlfriends I'd begun with were lovely. And the powerful friendship bond that began the first day of law school with Suzanne continues today, and we consider each other sisters. She coordinated our group of girlfriends, and they organized a wonderful lunch, presented me with some small gifts, and we just laughed and had good girlfriend fun. Husbands and extended family were not invited. And that was my graduation. My parents generously gave me a check for ten thousand dollars after I passed the bar exam, and I bought myself my first car. I was on my way.

Of course, my father prodded me. "So, when are you going to be a real lawyer?" Did I detect a hint of pride in his voice or was it something more sarcastic? Either way, my path ahead was clear.

"Yes, Pa. I am a real lawyer and I'm going to prove it."

chapter six

How to Listen

You would think that I'd want to relax and take some time off now that I had finally finished the bar exam. But that was not the case. Instead, I filled my time between job hunting by taking short classes in things like drawing, painting, and cake decorating. From taking macramé and other art classes in high school, to being a writer, creative outlets have always allowed my brain to unwind; they keep me sane. This was especially the case now. We didn't have the budget for massages or manicures, not to mention family vacations. But I always found funds for local classes—money I scraped together by returning bottles, saving my birthday money, and couponing. I didn't want to ask for money. I've never needed anything special, and the local classes were all I wanted anyway. Time out of the house also gave me a break from the kids, which as much as I love them, was very welcome.

It was extremely helpful to have away time for myself mastering something like candy making and then be able to come home fresh to the kids and the challenges of the house—not to mention fresh to my husband. Truth be told, he wasn't around much to relieve me or understand my desperate need for a break, an adult break, but he was surprisingly supportive of the classes because they fell under my "domestic" role. We all enjoyed the fruits of my labor, and my husband was prouder of what I learned in those classes than of anything I learned in law school. The skills I was learning *served* the family. If I had wanted to take photography or writing classes, he might have had a different reaction.

I loved the classes, and they filled my time, but my top priority was looking for work. Again, Dave was all for it, which might sound like a surprise. He seemed like the kind of guy who would want his wife to be a stay-at-home mom full time, but here was the thing about Dave: money never got in the way of his old-fashioned sensibilities.

It was a good thing he was on board with me working because I was lining up interviews all over town. Soon enough, I got an interview for a staff position with State Senator John Kelly who represented the five Grosse Pointes, Harper Woods, and the east side of Detroit. He was looking for someone with legal experience to serve as his administrative assistant and help manage his Lansing and Detroit staff and his campaign team. The interview went really, really well. To start, Senator Kelly and I had a lot in common. He had small kids, *I* had small kids. *He* had just graduated from law school; *I* had just graduated from law school. I had applied to the National Guard (something I had thought about doing from the time I was very young) and he was already *in* the National Guard. On the professional front, he wrote newsletters for each of the districts he represented, and I had been an English major with a journalism minor trained to write newsletters. To me, it seemed like a perfect fit.

Most people didn't understand or appreciate my eclectic background, but he did. I was creative. I was a hard worker. I had an enduring obsession with the law, with the military, and with doing things right and working hard to succeed. I put my family above all else.

Everyone, even my husband, my parents, and my friends, always questioned my ability to get it all done. But Senator Kelly was involved in diverse arenas the same way I was. So not only did the position with Senator Kelly feel like a better fit than working at a more traditional job like a law firm, but I felt he *understood* me.

Not many women were lawyers in the early to mid-1980s, and a lot of the places where I applied were on the lookout for women, which gave me a bit of an edge. If they hired me, I would be their "token" female. Indeed, quite a number of job offers began to come in, but I still hadn't heard from the senator. And I had decided that was the job I wanted. It was the job I was most curious about and the one that seemed to fit best with my background and interests.

When I didn't hear from him, I decided to call his office and make a follow-up interview with him. Scheduling your own follow-up job interview is not exactly typical—but that's what I did. I've never been accused of having a lack of tenacity. And oh, was it agonizing. Not only did he reschedule the meeting multiple times, but when his secretary called to reschedule, yet again, this time she also made it a phone appointment. Then to top it off, he was almost an hour and a half late for the call.

Finally, his voice came over the phone, sounding incredibly surprised. "I hear you want to meet with me? Why?"

And I was clear about it. I didn't hesitate at all. "Because this is *my* job," I told him. "I know it's my job. I have everything that you need in terms of background, and you said you could teach me the rest. I'm getting other job offers, and I need to know now if I'm hired or not."

His response: "You can start Monday."

Stunned, I thanked him, and hung up the phone. I got the job.

People have asked me how I found the confidence to make that phone call. It was a gutsy move to tell him that the job belonged to me and that he should hire me. But I knew this was my job. The way I saw it, I could open my mouth and say, "I need this," or "I want this," or "I'm the one who will get this done," or simply be up front as I did and say, "This job is the right fit, it's mine." I figured, *What's the worst that can happen?* Either I had the job, or I didn't have the job. End of story. With job offers coming in, I didn't want to turn them down while waiting around for the senator to get back to me. I had nothing to lose.

On the first day on the job, I asked him flat out why he waited so long to tell me I was hired if he knew he was going to hire me. He was truthful. "Because you're a woman," he said. "The lobbyists are mostly men. The legislators are mostly men. Most everyone you'll encounter will be men. I needed to make sure that you could handle yourself in this male environment. The minute you called me and you persisted, I knew that you would never let me down."

* * *

Going into the workforce was eye-opening. Senator Kelly was absolutely right. The legislature was completely male dominated, with only a few brave women fighting to be heard, sometimes literally shouting into the microphones above the male chatter: Senators Lana Pollack, Debbie Stabenow, Connie Binsfeld, and Lt. Governor Martha Griffiths. Law school had been somewhat similar in that I only had one female professor, but at least there were women in my classes! Here, it was like a scene out of *Mad Men*. The women were secretaries. The men were in charge. I was left floating somewhere in the middle.

The first day was a whirlwind. As part of my administrative assistant duties, Senator Kelly expected me to sit with him on the senate floor to assist with bills that were coming up, meet with lobbyists, talk to other legislators and staffers about bill amendments, and obtain cosponsors for his proposed amendments and legislation. I was one of very few women on the senate floor, and I was learning the legislative process right there in the trenches. Within the first fifteen minutes on the senate floor, Senator Kelly was explaining some votes that were coming up and some of the etiquette rules on the floor, but we kept getting interrupted by the phone ringing from his desk. Each time, he'd pick up the phone, he'd look at me, and he'd laugh at what the person was saying. This went on more than a few times. The phone would ring, and he'd laugh. I started feeling insecure. I had the real sense his smirks and laughs had to do with me.

"Did I do something wrong?" I finally asked.

He smiled. "They want to know if you're my new secretary or my new girlfriend."

The implication was that the only role for a woman in the legislature was as a wife, girlfriend, or secretary. These men never assumed I was a staff member. They never assumed I was a lawyer. They never assumed I was qualified in my own right.

"Oh," I replied.

And then we got back to work.

Look, I had plenty of experience with sexism. My own father would sometimes take me to the hospital with him to do rounds, and I watched him treat the nurses around him like his pets. I also saw the respect they had for him. It was part of the culture. It was confusing to me because, while I wanted the respect I'd earned, it came with the price of accepting being simultaneously diminished. Women were objects. They were sweet little accessories. They were meant to serve and be silent about it. And though it was something I was used to (did I have any other choice?), I didn't feel incapable because of it. And I didn't feel insulted. At that time, sexism was extremely challenging to battle head on, so I adopted an *I'll-show-them* attitude. It is a mantra that streams through my brain almost daily to this day. The hurdles still very much exist despite how far we've come.

Eventually, I got to know all the senators and representatives on both sides of the aisle, their staff members, and most of the lobbyists. Regardless of whether they were on the Democratic or Republican side of the aisle, most people learned to trust me and ask me for legal help or a legal opinion. Not because I was a woman or because I was somebody's girlfriend—but because I was capable and trustworthy and I finished all tasks. I loved learning how laws were made, and I respected procedure. Yet there were still moments where the line blurred. I'll never forget the day the minority leader, who we shared a suite with, asked me if I could sew a button back on his jacket. It took less than five minutes, and I did it without question. But his female secretary and administrative staff, one male, one female, weren't happy about it at all. "Why would you cater to him like that?" they asked.

I get why they took it as sexist and why they were offended. I knew damn well that I was being asked to sew on a button because I was a woman and maybe because of my ethnicity. Would he have asked a man to sew his button on? No. But from my perspective, my grandfather was a tailor and my grandmother was a seamstress. For me, sewing a button is like putting on a Band-Aid. And I operated with a get-it-done-for-the-team military attitude that many people do not understand. We must have each other's back for the good of all.

But look, this wasn't a situation where the boss was blatantly disrespecting me on a regular basis because I was a woman. I was treated with respect in the state senate; I wasn't barraged by "women's work" requests, and I didn't feel demeaned by it when it did happen. I take pride in my work—even if that means sewing a button on someone's jacket like my grandparents did. I take pride in teamwork and believe we succeed because of teamwork, not labels. I don't think there's a male or female category for anything in this world except maybe for having babies. I don't like those categories, I didn't abide by them when I was a child, and I didn't abide by them when I worked in the legislature. I'll never abide by them.

Plus, how could sewing on a button for a senator who was the minority leader have possibly insulted me? At least at work I was *asked* to sew on a button. At home, I was *expected* to do it. Sexism wasn't just present in my workplace (and let's face, it was everywhere I looked back then) but in my marriage. From the moment I met Dave, I was a fully actualized person. I knew what I wanted. I knew my potential. I knew that I mattered. That's who I was. That's who I am now. But Dave never caught on. Despite being married to an independent, strong lawyer, Dave never moved out of his Old-World mentality. At one point, Dave handed me a sock with the heel ripped out. He asked me to darn it. I nodded and took the sock. I faced him holding up the sock and said, "Darn it." I ripped the whole sock as I spoke. And I threw that darn sock away. He never asked me to darn anything again. Sometimes even a domesticated, hard-working, Maltese/German woman who knows who she is must take a darn stand! And darn it, I still feel good just at the thought of that darn moment. And it was another moment I realized that I needed to deal with my marriage, but later—darn it. Okay, enough, you get the darn point.

* * *

I worked for State Senator Kelly for almost ten years. I ran the staff and issues in both offices, the Lansing one and the Detroit district office. I attended committee meetings; testified on bills; worked with lobbyists, the Legislative Service Bureau, and individuals on drafting legislation and amendments; put in five bill requests every month; and drafted letters to constituents. I dealt with many state and local offices helping problem-solve constituent issues. I wrote regular articles and put together quarterly newsletters. I spoke to community groups. I regularly presented senate tributes and resolutions on behalf of Senator Kelly. I ran his campaign and fundraising and prepared and filed his campaign finance reports. I did everything I could for him and sometimes fulfilled requests on behalf of his family so he could accomplish even more. I was his right-hand person. It was an incredible job, education, and opportunity.

But it also gave me the ability to hear people's stories and what struggles they were facing. Juggling multiple responsibilities had always been a strength of mine. But public outreach, especially at this level, with these numbers, was new. I thrived on hearing constituents' stories and putting a team to work to problem-solve. I tried to do what I could with the resources we had. It wasn't easy.

Constituents are always calling and screaming about what was wrong and what they needed. And, most of the time, it's out of desperation. I mean, when people are calling the state senator's office, they're not calling to say, "Oh, have a pleasant day. Tell the senator we think he's great." No, these people are losing their houses. They need emergency funds. They need diapers. Food. Part of our district was in Detroit. Detroit's poverty rate was very high in the 1980s and continues to be very high. My best way to calm them down was by asking, "What would you like me to know? How can I help?" When you talk to someone who is going through a traumatic situation like losing their home or not having enough money to feed their kids, the question "how can I help?" stops them in their tracks. It calms them down. It gives them a chance to tell their story.

Usually by the time a troubled constituent reached me or my staff, they were at the end of the line. No one had listened to them. They'd called every department. They'd waited in lines. Asking them this simple question really taught me the power of creating a space for a person to speak and the power of listening. When they knew I truly was listening, and I not only heard them but got the full story, I was able to cut through the red tape and find the right answer and real help. Once I saw how effective it was, I asked my staff to do the same.

But it wasn't all hardship and crisis either. One call I'll never forget required me to get creative. A troop of Boy Scouts from our district was travelling out of state, meeting troops from all over the country. They were tasked to bring something unique to Michigan for each of the other troops. They wanted something more than just a Michigan flag or senate resolution, both of which I made sure they had. I suggested the stone of Michigan, the Petoskey stone. The troop leader was ecstatic. "Can you really get those for us?" they asked. I didn't know but promised to try. I contacted a group of Forest Rangers up north who worked in the Petoskey area and explained the situation. A week later, I received a box of over fifty Petoskey stones that the Forest Rangers had collected. Senator Kelly mailed them the box with a lovely letter. They were thrilled.

In any situation, "What would you like me to know?" became a mantra for me—followed by "how can I help?" And with that, I was able to reach out to the constituents and assist them as best I could. I thrived in this role and learned that troubleshooting and thinking outside of the box came naturally to me. I respected the people I worked with and the people I worked for. Ultimately, my experience working in the state senate gave me many useful tools and worked well with both practicing law and what has been one of my most rewarding careers: the military.

chapter seven

How to Serve Your Country

There weren't many photographs in our house when I was young. However, there was one, black and white, displayed in my grandmother's house, of my father in his army uniform from the Korean War. He wore a brown military jacket adorned with medals, and the words *US Army* emblazoned over his heart and *Aquilina* over the right pocket. He looked so distinguished. Next to it was a black-and-white picture of my Uncle Chuck in his navy-blue sailor uniform with its bell bottom pants and white sailor hat from his service on the *USS Bainbridge*. The back of the shirt had a white trim flap, and he wore a white sailor cap like Popeye. I loved that hat and thought it was perfect for me. (In fact, years later when I attended college, my grandmother gave me my uncle's old wool sailor's uniform. I wore it on cold winter days in college, then returned it to him for his sons.)

I spent my early years staring at those photos of my father and my uncle. I thought the uniforms were simply majestic, the prestige of it, the serious stature. *Look how pressed the uniform is,* I would think. *Look at the medals shine.* While my father had retired before I was born, my uncle would return from duty bringing me and my brother Joe wonderful toys from ports across the world. And cemented in my mind was *I want to wear that uniform.*

The uniformed photographs of two strong male figures in my life stayed alive in my mind as I grew. Here were two people who I loved and respected in military uniforms. These uniforms became the ultimate symbol of structure and control to me. They meant taking change of your own destiny, being in command. I had grown up with so much internal chaos from feeling kidnapped from my grandparents' home and moving from place to place with my parents, to the challenging relationship I had with my father as a teenager, the military beckoned as an antidote to all that. Even as I pursued my dreams of being a lawyer and then a judge, getting married and having children, I remained true to my conviction that one day, I would serve—and it honestly didn't occur to me that anyone would be less than fully supportive.

I remember my grandparents always saying to my brother and me, "There's no place like America." As immigrants, they believed that America was the land of opportunity. In America, you can be anything you want to be. I took that message to heart. *They* felt blessed to be here, so *I* felt blessed to be here. What's the best way to show your love for your country? Join the military. For that and so many other reasons, I wanted in.

Just as a side note, before I even passed the bar, I decided to fill out the paperwork to join the Navy. I knew I was going through some medical issues, but, as I'm sure you can imagine, that was definitely not going to stop me. However, I soon discovered the Navy isn't exactly family friendly. They wanted me to commit to moving anywhere in the world for two years, and while the opportunity sounded exciting, I couldn't do that to my children.

But this obstacle wasn't going to stop me. I started

investigating all the options the armed forces had to offer and was delighted to discover the perfect solution: the National Guard. I learned that the Michigan Army National Guard was a more family-friendly option. You only needed to commit to one weekend a month and two to three weeks in the summer. If we were called up for extra duty, for instance, as I was during Hurricane Katrina and during Operation Desert Storm, I would only have to leave for an extended period of time. It seemed entirely doable. So, I applied while I was waiting for the bar results. The time was right. I just needed my results for the final application steps. And then when I interviewed with and began working for State Senator Kelly, who asked me what other commitments I would have besides my family and working for him, I explained my plan. Senator Kelly was not only supportive, but he was also in the National Guard, and he encouraged me to continue the process, even offering to help. He told me I'd made the right decision. I was even more certain my long-time goal would be accomplished. It helped that my enlisting wasn't a problem for him nor a roadblock to working for him.

I had never been shy about my passion for the military—that's for sure. But it was time to finally have the conversation with my husband. One night after I'd filled out the paperwork, I sat with Dave after the kids were finally in bed. "Dave," I said, "I've decided it's time for me to enter the military. I've decided to enlist in the Michigan Army National Guard. I'm sending the final paperwork in."

He didn't have much of a reaction initially—except for a bit of a surprised look and a frown. I don't think he believed me.

But when he saw my paperwork in order, Dave became more concerned. "You are a mother. I didn't think you were serious about joining. You have a job with the senator, you don't need to join," he said. "What if you get called to war?" Sure, that was a reasonable fear, but it was also true that the kids would have Dave. And my parents weren't that far away. Plenty of parents go off to war and the families survive. My own family had survived it. "You watch football games on the weekend," I told him. "You go to the golf course. I'm serving my country on the weekend. One weekend a month. It is not a burden, it's a privilege. And it's my choice."

"What if I join?" Dave said to me, thinking that that would somehow deter me.

"Great," I said. "Extra income." He didn't expect that response. Truly, if he wanted to join, I would have welcomed it. I saw it as a plus. And something we could finally share.

But Dave didn't join. He got angry. In fact, Dave got so very, very mad at me he did something I hadn't expected. Furious that I didn't listen to him, believing I was leaving him, leaving the kids, he called my father. (As if *that* would change my mind!) The pair who had never bonded joined together against me, trying to control my future. *What are you doing? What if something happens to you? What are you thinking? You're a woman. You're a mom. You just recovered from a major illness. You're working. How are you going to do all this?*

I explained to my parents, my siblings, my entire family, and over and over to Dave, that it would be one weekend a month and a few weeks in the summer. It wasn't going to change anything about my daily life with my children. It wasn't going to change anything with my job. Senator Kelly was supportive! But their arguments wouldn't end.

"You never talked about this!" my parents said.

I explained to them that it had been a dream since I was a child. That my father's and my uncle Chuck's military photos, honorable service, and stories inspired my decision. That the military had helped our family thrive. They didn't care. They claimed I never spoke about it before. And there was the root of the problem: They never heard me. They never listened to what I wanted.

"I have wanted to do this since I was three years old," I cried. Not that it mattered. If I had just thought of it this year, that would have been my prerogative, but I thought maybe giving them insight to my process about how strongly and emotionally attached I felt to the army because of our family history, that they would understand a little bit better. Clearly, that wasn't the case. Not only did they not believe me, but to this day, they still don't. They reminded me that I never listened to them and that I always did what I wanted despite their counsel and their mandates. On this point, we simply had to agree to disagree.

The only two people in my family who supported me were my brother Joe and my grandmother. My grandmother laughed when I told her. "Oh, Rosie, that sounds like you," she said. Joe was encouraging because he and I have always been in sync. We've always supported each other's career decisions. Other than that, there was no one in my life who said, "Good for you." My mother voiced her worry for my safety, and I knew she wouldn't cross my father to voice her support, but I felt that despite her silence, there was a female voice in her that said to me *go for it*—at least that is what I hoped.

Everything my parents and Dave said was negative. I had heard it my whole life. "Why do you think you can get into law school?" "Why do you think you're going to get the job for the state senator?" "Why do you think they want you in the military?" "Why did you get married and become a mother if you were going to join the military?"

My inherent response: *just watch me*. Anyone might wonder how I'd juggle it all. And yes, I'm sure they were concerned for my safety to a certain extent. But this wasn't about that. This was about me as a woman, as a mother, and that I wasn't doing what they and society "expected" of me. And there I was, once again going against the grain, fighting for support and to be heard—even encouraged—in something I felt strongly about. My family's questions and concerns felt combative. And, of course, they were. A wife isn't supposed to be a leader. She's supposed to be subservient. She'd supposed to consider everyone else's needs before she considers her own needs. She certainly isn't supposed to join the Army National Guard.

Furious about my choice, my father refused to talk to me for an entire year. It was extremely hurtful, yes, but it was more of the same and it wasn't going to change my mind. And, by the way, I wasn't anxious to talk to him either. The deafening silence was okay with me. The military was my dream, not theirs. My life had really come full circle. When I was little, my grandparents always said to me, "You can be anything in America. You can do anything in America. We live in the best country in the world." I came here stateless to this country as a child, and once I joined the military, I belonged somewhere, somewhere I would be heard, somewhere I would be equal. Soon I was serving in the Judge Advocate General's Corps (JAG for short) as part of the Michigan National Guard in which I would experience some of the most meaningful moments of my life.

* * *

I knew that I was qualified. I knew that I had filled out the paperwork correctly. I knew that I not only passed the entrance physical exam but I had also been granted a waiver for a modified physical training test because of the weakness that remained in my arms from the removal of my first rib on each side. What I didn't know was that months would pass and my completed packet wouldn't move from the corner of a colonel's desk. I began to call and ask for answers and demand a specific date I would be sworn in on. More months passed. Tired of excuses I designed a plan. The military, like most governmental agencies must need volunteers. Who turns down free help? Right? I contacted Colonel Ralph Wilbur, commander of the Michigan Army National Guard JAGs, and offered to volunteer, arguing that I wanted to not only help but also learn what I would eventually be paid to do. He quickly agreed because there were several court martials, in addition to a few cases, that would soon be argued before the Michigan Military Tribunal.

The JAGs were on deadline. I was about to become immersed in the Uniform Code of Military Justice. I was thrilled. The morning I was to begin, not having a uniform, I donned my best and tightest jeans, my blue cowboy boots, and a blouse that I carefully buttoned to the top. These were the clothes I was most comfortable in. These were the clothes I knew would receive attention—not for a date, but for a uniform.

I arrived at 700 hours (7:00 a.m.). Around 1000 hours (10:00 a.m.), many officers took their coffee break. The JAG office was on the second floor in the building we were in at that time. I wandered downstairs to the break area where there were snacks, donuts, and coffee. Once inside, I took my time. I introduced myself to a few people and made small talk, including with General Andrews who I recognized from pictures and from his rank. Everyone was very kind. But by the time I returned to the second floor, coffee in hand, Colonel Wilbur had the phone a few inches from his ear with one hand, and with the other, he pointed at me. I walked toward him and heard their conversation which went something like this:

"Why is that girl not in a uniform?" General Andrews asked in a raised voice.

"She has her paperwork in order. She offered to volunteer while she waits to be sworn in, and I agreed," Colonel Wilber said. "No date has been set."

"Where's the paperwork?" General Andrews asked.

"Sitting on the desk in the Colonel's office next to you."

"Get that girl in a uniform!" General Andrews ordered.

I was sworn in the following weekend. Just before I was handed the contract, the commitment of six years was crossed out and replaced with eight. I laughed and said, "You can write down twenty. I'm staying the full twenty." Then I signed it.

I was sworn in, and while the General shook my hand and welcomed me, he said "Aquilina, the only thing that would have been better is if you would have been black." Was that inappropriate? Yes. Shocking? No. Nothing has come easy for me, for women, or for any minorities. In that moment, I learned I was the first and only female JAG officer in the history of the Michigan Army National Guard. We did, several years later, and thankfully, welcome other minority JAG officers who I had the privilege to serve with.

My first military lesson after I was sworn in was this: The uniform doesn't come free. I was going to have to buy my own clothes, and it was quite an investment. Luckily a female officer, a nurse, who became a friend of mine, and who later became a client, took me to the Selfridge Air National Guard Military Base PX, the base military store. It was good to have a female friend walking me through this whole new world. That's where I got my first boots, my uniforms, my rank, and ordered my name badges. So many years after admiring pictures of my father in his military uniform and looking up to my Uncle Chuck in his Navy uniform, here I was, gazing at my own reflection in the mirror of the tiny PX dressing room. I was a real life, in the flesh officer of the United States Army, Michigan Army National Guard. It was *exhilarating*. And worth every penny. Some people might feel that way about a new car. I felt that way about these clothes. I finally felt empowered.

There's a slew of tiny details that go into basic training. But back then, that kind of training wasn't available to JAG officers. Today, JAG officers go to what we call a "Knife and Fork" school so that they can learn the basics in a few weeks. Instead, I had to rely on other officers to teach me and on boxes of correspondence courses we were required to take. I was lucky in that I met a fast friend in Captain Mark Welch, who showed me the ropes. Here's how to spit shine your boots, here's how you burn hanging threads off your uniform, here's how you tie your boots and make sure that the shoelaces aren't fraying, and here's how you salute. We went out in the field a few times where he showed me ground rules like you don't ever leave a trace of a cigarette butt or a gum wrapper because an enemy can see that from the air. These seem like small details, but in the army, the tiniest of details count. And in my free time, I flew with our pilots in various army aircrafts when they needed to get flight time in or when they were scouting as part of *Operation Green Sweep*, which we loosely termed *Operation Hemp*—locating marijuana fields from the air. I saw firsthand how the enemy can track wet footprints, broken branches, and paper of any kind left behind and just how visible red and white are and how invisible camouflage is.

The greatest gift Captain Welch gave me was that he treated me like one of the guys. Other male officers saw that and followed accordingly. It's rare in life to have a man in your department say, "Here's what you need to know because we want you to be all you can be." From the time I was sworn in, to putting on that uniform, there were men who helped me be all that I could be. I don't have to tell you how unique and special this experience was. To this day, in my role as a judge, there's not one man who's come to me and said, "Hey, let me help you around." But can you imagine if every industry worked this way? Where women were welcomed with open arms. Captain Welch treated me like his buddy, no more no less. So did the other JAG officers.

Look, I know there are bad people in the military, and I ended up representing many of those people. I'm not going to pretend that bad things don't exist in the military, because yes, they certainly do. But that wasn't my experience. The men I was surrounded by were not just good people—they lifted me up, went out of their way to help me. I never felt so unconditionally and completely supported. It was not a chapter in my book of experiences until then. And I am not convinced many women, even my *daughters*, have ever experienced anything like it.

In the military world, we're not seen as humans but as assets. I don't mean that military folks aren't warm. Quite the contrary. When I put that uniform on and entered the military building, I immediately felt like I was part of the family. Even though I was only reporting for duty one weekend a month and two weeks in the summer, it always felt like I was going home.

* * *

I had the men on my side, but I still had to pass my most daunting test: receiving the approval of the general's wife. The Michigan Army National Guard, especially back then, still rested on some Old-World traditions. There was a certain hierarchy where women in pearls and white bouffant hair, their husbands smoking their cigars, were important to the social structure. And in this social structure the general's wife was a very big deal. "If you pass muster with the general's wife, you're good to go. But if you don't, there will be a problem," Mark warned me.

The general's wife, Grace Marie Andrews, who we fondly referenced as Gracie Andrews, was like Queen Victoria reigning from her throne on the porch of the officers club. With short blonde hair, perfectly done, her outfit prim and proper, her perfect makeup and nails, she would sit there watching as we filed in. If we didn't have our hair just right or our uniform just perfect, if there was one reason she didn't think you were up to snuff, then she would discuss it with her husband, General Vernon Andrews—the two-star general. Obviously, I didn't want to start my first experience in the army on the General's bad side.

There was an element of irony to this situation. I didn't feel guilty about leaving my kids for the weekend or for the summer camp weeks. I didn't feel worried about my uniform. Captain Welch had my back. The officers liked me. Yet here I was trying not to offend a woman who wasn't even *in* the army! The truth was, I just needed to be myself. Respectful, polite, my hair in place, my uniform straight, following the rules. And that's what I did. Not only was she lovely, but she told me that she liked my hair.

Past Gracie's review, we swiftly headed into the officers club, and Captain Welch gave me a pat on the back. "Well, you've just made it. You passed muster. She was nice to you, and she didn't have anything negative to say." I had passed my first test.

chapter eight

Rules of the Court

During annual training for the National Guard, which is the two weeks of summer duty where you emulate wartime, there are always a number of people who decide not to show. No-shows or those absent without leave, AWOLs as we called them, happen during the once-a-month training as well, but it is usually most egregious in the summer. During the mid-1980s, this was especially rampant.

People don't show up to service for all sorts of reasons. Most commonly, an employer might threaten to fire the soldier if they left for National Guard duty. People were not educated about their military rights, and they often felt they were left to decide *Do I go AWOL, or do I lose my job?* In actuality, it's against the law to stop a military person from showing up for duty. The Soldiers and Sailors Civil Relief Act, enacted in 1940, renamed and amended in 2003 to the Servicemembers Civil Relief Act (SCRA) specifies that soldiers called to duty to serve our country, regardless of whether they are called for military training or for active duty, cannot be fired or demoted or suffer the loss of any benefit that they are entitled to receive because of their service. Soldiers must be free to serve without worry of loss of employment, promotions, tuition or college placement status, the inability to pay bills, etc.

Despite all the education and outreach that was done, public awareness of soldiers' rights was really at a low ebb at this time, partly because of the large stretch of time, about twenty years, between Vietnam and Desert Storm. Military cuts were rampant and a lot of education and reeducation around the legal rights of soldiers and the immediate families they leave behind was needed. This wasn't just a learning curve for the public, it was also a learning process for the soldiers.

There had never been a formal program to address the problem of no-shows and accountability, but Major General Andrews directed our JAG Commander, Colonel Ralph O. Wilbur, to form and execute a state-wide plan to collect the soldiers who were AWOL. It was called "Operation Recovery." And I was put in charge. It was now my duty to handle Operation Recovery during my annual training with the Michigan Army National Guard and my weekend duty throughout the year.

Why did this duty fall on me, the newest JAG? Because no one else wanted to do this job! I saw it a different way though and was thrilled to have the responsibility and the exposure to the brigades, the commanders, and the soldiers I served with. It was a tremendous learning opportunity and a time of cohesion, team building, and verification that this woman—all women—belong in the "man's" army.

Keep in mind, I was also the only female JAG officer at the time. We had one very competent female law clerk, Sergeant E5 Joan Kirby (Burke), and the two of us quickly set up a complex system using maps, teams, check-ins, and documentation. I regularly had to brief over a hundred soldiers and military officers in an area half the size of a high school gymnasium. I also did briefings at the headquarters building, once or sometimes twice a day. It was exhilarating.

There were also moments of real levity. During one particular Operation Recovery, a soldier had been accidentally given General Andrews' jeep. It was about two o'clock in the morning and my commander, LTC Charles Palmer, and I were on duty. General Andrews had been calling us nonstop: "Where is my jeep? How dare you give someone my jeep?" Look, there are certain rules in the army. One of them is that you don't touch the general's jeep. Plain and simple. And yet, it had somehow happened.

Of course we apologized and promised we'd recover it, but it was also really funny. How did a soldier accidentally drive away in the general's jeep? Luck chimed in its humor in that the soldier who had taken the General's jeep was absolutely the *last* one to come in, near midnight. Thankfully, he and the military police returned with a recovered soldier.

Nevertheless, when you take a general's jeep, even accidentally, you have to take some heat. "Soldier!" Colonel Palmer commanded, "Look under that hood."

The kid shit in his boots as quivering arms lifted the hood. Vehicles in the Michigan Army National Guard that belonged to generals were marked by one big star under the hood. The quaking soldier raised the hood of the jeep. There it was. The star. I recall the whites of his eyes staring in silence at the star, then at us, then back at the star.

"What is your name, sir?" LTC Palmer asked. LTC Palmer was a good man, but, at over six feet tall, he was intimidating. It's never fun to have an enormous and powerful guy breathing down your neck. The soldier was still shaking. LTC Palmer took it a step further. "Soldier," he pointed a firm finger at that star, then launched it toward the soldier. "You stole the General's jeep! What is your name, soldier?" LTC Palmer leaned toward him, piercing eyes, solemn face.

The soldier was a young, skinny kid. He swiftly yanked off his cap and placed it over his heart, obviously intending to hide his name. This soldier was so nervous he forgot that the US Army tag is always worn over your heart on your left side. Not your name. Your name tag is always worn on the right side. He didn't cover his name at all. *Harris*, it read, clear as day in the beam of the moonlight.

LTC Palmer bent over him screaming like one of those drill sergeants you've seen in the movies. He stared at his name tag, then met his wide eyes. "Harris!" he barked. "You've stolen the general's jeep and he's very upset."

At this point I thought the guy was going to wet himself. Maybe he did and I couldn't see it in the dark. He couldn't get the words out. "Yes . . . yes . . . sir. Sir, I didn't know . . . sir, I'm sorry. Ahhhh, sir . . ."

And then LTC Palmer relaxed his stance and face, then burst out laughing. He patted Harris on the back in a comforting gesture. This confused Harris until he saw LTC Palmer and I grinning at him. Harris was visibly relieved. We shared a hearty laugh. Scaring the daylights out of Harris was tremendous fun. The kind of fun you have with your family or your best friends. It wasn't all darkness in the military; in fact, it was the best comradery I've ever felt. Everything in the military is so serious that, sometimes, you have to have a laugh at the most ridiculous things. In later years, LTC Palmer became my commander, and while we each have retired, we remain the best of friends and often share a laugh over our time in the service. And the thing about the military is that all the while, regardless of rank, regardless of gender, regardless of color, regardless of nationality, regardless of age, or regardless of anything else that usually divides people, we are bonded. We wear the same uniform, serve the same country, and join together working toward common goals that promote safety, respect, honor, dignity, with a familial-type bond.

Operation Recovery was ultimately effective because soldiers learned that they would be arrested for being AWOL. It served as a motivator to deal with problems in advance and a deterrence to those who might consider not showing up. After about five years, the program ceased because the number of AWOLs throughout the Michigan Army National Guard had declined and it was decided that individual units could handle their own AWOL issues as they saw was ncccssary.

Overall, Operation Recovery was a twenty-four-hour, five-day operation. It was intense. It was consuming. It was a time for Colonel Wilbur and the JAGs to shine. It was largely on my shoulders. It was successful.

* * *

During Operation Recovery—our big AWOL recovery—a team brought in a woman in her early twenties who looked horribly beaten down and sullen and was shaking. Let's call her Lucy. Lucy's face was raw from crying. "I have children," she sobbed, "I have children."

Instead of immediately detaining Lucy and debriefing her later when I was finished with other debriefings and tasks, I debriefed her immediately because I could hear the urgency, feel her distress. We truly weren't out to just punish people. The military does care about people, especially their trained assets. We wanted to hear their side of the story to determine what the issues were that led to being AWOL—maybe there had been a misunderstanding, maybe their vehicle broke down, their childcare provider didn't show up, or they were ill. Maybe there was an emergency. Life happens.

But Lucy didn't want to talk to the men. She

wouldn't tell them what was happening. So my female clerk, Sergeant Kirby, and I sat down in a room with her behind closed doors in a judgement-free zone with communication open. I wanted her to feel heard. I wanted her to feel safe. No crowds. No men. No one to overhear anything personal she needed to share.

I spoke to Lucy mom-to-mom rather than soldier-to-soldier. "I will help you. But the only way I can help you is if you talk to me," I said. "What would you like me to know?"

And then I listened.

Her story came tumbling out. Just as Lucy was about to report to camp, her husband called to tell her that he was involved with some extremely bad people and that he'd taken their two kids down to Texas. Unless she transported illegal drugs from Michigan to Texas and across the border, he'd sell the kids. He told her not to tell anyone. She had to do what he said. A vehicle would be delivered to her house with drugs hidden in the vehicle's tires. She had to wait at her home for it to arrive.

I heard awful, disheartening stories at the state senator's office, but this was the worst thing I had ever heard. It was like right out of an action movie. Completely unreal. I stared at her from across the table as she told me her story. I felt the horror and pain and kept thinking that I wasn't that much older than Lucy. I put myself in her situation. If this ever happened to my kids, I would do whatever I had to do to get them back without worry of consequence to me.

She felt the same way, which is why she didn't show up for duty. She was about to go through with it and leave in the vehicle that had just been delivered when our recovery team just happened to arrive and intervene. They stopped her from leaving. They didn't even let her collect her gear. She was hysterical when they arrested her as anyone would be. The lives of her young daughters were at stake.

Lucy was terrified to call law enforcement. She begged me not to. Look, when you're in a gang, which is what this was, a gang situation, and if you're told "we're going to sell your kids," you better believe them. She was understandably terrified. She didn't trust anyone—but thankfully, she decided to trust me. "I'm going to help you," I told her.

Sergeant Kirby stared at me. "What do you think you can do?" she asked, wide-eyed.

There I was, only a little first lieutenant at that point. But I was fired up, ready to get in a jeep and chase this guy down myself, but I knew that wasn't literally possible. However, I knew I could get the right kind of help. "I'm going to call the Texas Rangers," I announced. "I'm going to call the FBI." Lieutenant Aquilina to the rescue! I knew my worth. I knew I could make the calls I needed to make to get the job done. I'm a soldier. I'm a lawyer. I work for a state senator. This is America. "I'm going to contact the right people to get those kids back, right now," I told Lucy and Sergeant Kirby who stood ready to assist me. And I did.

As much as I'd like to believe I'm a one-woman army, I know that I am not and that I had to follow the chain of command. I immediately spoke with my commanders, who, by the way, were very supportive. They said, "Lieutenant, do what you need to do." They could have held me back. They could have said "let us take this over" or "you're just a woman" or "who do you think you are?" It was the 1980s. In the civilian world, someone like me would have most likely been told "we'll take it from here." There was none of that. Here in the military, my outstanding commanders just said, "Keep on doing what you're doing. Keep us informed."

And that is exactly what I did.

It was a powerful moment in my life. I learned that if you do the right things, then good things will come back to you. Not everything works as smoothly as it did in this situation, obviously. But it gave me hope.

I contacted the local law enforcement. I contacted the FBI. I contacted the Texas Rangers who I understood had jurisdiction to handle such a situation. Very soon, law enforcement and the FBI arrived on base in the JAG office. They interviewed Lucy and quickly set up a sting operation in Texas. She went with law enforcement not only so she could be there for her children but also so she could identify the people who the kids were with. And ultimately, with the various law enforcement agencies working together very quickly, Lucy got her kids back. Because of the circumstances, she was allowed to do a makeup annual training. Further, the members of the Michigan Army National Guard at annual training who learned of this through her unit set up a collection fund for her to travel to Texas and to return with her children. Almost every soldier who heard about these horrific circumstances donated something. It was miraculous, it was cohesive, it was moral building. It was a horrible situation with a happy ending.

While I had been asking this question—"What would you like me to know?"—to assist Senator Kelly's constituents, it was the first moment I realized just how strong its impact really was. People in crisis shut down the minute they feel that you are not listening, that instead you are blaming or shaming them. It makes them feel helpless, invisible, and guilty. It's simply not useful. When you ask an open-ended question, on the other hand, you are allowing someone to tell their story without judgment. You help them feel seen and heard. And without that, Lucy wouldn't have talked, her children may not have survived, and a lot of bad people may not have been arrested. Look, this woman could have hidden the truth and come up with any excuse like "my mother is sick" or "my kids are sick." We let plenty of people off for family issues. Instead, she felt believed, heard, and not judged. She looked to us for mercy, and thankfully, we were able to help her.

First and foremost, this takes a different mindset. You have to want to ask the question, "What would you like me to know." And then "What can I do to help you?" rather than "What can I do to punish you?" Or the blaming *why* questions: "Why didn't you . . .?" "Why did you . . .?" My opinion is that *why* needs to remain with researchers, not deployed when trying to help someone. *Why* is a blaming word by its very nature. And if you don't believe me, ask a few *why* questions and think about them: "Why were you late? Why didn't you finish your homework? Why do you work so many hours? Why didn't you call? Why did you buy that? Why are you wearing that? Why are you eating that?" I don't think I need to go on. You see the point.

The legal system can often be backward for this reason. We can be seen as punishers. That's not what we are. We are here to serve the public first, in the best, safest, and most efficient way we can. And sometimes it is punishment, and sometimes it is just getting people to the right services they need. But you can only do that if you're ready to listen.

After the situation with Lucy, became not just a conscious decision but my mantra. It became my absolute practice to ask open-ended questions, including "what would you like me to know?" It's about treating people with respect and wanting to get to a solution to resolve their issues with the best possible outcome—that includes healing.

I've made it a point to do this in all factions of my life: in the military, as a lawyer, as a judge, and, for the most part, with my children. And as I've said, I hate questions that start with "why" unless it is for cross-examination purposes because only antagonizing questions begin with "why."

The biggest mistake you can make is to impose your preconceived notion onto someone. Instead, it's so much more crucial to say, "What would you like me to know?" or "How can I help?" or "What is the best thing I can do for you right now in this moment?" It makes a world of difference and changes lives, one at a time. And sometimes you get very lucky and it saves a life.

* * *

Once Operation Recovery was complete and my mission of accounting for the teams with as many AWOLs as they could recover was done, it was time for me to go back to my regular JAG duties. JAG officers could serve as a judge, prosecutor, or defense counsel, depending on the situation. Indeed, it so happened that in those early military years that I was often the defense counsel for the soldiers I had helped bring in. As I had found with Lucy, not every case was cut and dry. We had hearings to determine if the soldier would be retained, punished, or discharged based on military law, rules, and regulations. There are many types of hearings. Regardless of the kind of hearing, there were multiple times when I, acting as defense counsel, argued that the soldier in question didn't have proper notice, particularly if the schedule changed. My line of questioning on cross-examination, once we got to hearing, looked a lot like this.

"Commander, how did you contact the soldier to let them know that the date of the drill practice would change?" I would ask.

"I called him."

"Did you leave a message?"

"Yes," The commander would respond.

"Did you recognize the soldier's voice?" I'd retort.

"Well, there was a recording, and I left the message there," the commander would say.

"And, you are required to give personal notice, correct?" Personal notice means that the soldier is entitled to get instruction directly from their commander.

"So, you never talked to him?" I'd ask.

"I left a clear message."

"It's fair to say you didn't recognize the soldier's voice on the recording?"

"Yes."

"So it could have been anyone, even a wrong number?" I'd ask and stare the Commander in the eyes.

"Yes." The Commander's voice would be angry, and his face would begin to redden. "But it sounded like him."

"But it's fair to say that you can't be *certain* it was him, true?"

"Yes."

The commander wasn't certain. And that sort of practice is sloppy and doesn't belong in the military. You have to give a soldier *actual* notice. You can't just make a phone call to some number and hope it's the right one. That might not be his number. It might be a machine. It might be a kid who answered. It might be a spouse who answered. You have to provide actual and *direct notice* to the soldier. And honest to God, I won all those cases, and after I did, they had to follow the rules and ensure they gave soldiers actual notice. And I upset a lot of commanders because if they could not prove proper notice, those soldiers were retained. My tough stance on this even helped secure a nickname I earned in the military: the barracuda.

The military is a different world, sure. We do things differently than we do in the civilian world. But not when it comes to the constitutionally protected right to a fair trial and fair process. In both worlds, civil rights, fairness, and the constitution speaks volumes.

In the military and in the state senator's office, I began to understand my worth. That I mattered. That what I contributed mattered. I looked at myself in the mirror, just as I did when I was a teenager, and said, "You earned that." There wasn't anyone else saying this to me. Not one person in my life was telling me, "Good job." I might hear "good dinner." Or "your hair looks nice." But what I was doing in the state senator's office and in the military were real accomplishments. Important accomplishments. And if I were the only one who knew I was doing that, it was fine with me. I discovered that before I could uplift someone else, I had to uplift myself. And I did.

My years in the military were really special. As I got older, there were a lot of women coming up through the ranks in various fields, and we all worked well together. I had a wonderful female role model, Brigadier General Mandi A. Murray, at the head of our brigade who I greatly respected and a female military police officer who also served as a civilian police officer, MAJ Carrie Ann Thomas, and countless other women in varied positions. I never met a woman I didn't get along with in the military and that's unusual for a workplace situation. Very often, workplace politics can be tricky between women. Here, we were on the same team. A team that not only supported each other but also boosted each other up.

The truth was this: my experience in the military was key to how I evolved as a person and became someone with control, influence, and compassion. After a weekend of working in JAG, I felt refreshed, not overworked—despite not having a day off for two weeks or sometimes more, especially once Desert Storm hit us. My service took me out of my daily routine with my job and my kids and my husband—pure gold to a working mom. I didn't realize how important such time was until I began serving. Not only did it give me confidence and a bit of an escape, but it also gave me training as a defense attorney, a prosecutor, and a judge. It taught me organization, leadership, and the importance of cohesion and morale building. It taught me how to speak in front of hundreds of people from all walks of life. It taught me to trust those people who would always carry me into safety, and I learned that I must always be that kind of strong, protective leader. There is no other arena in America where you can wear all three legal hats, be trained in so many areas, and always be respected as a valuable asset. Especially as a foreigner and a woman.

The military never felt like extra work or a burden. In the civilian world, my life often felt like chaos. Two small children. A marriage that was constantly on the brink of falling apart. Fighting with my parents for one reason or another. On the contrary, the military brought me calm and structure, and most importantly, the realization that I could be part of meaningful change. Any problem I had in the civilian world melted away when I reported for duty.

My one weekend away each month was giving me a clearer perspective on life. Soon that new perspective would cause me to make major changes in my life, starting with my marriage.

chapter nine

How to End a Marriage

I couldn't have asked for a better professional life. I was busy. I was learning. I was moving forward. I was a successful JAG officer in the Michigan Army National Guard. I was on staff in the State Senate. I was earning the respect of those I worked with. I was even taking on the occasional law client. But I had to admit that my personal life was falling apart.

Dave and I fought constantly. It wasn't good for either of us, and it certainly wasn't good for the kids. No matter the subject, every fight ended with him telling me I argue like a lawyer, to which I would respond "thank you," then threaten to leave him. "You weren't the person I was supposed to marry," I'd tell him one day. Another day I would say, "I made a mistake." It wasn't a good situation. Instead of working things out with me, he was more and more absent, oblivious to what was happening. His rationale and cure was that I'd be happier with him if he made more money. My rationale and cure was that we needed to learn to be in sync by spending more time together. The result was that I threw myself into my work and our children. Any reflective time was spent with regret. The more I complained, the more he poured himself into work and the misconception that more money would make us happy.

I became increasingly distant. Money does not equate to love. It is not a cure, nor is it a replacement for talking. Love is about two people being on equal footing. Love is about partnership. Love is about communication. Dave and I had none of that.

It certainly didn't help that we were still living in the "money pit"—the house we moved into when I was pregnant with our son David. The house was one of the many problems in our marriage. David was about four years old by then. The house was mostly finished but still needed work, and the basement was only good for housing the washer and dryer—and the children were growing. We were outgrowing our starter home.

We delved into the advice from our couples' class that we should continue to "date" each other. That the only way to spend time was to make time. So we planned a few dates. We started talking. I began to have hope.

Now that I was employed with benefits and a steady paycheck, both Dave and I spent much of our date time discussing the possibility of moving to a bigger home. On this, we both agreed. Since Dave was in real estate, we were quickly able to find a house in a neighborhood near where the children would attend school and where we each worked. It was a two-story colonial, and we both liked it. One night at the kitchen table, we had a serious conversation about moving, money, schools, and day care. Everything. Dave agreed to buy the house, but he had one condition.

"I'll buy the house if you promise to stay with me," he said.

I had promised myself to get my marriage on track now that school was over, I had passed the bar, and I had a job. So, despite not liking ultimatums, it was not an impossible proposition under my *let's move forward* attitude. As unhappy as I was, I didn't want to *leave* Dave. I wanted the marriage to work. We had two young children. And we wanted more children. We had a comfortable life outside of all the fighting. I didn't want to be a divorced woman. I never saw myself as a divorced woman.

But that wasn't the only reason. Look, I'm not going to lie. I also wanted to move! I didn't want my kids living in the money pit on a road that was too busy at times and with a yard that needed fencing. Despite having fixed all the holes in the walls, having replastered all the ceilings, repainting and carpeting every room, and fixing all the plumbing throughout the house, there were endless repairs and very little space to expand into. I was working, and Dave was working. There was no reason we needed to stay there. If promising him that I'd stay with him was what I needed to do to get out of that house and move forward, then that's what I would do.

I told myself that the new house would be a fresh start. Moving would give us a chance to start over in every way. Women can convince ourselves of anything if we try. We have endless hope. And that's what I did. I convinced myself that a new house would make everything better.

And if it didn't get better? Then I still had an exit strategy.

"Of course, I'll stay with you," I told him, but I was really thinking *if it doesn't work out, then at least I tried.* It was like my thought process the day of my wedding when I told myself *if it doesn't work out, I'll just get a divorce.* One foot in. One foot out.

* * *

The new house came with its own set of problems. It needed work, updating mostly, some of which I wanted to take care of before we moved in or immediately thereafter. Instead, Dave used $5,000 to have insulated wall panels installed that would prepare the basement for finishing. It was a new product that he'd learned about as a realtor, and he got a "deal." His plan was that, eventually, we'd make a family room and playroom in the basement that we would all enjoy. He thought he was doing a great thing by preparing the walls for renovation. I thought it was a ridiculous waste of money on a room we weren't even going to use because the only plan was wall preparation. When would we have the money to finish it? How were we going to afford the other updates, like new carpet and paint in the living areas of the main floor? And how long could we live in rooms without furniture? Shouldn't all that have come first?

It felt like our honeymoon all over again. Here he was, making decisions without even talking to me. The idea that this house was going to be a fresh start for us went down the drain almost immediately.

But in the spirit of moving forward and of continuing to "date," one day I bought a wicker picnic basket I found on clearance because it sparked an idea for a surprise. I planned a meal, packed it with some of our favorite foods, and included a blanket and a camera to memorialize our time. I decided to take it to Dave's office and surprise him, thinking we could go to a nearby park, sit on a blanket, and connect. To me, it seemed like the ultimate romantic gesture, something small and inexpensive but nonetheless meaningful. *If someone did this for me*, I thought, *I would think it was incredible.*

I carried out my plan to spend an hour with my husband. I arrived near the lunch hour to Dave's office. When he saw me, he was kind enough, but it turned out Dave didn't think it was so romantic. He was too busy, he explained—even if we shortened it to half an hour, which I offered to do. Instead of a picnic, I got the brush-off. So, I left his office by myself with a fully loaded picnic basket, dismayed, disappointed, and dismantled. I understood him being busy. I got it. I was busy too.

But there's nothing worse than putting yourself out there for someone only to have them turn you away, turn you off, and tune you out. This was only one heartbreaking example. Despite everything we tried, we somehow ended up just falling back into the same patterns, both of us wounding each other. Nothing was working. The distance grew too wide, the crater too deep.

My hope was sinking. My heart was breaking. Many times, I coped the same way I did when I was a teenager. After a fight, or after simply being ignored or discounted, I'd retreat to the bathroom, lock the door, and turn the shower on so I could drown out all the sounds. I'd look in the mirror, directly into the light of my eyes. We all have light in our eyes. That light comes from the intuitiveness that we've developed over time. I'd tell myself what I needed to hear:

You're worthy.

You're going to do things.

You're going to be somebody.

You'll get through this.

You'll make it through what comes next.

You can do everything alone.

You don't need anyone, except your kids.

You're a lawyer.

You can make and spend your own money.

You're going to have your own voice.

You can raise the children on your own if you need to.

You can do this.

You can accomplish so much more.

I saw a therapist during that time, too, because I thought I was going crazy. I felt like I had one foot in the marriage and one foot out. Plus, I had my kids to worry about. I didn't know what to do.

During this time, I came to learn that the only person I can really count on is myself. There are other people who can help, who you can talk to, who you can gain wisdom from, but ultimately, that love and strength must come from inside yourself. I'd remind myself of what my grandparents had told me: I can do anything.

In a lot of ways, I think Dave and I kept this cycle going because we didn't spend a lot of time together. I was away one weekend a month with the military, plus I was busy working in the state senate. He was always working, often late into the night. When we were home, we were with the kids. We didn't have time to bond or connect. When we were away from each other, we'd forget about the fighting because absence makes the heart grow stronger. I think, in many ways, that's how Dave and I survived for as long as we did. We were on a roller coaster, and we needed a real intervention. A marriage counselor.

Dave found a marriage counselor through a friend. When he asked me to attend with him, I confessed I'd already been seeing a therapist but that I would be happy to switch to his. His suggestion to see a therapist finally felt like a signal that he was committing to making the marriage better, recommitting to me. The therapist gave us lots of helpful suggestions: write letters to each other, go on dates, talk to each other—the textbook treatment. We'd tried dating before. I was open to dating again. These ideas were okay, except that I'd learned from the picnic episode that we no longer knew *how* to go on a date or *how* to communicate. Dates wouldn't solve the biggest issue in our marriage, which was that I didn't feel like I counted, was listened to, or valued as a woman. I knew Dave thought I was a good cook, a good mom, and a good woman. But I wanted my voice to matter. I wanted my opinion to matter, my needs, my desires, my interests. I wanted him to make decisions *with* me, not for me. I wanted to count as an equal and as a valued human.

Marriage counseling is not for the squeamish. You have to bring up a lot of negative things about each other. It's very slow and painful. Dave wanted quicker results. I was getting frustrated too. After we'd met with the therapist several times together and separately, we seemed stuck. We voiced our concern at a joint session, and the therapist asked us to draw shapes that represented our marriage. It came to me very visually. I saw us as two separate circles that overlapped in the center. I was one circle. Dave was another circle. Where we overlapped was the family—our two children and us. He has room to make his own decisions about his life. So do I. And in the overlapping space, we connect about the family, about our relationship, and about the life we are building together. We each have equal voice and decide things together. Dave also saw us as two circles. *Wow, maybe he agrees with me*, I thought. But then he showed us his drawing. Dave drew one large circle with another smaller circle *inside* it. Do I have tell you who represented the smaller circle and who represented the larger one?

My heart sank. The therapist saw the disconnect and immediately recognized my frustration. "Look, I don't know how to fix this for the two of you," he admitted.

"You see marriage as a true partnership," he said to me. "And you see marriage with you as the head of the family in every way," he said to Dave.

He gave us time to process and then announced, "It would have been best to discuss this before the marriage because these two models don't work together."

I applauded our therapist for saying that, for being

honest, because most therapists don't give you that kind of frank answer.

After hearing that, Dave was done with counseling. He wasn't going back.

As for me, I told Dave that, the way I saw it, we were finished. I proposed we could just live together under the same roof for the sake of the children. Stay married but live two separate lives. And all the while I stayed in therapy for almost three years. Regardless of how this was going to play out, it was clear that I needed an outlet, a support person, and a place to put all of my thoughts. My priority was to keep my head on straight and make sure our kids emerged from this situation whole and well.

In one session, I put it to the therapist straight. "Okay, what am I going to do here? Because I have one foot in and one foot out of this marriage."

"Something defining will happen," he said to me, "and, it will push both feet in or both feet out. I can't tell you when it will happen or what it will be. But I can guarantee it will happen."

* * *

One night, I was making dinner for my family as usual. That night, it was mashed potatoes and gravy, corn, and oven-baked pork chops. I had just worked a full day at the state senator's office. I'd reviewed spelling words with the kids. We'd watched an episode of *Scooby-Doo* while everything was cooking. Dave had returned home from work just as dinner was about to be placed on the table. He entered the kitchen, hearing me call out for everyone to come sit down. The kids were young and scrambling around the kitchen. The pork chops were ready, and I was just pulling them out of the oven when David, six, demanded Tang to drink with dinner.

Tang, if you don't know, was an orange powdered

sugar drink that was popular in the 1970s and 1980s. You mix the water and the powder together in a pitcher and voilà, Tang. I asked David multiple times to please sit down at the table and promised that once I placed the hot food on the table, the Tang would be made. It wasn't a big request. I was teaching my son that we all sit at the table to eat the meal. It was about manners and patience and respecting Mommy's wishes.

Dave waltzed in the kitchen, hearing the conversation and my request. He didn't care about what I had just told our son. He simply said, "Don't worry, I'll make the Tang."

It was one thing for Dave to disagree with me. But it was a completely different thing for him to override me in front of our children, even on something as small as this. No one was seated. The oven was open and hot. It was chaos. It was my life. It was me being invisible. Again.

I saw that moment as a metaphor for how the rest of our lives would be. Not only would Dave not listen to me, but he would also teach my children not to listen to me. It was as clear as the shriek of the high noon whistle. To be overridden in front of my children, even on a small thing like that, meant that bigger things were coming.

Dave didn't come in to say, "Hey, I'll help you place dinner on the table." He wasn't offering to help seat the children. He didn't care that I had just worked a full day, that I had gotten the kids from school, that I was making a full dinner for the family. If we traded places, I would have said, "Honey, how can I help you?" Instead, he nullified me.

Look, it wasn't about the Tang. It was about our partnership not being valued. It was about not being listened to and being dehumanized and demonized for so many years. I felt like a servant in my own home. He had no respect for me, and now, I felt that he was teaching my children not to have respect for me either.

In that moment, I realized I had enough. All my bottled-up feelings came out in that moment and spilled out into that kitchen.

Literally, spilled out.

I took the five-gallon container of Tang and dumped it all over the pork chops.

"There's dinner," I screamed. "Get out of my life. I'm done. We're done. I want a divorce."

I have not bought Tang ever again since that day. And yes, my kids still remember the Tang incident. I'm sorry it happened in front of them. You want to protect your children from emotional turmoil, but sometimes, you just can't. And that night, it was Tang on the dinner and the end of their parents' marriage. I immediately went upstairs and started emptying his closet. Very shortly after that, we started seeing lawyers to begin the divorce process. There was no going back. Both feet were out of the marriage.

* * *

After we split, Dave and I had a few rough spots but overall ended up being good co-parents. He bought a condo in the same neighborhood. The children could bicycle back and forth when they got older. We each had the kids every other weekend. Dave had the kids on Tuesday and Wednesday nights because I often had to stay late when I worked in legislative session or attended legislative functions. We helped each other when the other person needed it. We traded days, and we sent things back and forth when someone forgot something or needed something extra. I occasionally sent a meal or cookies. We communicated. We got along better in divorce than we did in marriage.

My one mistake: I should have taken child support.

Child support is the *right of a child* and it's the *obligation of both parents*. At the time, I had a crappy lawyer who didn't help educate me and who didn't help me think clearly. That was his job—to protect me. Yes, I was a lawyer, but at that time, I didn't practice family law and I wasn't thinking clearly. I simply wanted out of the marriage. I wanted control of my life returned to me. In my law practice, I used my life as the example of what not to do, and I didn't let my clients make the same mistakes I made. I never recommend not letting the other parent pay their share of child support, no matter how much you want to get rid of the person or how much you hate them. Dave was not a deadbeat dad or anything close to that, but he was worried about paying consistent child support because he was in real estate and his income varied. He had a goal of buying multiple rental properties and didn't want child support to go against his ability to qualify for whatever he wanted to purchase. Look, he's a great dad to my kids and always split the bills with me. But if I spent a hundred dollars, I would give him a bill and then I might see the fifty dollars weeks or months later. And he never paid for the extras or the essentials like heat, water, electrical, and all those things that child support is meant to assist with—the necessities of life. He paid half the uninsured medical, but I paid for the medical coverage; he paid for half the school tuition, clothing, and sports. But with children, there is always so much more, and I was like the bank: I usually fronted the money—he paid when he could. On occasion, if the children were with him and he fronted the money, he would simply offset the amount against what he owed me. Regardless, I paid for the necessities of life that are normally considered when calculating child support. He paid for his house; I paid for mine. However, there was a disparity of income between us, and I was the primary parent who had the children more often. This left me frequently living paycheck to paycheck. It's not a great way to live. I was paying interest on my credit cards. He was buying rental property.

I want to be clear: I could have asked the court for a child support modification to formalize it more than just splitting the bills. At any time, I could have asked for calculation within the child support formula that was fair to both of us, but I chose not to. I never asked for modification. I kept the agreement that we had made as stated in our Judgement of Divorce. He didn't want to formally pay child support. I wanted custody. It was a great deal in that way, but it shorted my wallet every month. I don't recommend it.

Years later, Dave said to me, "I have a lot of clients who pay child support. First of all, thank you for not making me pay. Second of all, I probably should have been paying more all along." He felt genuinely horrible about it. All those years later, Dave wanted to *pay me* child support! At that point, the kids were near eighteen. "Well, it's a little late now, Dave," I said, laughing. But I did appreciate his recognition and his offer.

Once I started taking clients, I always insisted they take child support, alimony, or whatever they were entitled to. Lots of people felt like I did; they didn't want to fight over it, they didn't want to take it, they wanted to just be done with the marriage. But if you can't use the money, put it away for the kids' college. And think about this way: it's your children's money. If he doesn't give it to you, he'll be spending it on a girlfriend!

The truth was that Dave and I were both chasing different dreams. He wanted a wife at home who would defer to him. I wanted a husband who was an equal partner and best friend as we each pursued our dreams. We were both living outside the marriage. Neither of us was present. Neither of us wanted to be divorced, but we could not find a way to resolve our issues and move forward as an intact family that remained happily together. We have each found our way separately and successfully in the world. And despite each of us having had other relationships in the many years since our divorce, neither of us have remarried.

* * *

I got a lot of flak for divorcing Dave. The first thing my parents did was give me the I-told-you-so speech. "We told you not to marry him. This is your problem." It wasn't about me. They didn't ask if I was okay. They didn't empathize about what a hard [illegible] how painful it must have been for me. There was absolutely no compassion whatsoever for what I was going through.

Once they got through with the I-told-you-so speech, they accused me of harming my children by getting divorced. To put the icing on the cake, my father decided to join forces with Dave as he had when I joined the military and blamed the entire divorce on me. Everything was "Why is she doing this?" "How could she do this?" "She is crazy." It was all blame and shame. There was no listening, no asking how I was doing, and no asking what I needed help with or even asking what happened. I was the evil one. I was blamed. I was still the stubborn troublemaker. I was at fault.

But I didn't need my father's criticism. I was broken already. I was very good at beating myself up. I never planned to be divorced. I didn't want to be divorced. I never planned to be single most of my adult life. I didn't want to be single. My grandparents had stayed happily married for life; they were a true team. My parents were still married and remain married to this day. Why couldn't I do the same? Why couldn't I be quiet like my mother? I felt like a failure, which I could handle except that it translated into failing my children. It was gut-wrenching to me. It still is gut-wrenching to me. Night after night, I woke up asking myself, *What should I have done differently? What else could I have done? Why wasn't I better?* I went back through time and blamed myself. I failed to look at the reasons I was marrying him. I failed to be strong enough before we were married to say, "Yeah, this isn't working. I'm walking away."

It didn't help that I felt so alone. No one was in my corner. Not one person. (Except for my grandmother. My grandmother didn't exactly encourage me to get divorced, but she didn't dissuade me either. She told me how difficult it was going to be. She told me it would be tough for me to be on my own. She told me that it might be hard on the kids. But she also didn't try to talk me out of it and tell me it was the wrong thing to do.) When my father realized that I was going through with it, he gave me the silent treatment. He didn't speak to me for about a year after the divorce. Fortunately, my brother Joe always checked on me, and eventually my mother did too.

But ultimately, how unhappy does a person need to be before there has to be a change? I was absolutely miserable. And though divorce is difficult, I also didn't want my children to think that being married was filled with misery, fighting, and discontent. So, I chose being happy over being miserable. I'd like to say that I have no regrets, but the truth is that I sometimes still question my decision. It wasn't an abusive relationship. Dave wasn't a bad guy. And I do feel like it hurt the children in some ways. For that, I'll always carry some guilt, even if, looking back, I can't imagine doing anything differently. Although my daughter, Jennifer, will tell you she was a lot happier when we got divorced because the fighting ended. My son, David, on the other hand, has gone backward and forward. He was not happy when we got divorced. Sometimes he would blame me, sometimes he blamed his father, sometimes he understood. Overall, I think he would have liked to see us stay together. And I think he has some residual effects of the divorce. No one wants to see their children get hurt. I solely am the blame for that. I will always blame myself for that.

Forgiveness is something I'm always striving toward. And I needed to forgive myself about the divorce. It's taken me years, but I've finally been able to see that I made mistakes in the marriage that led to the divorce and that I needed to own them. I needed to forgive myself and try to do better. I wasn't perfect. I just wasn't. In fact, I've had friends confide to me that they want a divorce. I've used my life and my regrets as an example of what not to do, and most have stayed married and found common ground and a happier path.

If you never resolve the things that you've done wrong in life, then you'll repeat that pattern until you do forgive yourself. Until I really forgave myself, forgave him, broke out of the mold of my own negative patterns, I couldn't move forward. I'm human. We make mistakes, and all we can do is learn from our mistakes, move forward, and try to do better.

chapter ten

How to Be a Single Mom

Divorce is never easy. It affects everyone. The kids, the parents, the entire family. Despite all the challenges we had while we were married, Dave and I surprisingly did a good job co-parenting together following the divorce. After so many years of living life by the seat of my pants, things didn't feel as chaotic. My children weren't babies anymore. They were more independent. And it was certainly easier not having Dave in the house. Our divorce meant it was one less person to fight with, one less person to ask permission from. Dave and I always battled, but the war had ended. Now I made my own decisions. I'm not saying being single was easy. It certainly wasn't. But in many ways, I felt like I had one less child to worry about. I didn't want the man I'm with to also be my child.

Shortly after the divorce, when my children were about fourteen and fifteen, Senator Kelly decided not to run for office again. At that point, we had worked together for nearly ten years. I knew I had to be very thoughtful in planning my next move. Between Senator Kelly's office, the military, and being a single mom, I was used to being in charge and having a lot of responsibility, which I loved and was an environment I thrived in. The last thing I wanted to do was go backward, taking a full-time job teaching at a law school or working for a firm and having to answer to someone else. I'm too independent for that. Plus, I didn't want to work the long hours dictated by some firms that wouldn't financially benefit my family. I wanted to be with my children at night. I wanted control over what I did. But first, to show my true independence, I also needed to set myself apart from Senator Kelly. I thought back. Two years prior. Governor John Engler had asked me to switch parties and run against the senator from Saginaw, where my parents still worked and lived. If I lost, he guaranteed me an appointment as a judge. But he told me I would win, and he guaranteed all the money and help I needed to win. I declined. I'm loyal. I wouldn't switch parties. I wouldn't bring shame on my boss. So Governor Engler found someone else to run and who did win. Two years later, when Senator Kelly was deciding on leaving, I recalled the thought of being a state senator, a job I knew and loved. I ran. I lost. While I came close, it is difficult to run against an incumbent, but I had accomplished by goal: to be looked at on my own, as a capable human. And my parents were in support of my choice to run so much so that they financially supported me during the campaign. After I lost, I spent the next few weeks packing up the senate office and calculating how far my final paycheck would take me. The money would run out very soon. How would I pay my bills? I laid out my jewelry and anything else I had of value and laid them out in the order I would pawn them when my bills came due. What job did I want next?

Starting my own law firm was the most appealing option, but you can't just snap your fingers to make that happen. I needed a solid plan. I was working weekends in the military. I picked up all the extra days I could. And I agreed to teach extra law classes. I applied for unemployment to help pay my bills. I used that time to recreate myself and put my new working life together.

I found a few other people I knew from the legislature who were interested in joining me in a law practice, and we got busy. We started from the ground up with new everything. New clients. New proposals. New stationary. Somehow, we found office space in the basement of the Michigan National Bank building (it's no longer there.) Because it was in the below ground and people didn't see it as desirable, we hit the jackpot in terms of space and price. Office furniture was acquired from a lawyer upstairs who was relocating, and we borrowed the rest. Initially, we didn't even have a copy machine, though running out to make copies got old so I took a leap and used some of my meager funds to purchase one and was later reimbursed when we began making money.

The whole process was a struggle—tough to do. When you're a lawyer, you're paid by the hour, and that's not predictable at the beginning. The only money I had coming in was from the military, teaching, and unemployment. I needed an alternate source of income while the firm came together, so I decided to turn to lobbying. I charged a flat rate per month with lobbying clients so I knew exactly what money was coming in. It gave me the opportunity to pay my bills while I built the kind of law practice I wanted with enough leeway to be able to choose the kind of cases I wanted.

Lobbing pays well—very well—much better than lawyering in most cases. I represented all kinds of groups as a lobbyist, including the YMCA, the Michigan local chapter of the United Brotherhood of Carpenters and Joiners of America Union, and even a group of acupuncturists. And I enjoyed it. Spending all your resources and energy to convince someone to get an issue passed or killed is interesting and there's also an adrenaline rush to it.

A word about lobbying: it can be a very dirty business. Some people call it "legalized bribery." Dirty lobbyists put a spin on their client's needs just to win a legislator's vote, even if that spin isn't exactly accurate. And sometimes, elected officials are especially motivated by donations to their campaigns to offer political favors. While that's not how lobbying is supposed to work, it often does. Yet, if you take that element out, people have the absolute right to voice their opinion with the government, and, if you boil it down, that's what lobbying is. It gives people or organizations or a voice. You can't ignore it. And I tried to be a voice of good who was in it not just for the money but rather to help make positive changes, to give voice to important issues, and, in that way, to strengthen our state.

At the firm, things were going well. As much as my military family supported me and helped form my voice, they also became some of my first clients. When they needed a divorce or had an issue with a landlord or maybe had a problem with their employer—issues JAG officers didn't handle—I stepped in. I also had several clients who I met when I was working in the legislature, people who knew me and trusted me. Between those two worlds, my client roster grew exponentially.

One of our law partners wanted a steady paycheck, so she accepted a job in the Attorney General's Office. And shortly thereafter, the building where we rented space was sold. It was to become the new building for the Michigan Legislature. We were bought out of our three-year lease, and with the money, my law partner, Garry Goolsby, and I turned to Dave, and he helped us find and buy a building downtown a few blocks away. We were on our way.

About a year after we moved into our new building,

a large box arrived. I hadn't ordered anything. It was very heavy. Curiously, I unleashed it. Much to my surprise, it was a bronze cowboy riding a horse mounted on granite. It was from my father. There was no note, but I knew the artist was one of his favorites. He has always appreciated the arts. Perhaps this was a sign he appreciated me? I placed it in my office across from my desk as a reminder to work harder.

My clientele expanded to a point where I had to decide if I wanted to lobby or practice law. I couldn't do both. Though lobbying gave me a steady income, it was a high-demand job. Clients called me at all hours and needed me to drop everything in that moment, and when there was a late or all-night session, I had to be there. My goal was to be a judge one day. I had wanted to be a judge from the time I went to law school. I always wanted to be the person who enforced the rule of law. That feeling came about from an early age. I knew lobbying wasn't going to lead me in that direction. And I needed to prioritize my children. I couldn't keep dropping everything for lobbying clients much longer. I already spent enough time away during my one weekend a month in the military. When I was at home, I wanted to be present. So I decided to drop lobbying, continue to teach law, serve in the military, and pursue significantly growing my new law firm.

* * *

After Dave and I divorced, I really didn't date. Not only was I always busy working and with my kids, but I had also just come off a big breakup. I didn't see the need to dive back into the dating pool. With that said, I did start a relationship with someone: let's call him Jake.

Jake was an attorney, and I occasionally worked with him professionally. He was talented at his profession, possessed a photographic memory and an unbridled charisma. I had great respect for him. Jake and I would talk endlessly about law cases, politics, civil injustice, and immigration reform. He was finally someone who could meet me on my level. I was turned on by his charisma, how smart he was, how seasoned he was as an attorney, and how evolved he was as a man. I finally met someone who pushed me to think more about life in a different way, who respected my opinions, and though he was ten years older than me, the age difference didn't bother me. He had a more mature perspective, which I loved. I've always been an old soul, and Dave and I were too young when we married, so it was a pleasure to be with someone who knew more than me, someone who wanted to teach me, someone with great confidence in himself and in me. But more than that, we had, at least I thought we had, remarkable respect for each other. Jake never treated me like a woman who couldn't do something. He always treated me as a woman who could do *more* than even I thought I could. And it was so refreshing. He was so different from men like Dave and my dad.

I was still young, only in my late twenties, and had just gotten divorced. I didn't want to get remarried. For me, marriage meant signing back up for a patriarchal existence. I couldn't have that. I had come too far. Jake wasn't looking to get married either. We'd see each other a few times a week, only when Jennifer and David were with their dad. There would be many weekends where I was doing military service or when I was with my children that I simply wouldn't see him. It wasn't as if I brought him around my family. My father? Come on. He didn't want to meet anyone until I married them. Jake was my boyfriend, yes, and we had mutual friends through our work connections who we spent time with, but I kept my distance. I wasn't interested in introducing anyone to my children or my family unless I was serious about marriage, and I simply wasn't interested in marriage with Jake. Despite that, I thought what we had was special. And I believed he felt the same way because he repeatedly said he did.

However, my present-day self, my older, wiser self, sees now that there was nothing special about it. He was a classic abuser. Jake was grooming me. He had catch phrases that he would say to me like, "You're too much. You're all you can be. And no one can help you like I can." Frequently, he reminded me, "No one will love you like I do." And when he wanted me to help him with his projects instead of focusing on mine, he'd say, "You're more capable than any man around us. Everything you do is tremendous. No one understands you like I do." Everything was about what *he* could do for me. That no one else could understand me like he did. That no one else would appreciate me like he did.

Of course, that wasn't true. I thought I was so strong, so secure, so tough. But I was so naive. I had closed my eyes to all his negative behavior and only saw the good. He put me up on a pedestal. He put himself in the role of the only person I could turn to, the only person who understood me. All of it was his grooming technique. I didn't know about this type of grooming when I started dating Jake. I didn't have a name for what he was doing. I was too naive to recognize it and to understand it.

Domestic violence abusers groom their victims by isolating them. They come on heavy, like they're your savior. They want to be everything to you. Really what they're doing is isolating you from everyone in your life. They're setting you up so that you have to depend and rely on them. Because our relationship moved at a slower pace, I didn't start to realize something was wrong until at least two years into the relationship. Jake was supposed to come over for dinner. My children were with their dad. I had a great dress on. I made dinner. Candles. The works. But Jake didn't show up. It was so unlike him. No call, no nothing. I called every place, every person, I could think of, looking for him. And when it started getting late, I called hospitals. I was worried as any normal person would be. It wasn't as if I was getting stood up by a first date. I had talked to him earlier that day! I convinced myself something awful happened to him. That he was dead. That he was hurt or in an accident.

Finally, I went to sleep, praying that nothing happened to him—that I'd hear something in the morning. In the morning I did hear from Jake. He was furious. Furious at me for calling his friends. Furious at me for leaving urgent messages on his phone. Calling people asking if they saw him. He was upset I would follow him, check on him. More than that, he was angry. "I told you I wasn't coming. I told you that I had a late meeting," he insisted. He told me I was having a memory lapse. Memory lapse. It was a term I would hear hundreds more times in my relationship with him. He didn't care that I was worried. He didn't care that I spent the night crying thinking he was dead. Furious with me, he hung up the phone.

I was flabbergasted. I had just gotten admonished like a little girl. And so, I questioned myself. I thought, *Oh, my God. Did I create this? Did I do this to myself? Did I have a memory lapse?* Although my head was telling me no, my heart was saying *he wouldn't do this to you if it wasn't true*. It *must* be true.

These kinds of things started happening with more and more frequency. Jake and I would have a date. He wouldn't show up all night and then blame me, telling me—the woman, who he had once said was the smartest person he knew, the sharpest tack, sharper than everyone else around us, women and men—that I was having "memory lapses." He would become outraged. Look, if we were married, if we were living together, maybe I would have seen it differently. Maybe I wouldn't have questioned myself. But that's what abusers do. They make you believe that you're crazy. That you're the one with the problem. That you're at fault.

Back then, we didn't have social media or Google to look someone up. To maybe get a glimpse into their life. You had to take people at their word. When I met him, I did not know many things about him. And so back in the '80s, you had to go on trust. But if I could have looked him up, maybe gotten more insight into who he really was, I'd like to think I would have walked away and stayed away. But I don't know. Hindsight is 20/20.

I was so compelled to believe what he'd said that I asked a mutual friend if she thought I had memory lapses. I can still see what I thought was her stunned face, and she shrugged off the idea. Later, I learned she knew about him, his tricks, his bad behavior, and she chose to support him. I now know this is also common. People choose sides.

But I didn't stop with just her. I asked other friends. I had been through a rough marriage—maybe it *was* me. "Do you think I have memory lapses?" Each one looked at me confused and explained how that wasn't possible. "You? Memory lapses? Look at all of the things you juggle," they would say. "You have a law firm. You're teaching. You're writing. You're a single mom. You're in the military. If you have memory lapses, you would be failing. But you're succeeding. What's going on?" They wanted to know why I'd think this about myself.

But I couldn't say. I didn't want to admit to them that someone I cared about was accusing me of this. Because I believed in myself. I didn't realize it then, but I was in an abusive relationship with Jake. He blamed me for our problems. He blamed me for the arguments. He blamed me when he failed, and when he succeeded, he gave me no credit.

I bought every self-help book I could find, looking for answers. Research. It is what I know to do, how I think, how I was trained. Eventually, I got wise. I started asking him if he was cheating, which at this point I knew he was, and he told me I was crazy. He'd say the most horrific things to me. Emotional attacks. Attack my character. My psyche. Everything. And I believed it for a while because I was stuck. It wasn't easy to psychologically untangle from the male-dominated household in which I was raised. I didn't know to expect better. I didn't know how to look for better. Jake didn't want anything from me outside of our time together, so I rationalized that this made him a safe bet. I knew what to expect even if it was nothing good. I comforted myself that being with him actually gave me independence. We'd fight. I'd accuse him of cheating. I'd find evidence of his cheating, he'd challenge my loyalty, accuse me of making things up, of being a good storyteller. He'd tell me that I was crazy, that I was having memory lapses. He'd forgive me. I'd forgive him. He'd go back to telling me how wonderful I was. And that felt right. We would go back to supporting each other and enjoying each other's company. We stroked each other's egos. And then it was the same cycle over and over again. The cycle of abuse.

I see now that we don't always choose the right people; sometimes we choose the most *familiar* people. Even if the familiar is abusive behavior. Even if he told me I wasn't worth anything.

I should have gotten out, but I didn't.

Being with Jake gives me empathy for those I've represented and those who stand in front of me when I'm in my robe and tell me in their victim statements about their domestic abuse and the effect it has had on them. I relate to them because Jake was an evil person. I knew that, and I still couldn't extricate myself from the relationship. I'm compelled to encourage victims that they can get through a traumatic situation because I have been in traumatic situations. I tell them that they matter because I've stood where they stood. Like those abused victims, I've been emotionally fucked with. I've been there, and I've lived to tell the tale. I've not only survived, but I have also thrived.

Looking back now, I think one of the reasons I chose Jake was because I knew I wasn't going to have to make a commitment to him. I loved him, but it wasn't love that was appropriately reciprocated or that would get us through the tough times. I wasn't in love enough to be totally blinded by it. I wanted and needed to focus on my children. On the military. On my career. What I truly was in love with.

Then came Valentine's Day. I believed my thyroid medication and the antibiotics I had recently taken were interfering with my birth control. I was having breakthrough bleeding. And, so, in preparation for our romantic night, I bought condoms. I told him that I get pregnant if a man looks at me the wrong way. I joked and told him I get pregnant if a man just simply takes off his pants! Heck, I get pregnant on birth control. But he looked me right in the eye and said to me, which I thought, was with all the love in the world, that he wanted to do it anyway. No condoms. Nothing between us.

And of course, I got pregnant.

I thought about it, and I knew I wanted to have this baby. Jake didn't want the responsibility of having the baby. He didn't want to commit. He already had two children with his ex-wife. At first, it hurt tremendously. But not for long. I realized that Jake had never really been there for me. He never wanted to commit, even when I was ready to. (Later I would find out he only wanted to commit to being adulterous with many women. And, double-whammy, I learned that some of our common friends knew and covered up his lies with more lies to me. I detached from them. I should have detached from him as well, but it wasn't that easy.) Yes, I had my independence because I was with him. But being with Jake had kept me from other men, had kept me from having those other children I always longed to have. It was time to proceed. I knew what I had to do.

I told him, flat out, "I want nothing. No child support. No father-daughter dances. I'll raise this baby on my own." I always wanted another child. For me, it was fate. I figured this was the time, and I didn't need his support to bring a new child into my family. I could do it alone. After hours of discussion, with my feet firmly planted in my decision, Jake, not surprisingly, agreed to my proposal. It was the cycle of abuse all over again. We were in this sweet spot. I had my independence, which I wanted, and I was pregnant. Happy. Excited for a baby. Back with Jake telling me how incredible I was. Putting me back up on that pedestal again.

"You can do it all," he would say. "Lawyer, mom, everything." In many ways, it was just easier to keep it as status quo. Then I didn't have to think about what was really happening. That I was involved with a man who would never commit. Who was lying, who was cheating, who asked other people to lie to me, and who would likely never be there for this child. A man who continued to make me doubt myself to my very core and who continued to make my inner girl fight for herself.

As much as he said he didn't want the baby, I look back now and realize that it was part of his manipulation. He thought that by getting me pregnant he could control me, keep me in the house, and in the dark about what he was doing. As much as he told me how smart and capable I was, he clearly didn't realize I had the fortitude to keep going forward. And so instead of facing what was really happening, I just decided to do what I had always done in a crisis. I went inward. I focused on myself. I didn't worry about my relationship with Jake because I knew, no matter what, I had myself. I separated myself from my emotions, and my decision to go forward made me feel stronger. Would I have liked to find my real soulmate? Yes. But I had a career to build and children to raise. And I didn't have faith that there was a man who could offer all that and let me be the person I need to be. Despite their traditional background, my parents, my grandmother, and my siblings didn't shame me. They were quite supportive, actually, and were excited about the baby. They knew I was an independent person, an independent thinker, and that I was going to do what I wanted to do.

And right now, I was more than ready to be a mom to a little girl I already loved very much.

chapter eleven

How to Ask the Right Questions

So here I was, a single mom pregnant with her third child, working on putting my law firm together. And you can be sure I made it a top priority to hire pregnant women and moms. I was in charge now, and I got to do it my way. I was also so lucky that my sister Helen, also a lawyer, came to work with me. I adore my sister; she's brilliant, kind, and hard-working. It was a fortunate situation.

It was an easy pregnancy, and before I knew it, it was a few weeks before Thanksgiving, which was shortly before my due date. I was sitting at the conference table next to my sister Helen, working on a case for a client when I started feeling labor pains. With my two other children, David and Jennifer, my labor went on forever, so a few contractions didn't scare me anymore. I kept working, and when I had a contraction, I'd breath into the pain. It would go away, and I would continue to work.

Helen was worried. She already had three children, and her deliveries were quick. As in barely-made-it-to-the-hospital quick. "I think you're in labor," she fretted.

I brushed her off. "Oh, I know I am," I said. "I just want to sit here until I absolutely have to go."

My sister turned to me, her face dead serious. "I am not delivering a baby. You have to go *now*."

She started gathering my things, ignoring my protests. I tried stalling her, explaining that my labor goes on forever. I pleaded with her to let me just finish up my work. She compromised by packing everything up: the paperwork, the Dictaphone, extra tapes, and all. "We're going *now*," she said. "You can do whatever you want at the hospital."

* * *

My hospital experience was entirely different this time. First, Dave wasn't there telling me how to breath or complain about being hungry. Secondly, with this labor, I opted for an epidural. With my other two, my Dave wouldn't let me have any medicine, so this was a *huge* deal. Soon, my labor pains felt like a blip. I watched contractions on the monitor but couldn't feel a thing. I was feeling pretty damn good, and it was fantastic.

Still, it was taking even longer than usual because an epidural can really slow down contractions. But I don't wait for anyone. It was time to get back to work. So, there I was, hooked up to the IV, hooked up to the machines, doing billable hours with my Dictaphone, catching up on my work.

The doctor walked in and just stared at me. Clearly, he had never seen a woman in labor who was also working.

"What are you doing?" he asked in a shocked tone. "Could it possibly be billable hours?"

Billable hours are part of the work a lawyer needs to do that's related to a client's case. It's the labor, if you will, of the work.

"Yes, exactly," I replied.

"I've never had anybody do billable hours in a delivery room," he said, laughing.

I recall an episode of *ER* blaring on the television in the background. "Okay, just let me know when we're going to deliver because I'm going to keep dictating." It was a beautiful thing. Work was my meditation. You might listen to music when you're in labor. For me it was billable hours.

But eventually I had to put down the Dictaphone and deliver my beautiful baby girl, Johanna. When I first found out that she was going to be a girl, I told my mother I was going to name the baby after her. My mother was completely against it. "No, that's a German name," she said. "No one will understand it. She'll be looked at as strange." I told her I didn't care. That I loved the name and that it's a family name. So I named Johanna under protest. And miraculously, she could be my mother's twin. Blond hair, green eyes, fair skin. My mother took one look at her in the delivery room and declared in wonder, "How did you do that?"

Two days later, I was back at work. I had a case in front of the Court of Appeals that I wasn't about to miss. I brought Johanna to my office, and my secretary watched her. We had a portable crib, swaddles, wipes, and diapers—everything we needed.

I argued my case (yes, one of the files I was working on while I was in labor) in front of the Court of Appeals and won. I could just feel that the judgment would be on my side, and I was right.

"Counselor," the appellate judges said, "you can't possibly say anything better than you did in your brief."

Little did they know I crafted and practiced most of my oral argument in the delivery room!

Elated, I left the Court of Appeals courtroom down the center aisle beaming like a bride with pride while attorneys stared at me with looks of wonder. You see,

Court of Appeals judges rarely show their decision-making hand during oral arguments. I returned to my office and held my beautiful baby. I was so proud of myself. I felt invigorated by my drive. I had just proven that I really could do it all.

Look, I understand that not every labor is as easy as this one was for me. My other two deliveries were painful and difficult. I know it's important for a mother to take time after she has a baby. I also know that if it wasn't for my staff and their help, nothing would have gotten done. But nevertheless, here I was, launching a new life for myself, not only winning an important case for my client but also doing it as a brand-new single mother to Johanna.

There was a time after Johanna was born that Jake and I were close, bonding over her as people do after they have a baby. Babies are the great unifier. And we were both in agreement that we didn't want Johanna to be an only child. But the truth was, I could only afford one child at that point and Jake still wasn't up for contributing in that way or in any real way. Still, he saw Johanna regularly, about once a week, until about the time she began kindergarten.

That's what people don't understand about being in an abusive relationship. You can be a strong woman like I am and still be with a man who abused you emotionally for so many years. I kept returning to him because I believed what we first had together was so strong. The love that he had for me, the way he looked up to me, the way I helped him with legal cases and how he made me feel when things were good—all that was what I was coming back for. That was the grooming in effect. He was a master manipulator.

And when things were good between us, I dreamed Johanna would have siblings closer to her age than Jennifer who was eighteen and David who was twenty when she was born. And it was a dream Jake said he shared. I believed it just wasn't a reality just yet.

* * *

In the meantime, work kept me fulfilled in other ways. Legal advice doesn't come cheap. But I was always happy to lend an ear for free, and there were many people I met over the years who would just call for some advice, basic questions about child support, a will, or an affidavit. I had no problem taking phone calls and answering simple legal questions from people, regardless of whether I knew them and without payment of any kind. The power of putting good will into the world was taught to me by my grandparents, but also by my father who always said, "The good you do in the world is returned ten-fold."

One particular phone call I answered was a woman in an assisted living situation who had purchased a fancy electric wheelchair—paying nearly three thousand dollars. She'd changed her mind, cancelled the order, and requested a refund that was denied. She had limited income. She couldn't afford a legal bill. I told her there would be no charge, that I was treating her like my grandmother. A week later, she had a full refund. She sent me flowers and fifty dollars. I called her and thanked her and explained that I would be returning the money. She said, "No, please keep it. I'm treating you like my granddaughter."

One day, after fielding multiple phone calls, I turned to my secretary and said, "I ought to be Frasier." It was the mid-1990s and the television show *Frasier*, about Frasier Crane, a psychiatrist who had a radio call-in show, was extremely popular.

And then the idea occurred to me: I could do a radio show.

My secretary laughed. "Don't you have enough to do?" she asked. "How are we going to fit this in?" Like everything else in my life, I didn't listen to someone else's doubt, I listened to my gut.

Soon enough, after speaking to a few people about making a radio show, a local radio station gave me the opportunity to become the host of a call-in show, and we played around with time slots and networks. I had named it "Ask the Family Lawyer." Sponsors were found, and we learned what worked and what didn't. For several months, a station was interested in syndicating the show, and I learned that many radio talk shows were created in the hosts' home. Doing a radio show back then was a lot like doing a podcast now. You needed a studio, yes, but you could create one in your home. All you really needed was a microphone, headphones, and a basic broadcasting deck that allowed you to control the sound. My new producers got me movable equipment so I could do the show anywhere: on my weekends away in the military or even on vacation in our family home up in northern Michigan. Here it was a year later, and I was being broadcast throughout the United States.

I loved doing the radio show. I treated every caller like a client. It helped my practice somewhat, and it gave me greater name ID. But it was more about helping people one at a time, answering questions, or talking about problems they had and giving them some good advice and peace of mind. I'd recruit a diverse group of guests to join me on the show. Sometimes it would be my sister Helen, who primarily practiced family law in my firm; other times it would be a local judge, or perhaps a lawyer with expertise in a specific legal area we were discussing that day. On occasion, it might be a friend who was a therapist who would speak about emotional or relationship topics, especially if we were talking about divorce law and child custody.

One of the most common questions we got was from men who were being withheld visitation rights because they were behind in child support. I remember one man calling and saying, "I'm behind on my child support. She's not letting me see my children. I'm suffering terribly, and so are my kids. My kids call me and want to see me, and I'm not allowed to see them because I haven't paid. But I've lost my job, and I just don't have the money . . ." I always advised them to file a parenting time complaint with the court and that the law is that child support is the right of the child and the obligation of each parent. But also, that each parent has a constitutionally protected right to raise their children, and most important, that money and visitation are not related. If every parent who was late on, or didn't have the ability to pay child support, lost visitation, there would be a lot of children without parents. My stance was, and the law is, that we simply can't have a system where poverty dictates whether or not you see your children. If you are behind on child support because you lost your job or didn't get a bonus, you should still be able to see your child. It cannot be about the money. Otherwise, we would have two classes: one with money and who can raise their kids and another who had no money and no contact with their children.

It shocked some people about how many calls we received on the issue of child support and parental rights and that I took such a firm stance. Not only is this the law, but children also have rights too. They have the right to see their parents and should not be put in the middle of a financial fight between parents. And I remain hopeful that children will have a separate constitution that gives them a voice; the gives them the right to be believed, not abused, or mistreated; and protects them from being pawns between fighting adults.

Sadly, another common question was about reporting an abusive parent. A caller might say, "I know my neighbor's getting drunk. She has children, and

I worry about them. What can I do? It's disturbing to me." I always had the same response: report them to the authorities, the child protective service. Yet people feared retribution. They didn't want to be seen as the one calling the cops or child protective services. "Here's the thing," I would tell them. "When you call the police department to report child abuse of any kind, it's anonymous. Child protective services, even law enforcement, will not disclose who called. Once the call is made, police and protective services can do a welfare check to ensure the safety of the child or children. The court isn't looking to separate families. They want to help. They want to provide services. They want to get the family back on track. They want to help parents, keep families together. And that's not just the truth, that is the law. But, in some cases, the law finds that rehabilitation isn't possible, and families are separated for the protection of the children."

I was always very willing to answer these questions. They're the kinds of questions that make people uncomfortable. They don't want to necessarily ask that kind of question in a face-to-face scenario, or they don't have the money to consult a lawyer. I learned something about myself doing that radio show: I liked being a sounding board for difficult questions. I might have had my own problems that I was dealing with, but helping other people always made me feel good. It gave me a great sense of purpose. More than that, I know that knowledge is power and that it unlocks doors that are otherwise daunting. By sharing my power, I also began to really own, understand, and connect with the power I had within me.

* * *

I started getting more and more clients in my law firm. Things weren't good with Jake, but that was always the case. He started getting envious of how well I was doing in my life. Then he would go back to telling me how wonderful I was. How smart I was. Sometimes we'd travel together. We'd go to my parents' condo up north to spend time together. The relationship was far from over.

Despite my issues with Jake, I was happy.

My law firm was doing well. The firm continued to grow. Garry Goolsby left the firm to pursue his specialty as a worker's compensation magistrate. I was worried, and Garry said, "There's nothing to worry about; you are already doing it. You will continue to succeed without me." I was grateful for the confidence he had in me. And I did get busier. Very soon after he left, I was hiring new attorneys and additional support staff, expanding in every direction. Then, about ten years into my firm, one case changed the course of my life.

A decade after I had opened my law practice, twenty years after I'd passed the bar, a court-appointed case was assigned to me. It was a case that changed my entire trajectory. A mom of an almost seventeen-year-old teenage daughter entered my office. She sat across from me at the conference room table. We briefly discussed the child abuse case that was pending against her. I laid out the pictures I'd received from child protective services: the pictures of this child with vivid, swollen welts on her back, arms, and legs the size of mountains. She had bruises—marks that were white, red, blue, and purple. The mother's eyes grazed over the pictures without a hint of emotion in her face. She explained that, in order to stop her daughter from leaving the house, she would hit her with a belt buckle. This wasn't one time—not that one time is acceptable—but this was ongoing child abuse.

Once the school saw the welts, child protective services was called, and the court took jurisdiction of the family. I had also talked with the guardian ad litem (this is a person who is appointed by the court as an objective, impartial person to represent the child.)

I had come to learn that the mother had certain rules. She didn't want her daughter to go out with her boyfriend at night. Defiantly, the teen was sneaking outside through her bedroom window. When she would get caught by her mother, the belt buckle was her punishment.

I pointed to the bruises, reconfigured the pictures, holding up the close-ups. "This is not acceptable," I said, firmly. "We need to change this."

But the mother was adamant. It wasn't her fault, she told me. "It's my daughter's fault because she won't stay home. She won't follow the rules." The mother pleaded with me; she told me she did everything she could do. She nailed the window shut! Yet her daughter was still sneaking out of the house.

I could not get it through this woman's head that this was child abuse. I tried to explain to her that she needed to use other techniques like redirection. That she needed to ground her or use some other age-appropriate punishment. "Nobody deserves to be beaten," I told her and slid the images of her daughter's horrific bruises and welts toward her on the other side of the conference table.

She pushed the pictures back at me with anger. "None of this is my fault. It's her fault. She deserved the punishment," she said.

I was so upset at her response that I literally sat on my hands. You can't show your emotions as a lawyer. You're supposed to represent your client without judgment and with the best possible legal defense. I was trying very hard to be very gentle and kind, trying to be understanding. "Yes, that might have been your experience," I told her. "But you can't do this to your child."

No, no, no.

I can't believe I can't get through to her, I told myself.

I can't believe that I have to represent this kind of person. My gut just caved. This is the kind of person who needed to go to jail. This is the kind of person who needs immediate and intense rehabilitation. This was assault. This was child abuse.

I had always thought of being a judge, even when I first envisioned going to law school. But confronting this situation—a woman, pushing away photos of her damaged daughter who she herself beat—was the catalyst for something momentous in my life. I wanted to be in a position of power. To make sure people really took my words to heart when I spoke. And to help ensure the rule of law.

That's when I knew. It was time to run to be a judge.

chapter twelve

How to Make the Rules

Running for judge was going to be a whole new process for me. A renewal in faith. I certainly was going to need to believe in myself if I wanted to do this because no one was going to hand me anything, nor had they ever. I worked in the legislature and in private practice. Now I was ready to serve as judge. I was motivated on many levels, one of which had very much to do with me being a working mother. I knew the consistency that comes with being a judge would be good for Johanna. I could offer my young daughter stability while making the kind of impact I've always hoped to achieve. That was my thought process.

My sister, Helen, who left the firm a few years prior to become a Friend of the Court attorney referee, knew what being a judge meant to me. She knew that it would give the chance to really make a difference in people's lives, and she wanted to support me, but she was concerned. Not because I was divorced and a single mom of three, but because now, Johanna, fathered by a different man, and born out of wedlock, would become public. She was worried about what people would say against me during the campaign. She queried me about what my response would be and pressed me for answers. Helen didn't want to see me hurt. But I didn't give a damn. I had nothing to be ashamed of. I had a wonderful young daughter. A great family. A support network. Being a single mom had *nothing* to do with my capacity to be a judge. And I knew my sister knew this. She wanted just to have a chance to talk through all these obstacles with me, which I appreciated. She wanted to be my sounding board, and she still is to this day. She wasn't accusatory or blaming. She didn't ask me "why?"

My sister knew my theory had always been that "why" belongs in science, not in an open discussion. She didn't tell me that I was making a mistake; she didn't try to convince me I was wrong; she didn't tell me that I needed to change my mind, my focus, and my direction—all the familiar arguments I knew from my father and Dave. And having practiced family law with me for a decade before moving on to work for the court, Helen clearly understood the issues we needed to discuss. She also understood and respected my response: "With over half of marriages ending in divorce, people will understand that I am just like them." Helen agreed and supported me. She has since been promoted and serves as the Ingham County Friend of the Court.

My career and all my hard work were starting to really come to fruition while my father, who had always been the workaholic of the family, was just starting to slow down. It's remarkable how our relationships with our parents evolve as we get older. Here we were, both at a crossroads, and suddenly, the dynamic shifted. Suddenly, after all those years of fighting them, they needed me. Now, we had different things to offer each other.

When my father finally retired, my parents needed to decide where to live. They were still in Saginaw, about an hour away from me and my sister in Lansing. My brothers lived with their families out of state. My parents had friends in Saginaw but no family. They wanted to retire where their children and grandchildren were. I was eager to remodel my house, and they wanted to buy something new. So we came up with an idea: find adjoining properties and build neighboring homes.

We looked at plenty of lots and talked about building houses side by side. There was even a discussion about building a walkway between the two houses for easy access. Going along with that plan, we bought three side-by-side lots in a cul-de-sac, planning to build each house on a lot and a half. The best part about this plan was that it was just down the road from where my sister lived.

Even after we closed on the properties and began to put building plans in motion, something continued to feel wrong to me . . . I kept thinking about my grandmother. After watching what my grandmother had gone through—not wanting to live with me or my parents and refusing to leave the Detroit area where most of the family still lived and where her friends were, she decided to live in a nursing home. Despite the family visiting often, I saw her rapid decline. She called me regularly, unhappy and distressed. I would call the nurses station or drop everything and drive to her. Nanna quickly deteriorated in that nursing home, and it was devastating to me. I would never let that happen to my parents no matter what we had been through. I knew that what I really wanted, and what I was committed to, was that my parents would never live in a nursing home. And I knew that as the oldest child, and the single child, that meant we needed to live near to one another or together. I was also certain that I would be *babysitting* their home when they travelled because they never leave their home unoccupied. I also knew that when God took one of them the other would live with me. I knew that if one of them became ill, there were plenty of resources available in my community that would allow me to keep them at home and bring in all the services needed for their care. At the price of what my grandmother paid, I could do much better for my parents and save money too.

"Why don't we just cut to the chase?" I asked my mother. "We should build one house that is handicap accessible for when it's needed. If we live together when the time comes, I can take better care of you than a nursing home." It just made sense. My mother saw that. She spoke to my father who also understood and agreed. The one thing my father and I agreed upon was the lack of care his mother, my grandmother, received in the nursing home. And Nanna had been in the best, most expensive nursing home in her area. There was medical care, beautiful grounds, lots of amenities, and she had a private room. But it was not like being home. My father and I agreed that the food was barely tolerable and very different from our homemade cuisine. We sold the three lots and bought one lot in a different neighborhood. We designed and built one house to accommodate our anticipated needs.

So, nearly twenty-eight years after I left home, Johanna and I moved in with my parents. I had two grown children, a minor child, a marriage behind me, and multiple strong careers with many more I wanted to pursue. Although we moved in together, in many ways it was like moving back home because when I say I live with my parents, I mean that I *really* live with my parents. While we each have separate garages for our vehicles, there's one kitchen, one dining room, and one family room. It's truly shared housing. The hallways are wider in case they ended up needing a wheelchair or extra assistance. We installed handicap height toilets and walk-in showers. Could we have built a two-family house that would give each of us some boundaries? Probably! But I decided that if I'm going to build a new house, I didn't want to have to worry about dealing with two of everything, living between homes and eventually reconfiguring our lives again. We wanted to be there for each other. My mother helped with Johanna when she was not in day care, and we shared the household chores. My mother does most of the laundry; I do most of the cooking. And we all help each other in many ways.

A few years after our house was built, my sister moved down the road from us. She's a little over a mile away from us, and she comes over at a minimum every Sunday for a visit. When I call her for help, she arrives in minutes.

After everything I went through with my father, I know it might seem like an unusual, maybe even an insane decision to want to live with him again after creating a rich and rewarding life for myself. I had such a tough relationship with my father growing up. We *still* have a tough relationship. We have issues that I have accepted will never be resolved. But I learned to understand and accept the circumstances. While I'd learned that, to truly move forward, I needed to forgive my parents and my ex-husband, I also needed to be kind to my inner girl, and I forgave myself. It was freeing to finally lead my life unencumbered by the past and with my heart, compassion, and voice full and intact.

Is it easy for me to live with my parents? No. It's not easy for them to live with me either. Aside from our past, it's very difficult to live with people, even when it's your own family. The first ten years, we all threatened to move out more than once. *I'm moving out. No, I'm moving out!* We do not always live in a peaceful environment, and there are times when things get very heated, but ultimately, we're in this together. Yes, my father still has his ways. He doesn't like casseroles. He doesn't believe in eating sandwiches for dinner. He hates when the children want breakfast for dinner. He eats on china even when everyone else uses paper plates. Sometimes I'm making three different dinners just to please everyone. He likes to eat late. I prefer the family eats earlier so there is more time to prepare for the next day. Sometimes he refuses to eat with us, so my mother or I serve him dinner at a later time.

I've learned that I can't blame someone for being who they are. I've learned not to blame anyone for not liking who I am because what is important is that I like who I am. I've discovered that an even stronger, fearless courage surfaced the instant I accepted myself. I've learned I can't change someone else's expectations. I've learned that I can change my expectations and that I need to be more tolerant and accepting of others, even when they don't reciprocate. I honor what my grandparents taught me: we must learn to accept each other because family will always be family, and to me, that's the most important thing. At the end of the day, we're family. And I love my family. That's the only way I can explain it. They are everything to me. I want to be the kind of example to my children that my grandparents were to me. Like Nannu and Nanna, I will do anything I can for my family, regardless of any consequence to me.

I've seen so much in my practice. I've seen so much in court. I've seen children walk away from their parents; parents walk away from their children. Families opposing each other in court. Families taking sides in court and alienating each other, forever. And there's never any good to come from family division. If you don't have your family, there's a hole in your life. It's an easy visual for me. I picture myself on solid ground standing with my family. I see myself standing, sinking into quicksand, standing alone.

I think there's another reason I moved in with my parents. Emotionally, I knew that I didn't want to be in this cycle of emotional abuse with Jake. I couldn't do it anymore. I knew that if I moved in with my parents, there would be an irreconcilable wedge between us. We would never, and could never, be something more. My parents had chosen to live with me, and he was not included in the deal. They didn't want to know this man or any man I dated, at least that was still the mantra I heard in my head. They didn't want to be around him unless we were getting married, remember? Was this entirely true? They did have questions about him, but I'm so good at shutting down, at hiding my emotions and just steamrolling forward, that I simply didn't engage about this topic at all. Not with my parents, not with my siblings, not even with my friends. I made it clear to everyone: Johanna was *my* child. End of story. I didn't need a man in my life to raise her, not even her father. It was my way of protecting myself, and my decisions, without discussion and challenge. It was a way for me to guard myself against what was really happening.

Jake wasn't thrilled that I was doing this. But it wasn't his choice. I didn't ask him. I simply announced that I intended to move in with my parents to plan for the inevitable future. Jake and I did have several conversations about getting married, but either he or I would drop the issue every time we would discuss it. We'd just move on. I never pushed marriage. I never said, "Yes, let's do it." Deep down, I knew that I didn't want to be legally entangled with Jake. I needed to protect myself and Johanna. I didn't want to live with a husband I couldn't trust. Dave, my ex-husband, on the other hand, for everything that we went through, is the most trustworthy man. To this day, I know my children and I can and will always be able to count on him completely. I cannot say the same was true for Jake.

* * *

Instead of sorting out my relationship with Jake, I focused on building the house, settling in with my parents, and running for judge. Initially, I decided to look for a seat on the circuit court bench I ran. I lost in the primary, which I deemed a good thing. I'd gotten my name out there and publicly and solidly established that being a judge was my goal. I gained supporters. As we approached the next election cycle, a male attorney who stood next to me in the long courthouse hallway waiting for a hearing turned to me out of nowhere and said point blank, "I know you want to be a circuit court judge, but look who's running for the open district court seat. You can beat each one of them. You run? You win."

And sure enough, I reviewed the names of the eight other people running for district court who were all familiar to me through my legal practice. I went through one person at a time and, in my mind, eliminated them as competition. This one is without experience, this one has a terrible demeanor, this one has no name identification, and most candidates did not have the *breadth* of experience that I had coupled with the name I'd made for myself in the county through my practice, serving on boards and commissions, the military, my radio show, and teaching. Sure, there were few candidates who would be the real challenge, but I was up for that challenge. I knew judges with terrible reputations and politicians who shouldn't have been in politics in the first place. I knew how to run a winning campaign. My friend was right: I could beat all eight candidates. I would be the ninth name on the ballot. And I would win.

Being elected as a 55th District Court judge became my focus. District courts handle matters that include traffic and ordinance violations, misdemeanors, felony bind overs, and matters under $25,000. District courts are considered a "lower" court; circuit courts have much more power and handle cases with claims of more than $25,000 and all felony criminal cases. And until a few years ago, our circuit court was also the court of claims, hearing claims filed against the state. I saw being a district court judge as a stepping-stone—where I'd gain experience and prepare to work my way up to becoming a circuit court judge.

I had worked on multiple campaigns with State Senator Kelly, but along the way, I had run for a few local positions, which I had lost. So it wasn't as if I were going into this race blindly by telling myself, "Oh, I know how to run a campaign." Although I had been through this before and put in the hard work, there's nothing that I've done that's come easy to me. Nothing. I have always wanted to get credit for my own work, to stand on my own. And here was my chance.

I needed T-shirts, pins, magnets, flyers, and signs. I needed *everything*. All that takes money. My home, which I kept in the divorce, was paid off and was my only significant asset. I had no other funds to pull from and had to take out a mortgage on my house. I needed to recruit people to help get elected. No one gets elected without help. I ended up with a core group of five to six people including, but not limited to, Tom Mattern; Emma Malcangi; Susan Pitts; Joan Burke; my sister, Helen; and my two oldest children, David and Jennifer, and my now son-in-law Aaron, who faithfully worked by my side. There were countless other attorneys, clients, family members, and friends who joined in and helped. But the core group worked tirelessly and constantly.

Then there's a lot of groundwork. My entire campaign was built on touching one person at a time. I based it on making connections with people. I plastered magnets on everyone's cars. My kids, core campaign volunteers, and I walked parades, tossing candy and handing out flyers, campaign magnets, and nail files. I attended every debate, made speeches, and answered questions. Wherever I went—football games, homecoming events, festivals, craft shows, or holiday celebrations like the Fourth of July—I wore a T-shirt: AQUILINA FOR DISTRICT COURT JUDGE. I went to every single local commissioner's meeting in the district and spoke. I pounded the pavement; walked neighborhoods; knocked on doors in rain, shine, or snow; asked for votes; and asked for permission to place a lawn sign in their yard or business.

I went out of the city and into the small towns of my district. Like a politician, I'd show up for breakfast at local diners with my T-shirt on and introduce myself. People were shocked. "We've never had a judicial candidate come into our part of the county," they'd say. "We've never talked with a judge." I gave information. I answered questions. Provided lawn signs of all sizes. I didn't just put up a billboard and say, "Here I am. I'm larger than life. Vote for me." Believe me, there were plenty of people who did that. By meeting with all the people that I could, I showed them that I was just like them and part of our community and that I wanted to serve *them* and I wanted to listen to *them*. I not only wanted to follow the laws, but I also wanted to bring fairness and common sense to the bench and the judicial process.

I talked to so many people seven days a week during the long election cycle and met so many people that I got to the point where people were asking me, "Haven't you *won* already?"

Knocking on doors in one of the neighborhoods, one much older woman came to the door and took a good look at me. "You're not old enough to run for judge," she said.

"Yes, I am," I said. "I'm forty-six years old."

She came closer, squinting. "Oh, Henry," she said, calling her husband. "You have to see this woman. She's very well preserved."

What was I? A jar of pickles? To this day I still laugh

about that. But I was certain that, in those moments we shared, I had two more votes.

Aside from her, there were plenty of women who looked at me strangely when I introduced myself as the judicial candidate. "*You're* running?" they'd ask. "How? You're a mom."

"I'm a single mom too," I'd respond. "Hard job, isn't it?" People respected that I was straightforward about it. Especially single mothers, because they didn't feel that anyone paid attention to them and their plight. They didn't feel like a priority. They weren't paid equally because they were women. They were treated as last on the list. My sister had nothing to worry about. The people I met, both men and women, raised me up for being a single parent. They didn't hold it against me.

Sure, we had a few hiccups. Every campaign does. My biggest hurdle? My signs kept disappearing . . . obviously the work of an especially unscrupulous opponent. Signs are expensive. The wires they hang on are costly. The fence posts for the large signs are even more costly. We kept finding signs shredded, or just completely gone, and missing wires and fence posts. It was an expensive loss both in time and in money. It was infuriating. It was illegal. We were stumped about how to handle it. I complained about disappearing signs to my military friends while on duty. Several of the men wanted to borrow our military night vision goggles and set up a stakeout. We laughed about this and how much fun it would be. However, I declined because it was inappropriate to borrow military equipment for personal use. That is when one of the soldiers, who also hunts, came up with a great idea: spray the signs with skunk scent. Hunters use it to mask the human scent. Once you're struck with this scent, it just gets worse and stronger as it's exposed to air. It was the best idea I'd ever heard. While it is illegal to destroy or remove another candidate's signs, it's not illegal to destroy or tamper with your own signs. But first I had to buy it and develop the proper plan so we didn't skunk ourselves in the process of skunking the signs that kept getting stolen. Needless to say, everyone was delighted. Game on.

Tom Mattern, who worked tirelessly by my side campaigning every day, had put a lot of work into getting those signs up, and he wanted retribution! We decided to go out on a Friday night so we didn't have to go to work the next morning smelling like skunk if the worst happened to us and so that we could get up very early to check on our handiwork. We gathered around midnight, donning surgical gloves and masks. We piled into my van, armed with multiple bottles of skunk odor and the full rear of the vehicle filled with new signs and manual post hole diggers, and we got to work. We replaced all the missing signs, some of which were regular yard signs but most were 3' x 4' or even larger and mounted on fence posts. After the sign was replanted, the bottle would be opened, and skunk juice would be poured over the edges of the signs and onto the stakes and posts. When we were finished, we would toss the gloves and the resealed bottle into a plastic grocery bag that was tied on the end of a very long stick. We drove off with that filled grocery bag hanging out the car window. The more signs we sprayed, the smellier things got. We were dying here. *Dying*. There is no way to describe how disgusting the smell was.

At daybreak, Tom was excited to see the results of our evening. He couldn't hold back his curiosity to see if the skunk scent scared anyone away. Tom called me and reported that the signs were still there, not missing. "But," he said, "the signs have been taken off the posts, but instead of being ripped up or disappearing, they have been left partially hanging, tossed on the sidewalk or in the grass." No more wires or posts were stolen. Whoever tried to take them got skunked! Victory!

And a larger victory was at hand as well. I ended up being the top vote-getter in the August primary election and then beat my final opponent by miles in the November general election. Suddenly, here I was, a 55th District Court judge and in the position I had wanted since I first went to law school. I was a civilian judge.

I was in charge of my own future, and I was doing everything I wanted to do. I liked being a driven person. It was a characteristic I wanted to pass down to my children. It was a characteristic that I know my grandparents and parents passed down to me. Yet, I was a single mother. (I still am a single mother.) And ultimately, my children are the most important thing in the world to me. I had three beautiful children. My family was at my side. I wasn't in debt to any man—not even to Jake.

Our tumultuous, unsteady relationship really started falling apart when I became a judge. By that point, his law career was busy, but he was struggling to keep up. He became dependent on me to help him with his diverse projects, his teaching materials, and his legal career. It became clear that he hated that I was capable, but he needed me, and my being a judge got in the way of me agreeing to support his every whim. I helped him with his cases. I helped him with his ego. I offered advice, solutions, and listened to his rantings that every wrong thing in his life was my fault and, because of that, I owed him my time, my help. And I became more and more certain I wanted to leave him. But here we were in this codependent relationship. I was learning to say, "I can't help you now; I'm not allowed to do that as a judge," but a flat-out "no, I can't do that" was difficult for me to say. I still felt as I always had when I thought of simply walking away—that if I left him, I would be abandoning him in the woods.

I was someone in his life who he loved and hated at the same time. And he was someone who I loved and hated at the same time. Patterns are not easy to break, and I acted with Jake a lot like I reacted to Dave and my father when they tried to tell me that I couldn't accomplish something. I worked harder. I became more driven. I wanted to prove that all his negative attacks were wrong: That I had memory lapses. That I was crazy. That I was a stalker. That I was nothing without him. I wanted to show him, like I've shown every other man in my life, that I am not just better, but I'm also stronger and can achieve more. That I'm going to leave him in the dust. Jake never physically beat me, but he emotionally bruised me. To cope with that, I always repeated the mantra in my head and told that girl in the mirror what I wanted to say directly to him: *Just watch me. I'll beat you at your own game.* I knew I had choices to make. I chose to transform his every negative word into a nugget of inner strength.

Which is where we landed when I became a judge. It was something he'd always talked about and wanted for himself. My career had eclipsed his. He had become not only envious of me but had also become overly critical of everything I did. At times, he was very demeaning, and I learned to smile in the face of his negativity, which infuriated him. It was my way of emotionally walking away since I didn't have the courage to completely walk away.

"Congratulations" never came out of Jake's mouth. Not once. Instead, he said, "Now you're going to get everything you ever wanted" with recognizable evil gleaming in his eyes. It wasn't the kind of thing that you would say to your lover, to someone who you're close to. Rather, his response was one of envy, rage, and even accusatory disloyalty. I thought it was an odd reaction, but, like always, I let it go. Upon reflecting, I realize that he was telling me that he couldn't handle my success. That it was too much for him. That he was done.

* * *

Johanna was about five years old, and the world had changed dramatically since she was born in 2000. My family was glued to the news, watching reports on 9/11, and about the wars in Afghanistan and Iraq. Looking back now, I see that Johanna was very much aware that her mom was in the military and that all those events directly affected our family. Slowly, she recognized the uniform that mom wore was the same uniform that the soldiers wore on television. She would watch the stories about people in uniform who surprised their kids at the airport after not seeing them for a year and a half. She began to understand that people in that uniform were regularly getting killed. And because of the chaos in the world at that time, she was seeing me wear my uniform more and more instead of less and less. I was gone for more weekends than ever before. Yes, she had her siblings. Yes, she had my parents. But at that point, she started realizing that other children had their mommies and daddies at home and I was not.

Worry wasn't an emotion Johanna could verbalize. She was too little for that. But Johanna was a very smart kid. (And is now a very smart woman.) She started communicating in her own way.

It was about six thirty in the morning, and I had set my clothes on the bed. My socks, my boots, my hat, my holster. Everything. I went to the bathroom, and when I came back, it was all gone. I looked in the obvious places, but soon, finding my uniform turned into a full-on scavenger hunt. We all looked high and low. And no one, not me, not my parents, could find anything. But where was Johanna? Suddenly, I had an idea.

"Johanna," I questioned, "Do you know where my

uniform is?" At first, she told me no, but after a little more digging, she told me in her squeaky little five-year-old voice that she didn't want me to go to war. She didn't want me to go away anymore. She was going to hide my uniform every time I tried.

It broke my heart. I didn't realize the level of keen awareness this kid had about the world and my place in it. I was going along doing what I do, just barreling ahead. I've been doing this since I was born. I believe in myself. I do whatever I want to. I say fuck the world because *I can*. I don't care if I'm a girl. I'm a person in this world, and I'm going to pull myself up and do, do, do. Which was great for me. Except I didn't realize the effect it had on my kids. I felt, and still sometimes feel, badly about that. I can't go backward, and I don't know that I *would* go backward. I hate that we women always have to be apologetic about our life and career choices. Men don't have to apologize for being driven and ambitious, but women do. We feel guilt, and they simply do not.

I've always loved the military motto: "Be all you can be." I truly tried to embody that in everything I did and still do. I wanted to pass that sentiment onto my kids. I wanted them to know they can achieve whatever they set their mind to.

However, the alarm bells went off when Johanna hid my uniform. That was pretty serious for me. That message rang louder than anything else. I had been in the military for nearly twenty years. I had intended to stay for twenty-five years and retire as a general, but at that point, I had to back off and not go any further. Even though I knew it was the right decision and even though I knew without a doubt that it was the *only* decision, I felt like a failure. (And truthfully there are times I still feel like a failure for not serving longer and achieving my goal.) No one told me this. This was in my own mind.

But I knew my daughter needed me to step aside. And this was reinforced every time she hid my uniform or my boots, which continued until the day I honorably retired after twenty years of service.

Two years after I was elected to the district court, I retired from the military. I was able to focus more on my family while serving my community as a judge and a law professor teaching new lawyers. My last summer camp was especially difficult for me because something I truly loved and respected was coming to an end. My oldest daughter, Jennifer, knew my leaving would be difficult. She decided to come up to Camp Grayling and spend the last few days of training with me. It was such a joy to introduce her to everyone I cared about, to show her the camp, our headquarters, the barracks, the PX (post exchange), the mess hall, the officers club, and all the important places where I spent my time during training. We finally shared the place that kept me away from my children for weeks at a time over twenty years. Jennifer was grateful to experience this event with me. And, today, we have that shared final memory. Yes, there were tears on the last day of my final drill, but I am proud of who I was and my service to our country. I'm proud to be part of the military family. Proud that, to this day, I'm in contact with soldiers I served with, and I'm so very honored when they stop in and visit me because they were simply in the area, not because they had to. I'm grateful when they or their loved ones still think enough of me to ask for help or advice. And mostly, I'm uplifted because I served my country and honored Nannu and Nanna's words: "There's no place like America!"

* * *

Serving as a district court judge offered more stable hours than my law firm, and I could go home to Johanna without worrying about clients needing my attention at all hours. Further, I had been in that courthouse so many times over the years as a lawyer that I felt right at home. It might have seemed like a huge step-up, and don't get me wrong, it *was* a huge step-up and I was honored to be there, but I was comfortable wearing the robe and with all the responsibilities that came with it. And, I knew and loved the courthouse staff, most of whom I still have contact with.

Sobriety Court was one of the courts I was in charge of when I first got elected to district court. Defendants agree to enter Sobriety Court for a reduced charge upon completion. They would have committed an offense where abuse of alcohol or illegal drugs was involved, which can be anything from drunk driving to stealing to support their addiction. There are four phases that a defendant must complete when entering Sobriety Court. The first phase is the most demanding, and it includes everything from meeting with the judge every two weeks, to meeting with a probation officer once a week, and to attending substance abuse counseling. As you work through the phases and reach phase four, you're essentially learning how to create a support system and get your life back on track to include an education, a job, and a sponsor. It's an intense program, but the idea is to rehabilitate your entire life. Studies done on the program showed that with this four-phase program, the recidivism rate went down. But without treatment, studies found, a person is almost guaranteed to be a repeat offender. So it's a remarkable program that is worth the extra effort from all those involved. When I was elected, it was in its infancy.

Most of the people who came into Sobriety Court were in dire straits. When people lose their driver's license, they often can't work. While there is a lot of affluence in Lansing, we also have a high poverty rate, and there are many people living below the poverty line.

There were many people who came into Sobriety Court who could not afford an alarm clock or a bus ride. They could not afford a calendar.

They needed so many basics: food, shelter, transportation. We did what we could to help people scrape by. They needed to get to their therapy sessions, testing, and AA meetings to even have a chance. We would all bring in extra bank calendars, and we got grant funding for staff and it provided a few extras for the participants, like free bus tokens, and offset the cost of substance abuse testing and counseling. There was some community support, but money was a real issue and that made me more frustrated than anything else. I mean, how can we allow people to fail this successful program because they can't afford a calendar or if they can't get a ride to treatment, testing, or court?

When I first started, we had about a dozen participants. Maybe two years later, the program had grown to about 100 people. Sobriety Court was bleeding at the seams. Our grant funding would eventually lapse. Completely overextended. We simply needed more staff to help with all these people who were willing and eager to go through rehabilitation. I begged for another Sobriety Court probation officer for extra support staff and extra money to fund the program. The commissioners did what they could, but it wasn't enough.

We needed a foundation. And we needed it immediately. Look, as an attorney, as a JAG officer, as a judge, and even as a mom, I like to get to the heart of the problem. If someone is telling me that they want to go to AA meetings but can't afford to take the bus there, then I want to get them bus tokens. I want to solve the problem. Judges, at least the good judges, end up a bit like a preacher or a therapist. A good judge is supposed to do the community a service. A good judge wants to see rehabilitation and continued success. I treat every person who comes into my court as a human being. And when you treat someone like a human being, they feel that they've at least gotten a fair shake. If we treat people like garbage, they're just going to sink even farther. We have tremendous power as judges, and I intend to use mine to help people. I call it the power of the robe.

I recruited a group of lawyers, community activists, and fundraisers, and together, we formed a foundation. I named it the Ingham County Sobriety Court Foundation and ensured that it wasn't just for the 55th District Court but for all the Sobriety Courts at all levels in Ingham County. It's amazing what happens when you ask people for what you want and are straight forward, especially when it comes to social justice. The Sobriety Court Foundation has done very well, and it continues today. At the time of publishing this memoir, it is in its thirteenth year, and I am very proud of this accomplishment. The Foundation gets stronger every year and continues to serve those who are struggling and help those who need it most succeed.

Most people who are on probation feel it's just a trap and they will just be sent to prison or jail. That's not the case. Not with me. Sobriety Court, or any other rehabilitative sentence, is a gift. When I place someone on probation, I listen and I make sure they are set up for success, not failure. And I see this as a path to rehabilitation, not punishment. So if money is a roadblock in Sobriety Court, then let's get some damn money.

Because Sobriety Court was such a success, the Foundation's board decided to expand its mission to include all Ingham County Specialty Courts and renamed it the Ingham County Treatment Courts Foundation. Out of courtesy, they asked my permission to rename and expand the mission of the foundation. I was thrilled. There's a mental health specialty court. There's Drug Court. There's the Phoenix Court, which is for human trafficking. Domestic Violence Court. Specialty courts continue to grow as the needs of the community change. I'm proud of my contribution and of all those who have carried this forward.

At the end of the four phases of Sobriety Court, there's a graduation ceremony where I would speak and where I invited others to speak: the officer who arrested them, commissioners, other judges, probation officers, and family members. Countless families thanked me. "Thank you," one mother said to me. "I got my son back."

Probably the most profound moment was when a little girl, about nine or ten years old, got up to speak in front of the courtroom. Her father had been through the Sobriety Court program and was one of the graduates.

"Judge," she said, "I want to talk to the police officer who arrested my dad."

I asked the officer to please step forward. We watched silently as the officer came to the front of the room. And this little girl stood there while a full courtroom of people watched her.

"I wanted to thank you because you arrested my dad," she said to him. "I've always loved my dad. But now I like him."

There wasn't a dry eye in the place. Though I knew the effect of Sobriety Court, and I knew the great success rates, to see it in action, to feel the emotion-filled courtroom, with a little girl able to communicate how happy she is that her father is not only sober but that she can also have a relationship with him was an uplifting moment that I'll never forget.

chapter thirteen

How to Let Every Voice Be Heard

I believe the power we have as judges should be used to make a positive difference in people's lives regardless of why they appeared in front of us. Each person before the judge is not a case. They're not a docket number. They're a person. And I always make it clear that I do not believe in throwaway people. I choose rehabilitation whenever I can. I try to make a difference one case at time with the simple one-ingredient formula: listening.

I wanted to make a bigger difference in my community. I was about four years into my position as a district court judge when a spot opened on the circuit court. A one-time, beloved judge had been removed from the bench for bad behavior. Much had led up to this event, including a very public divorce and custody battle between her and her husband. I could see the writing on the wall. I knew she was going either to leave, or they would remove her. And if she wasn't going to leave, I was going to beat her.

I didn't have anything to lose at that point except time and money. I knew I would have to run while maintaining my district court seat. So, even if lost, I would still have my district seat to fall back on because I wasn't up for reelection to that seat for two more years. I went to work every day and I campaigned at night. My tireless campaign workers joined me once again, every day, including my extern, Luke Goodrich, (in law, an externship is a required internship) who donated all his extra time when he wasn't working or studying for the bar examination. Many lawyers also joined in to help my quest to move from district court to circuit court, and I was very honored and humbled by their efforts on my behalf. I talked to people, shook hands, got signatures, and knocked on over 40,000 doors. All the things I had the first time around, but this time, it was for the entire county, not just a third of it. And then I won.

Being a judge is different than being an attorney, and there are so many things about being a judge that are not taught in law school or in judge's school. Things like funding issues and the ins and outs of the judicial system, what I could do and what I couldn't do, and what people tried to get away with to interfere with or gain an advantage in their case. In a way, district court had been boot camp. The cases were smaller and shorter. I was able to see a lot of the problems people were dealing with early on because I was handling misdemeanors and serious offenses, traffic offenses, appeals from small claims court, preliminary examinations for felonies, and an endless stream of varied civil cases in controversy under $25,000. I worked closely with our court administrator, Anethia Brewer, and I credit her with helping to raise morale in the courthouse and for always paving the way for both myself and Judge Thomas P. Boyd (the other judge in the 55th District Court, to always shine and be both informed and ahead of where we needed to be. (Judge Boyd now serves as the state court administrator for the Michigan Supreme Court.)

Circuit court is where you face the most serious cases, which included felonies and the misdemeanors that travel up with them, civil cases in controversy over $25,000, and hearing prisoner appeals, administrative law appeals, and district court appeals. The criminal cases are anything over one year up to life with a maximum term of probation of five years, whereas in district court, the maximum punishment is up to one year in jail and, for most offenses, the maximum probation is two years.

I see people succeed, but I also see them fail over and over again. By the time someone gets to circuit court, they often have rap sheets that can wallpaper a bathroom they're so long. As a lawyer and then a district court judge, I had always seen faults in the system, but here I was seeing real judicial neglect up close. I would look at a case and think: *Why does this person have thirty-seven convictions and has never been to prison? Why has nobody ever listened to them and given them treatment? Why has this person been out on the streets doing the same kinds of things over and over without any investigation into what happened, what is still happening? Why didn't anyone see how this person's behavior was escalating, how it was a cry for help?* I asked myself those tough "why," blaming questions, and I blamed the legal system for missing very basic questions when we have the power to dig deeply and use our power for the good of a human and for the good of humanity. And in each case, I asked those questions that no one else had asked: "What would you like me to know?" "What have we missed along the way?" "How can I help you?" "What can the court do to help you succeed?" "How can we make this better?" "What can we do to help you break the cycle and start over?"

Neglect in the criminal justice system happens for a lot of reasons. Mostly because it's easy to say, "You're going to jail." It is also easy to say, "Pay money or go to jail," thereby making the system a debtor's prison with disparate treatment between the rich and the poor. Sending someone to be incarcerated based solely on money is something I do not do, and based on indigency, I forgive the payment of money, only ordering the miniscule mandatory fees. I focus on the rehabilitative aspect, which is what matters most. I don't allow affluence, poverty, or status to dictate the outcome. I always consider rehabilitation and what is right for all involved based on the case in front of me. I believe in individualized sentencing. Listening and allowing everyone to speak allows me to achieve that goal.

It is easy to toss someone away and say, "Go to jail" or "Go to prison." It's so very tempting to wait for somebody else to clean up the mess. On the other hand, it's hard work to listen to everyone at sentencing—victims, and defendants—to listen again during a probation violation, to listen to the sob stories and excuses, to listen to the trauma and discord that got someone to this place, and to listen to how failures were someone else's fault. And then to problem solve, to get it right, to keep the rights of everyone involved in the forefront. And, finally, to find something impactful to say to the individuals and, collectively, to all those involved with a goal of healing, change, and closure. It's very hard. It's even harder when the recommendation from the prosecutor or probation officer is to send the person to prison because they don't find them worthy of rehabilitation or capable of continuing probation. That is when the really hard work begins for me—looking at what I'm told is a damaged human and then discovering how to help put them back together without simply discarding them. I travel this rocky road over objections and naysayers because I have seen it turned into smooth pavement. It is part of my disposition to turn "no you can't" into "yes, I can, and with success."

I make it a point to listen to everyone effected by each case in my court. I listen to the victim, of course, but I also listen to the defendant. When you're listening to the defendant, you are listening to the problems that go on in your community, and we must ask ourselves *Where did we fail as a society with this defendant, and how can we fix it?* If you can fix it one defendant at a time, you will have less victims. And look, if someone comes in front of me repeatedly, someone who was using drugs, I'll address that. "You're shoving down problems with drugs that you haven't addressed, I'm right, aren't I? You won't get better until you share what's happening—not with me, but with a therapist—your secret keeper. Can you do that?" "You're blaming yourself—do you understand that what happened to you wasn't your fault and that this crime-spree is your cry for help?" And I reassure them that they can do great things by shifting their mindset and refocusing their energy. I'll put them in group therapy, individual therapy, anger management, cognitive therapy, parenting classes, GED, and trade school classes. Sometimes I send them to gun safety training because I know that, pleading to a gun charge, there is a high probability it won't be the last time they have a control of a weapon. I order them to whatever treatment and programming will help them achieve success. It is not a one-size-fits-all proposition. It is a listening, common-sense proposition that must be filled with belief and encouragement because they have beaten themselves up enough and everyone deserves to be given the gift of hope and the gift of knowing someone in power believes in them and thinks they matter. How do I know this registers with them? It's not just based on the success at the end, but the tears I see as they hear me talk to them like worthy human beings.

Living a joyful, productive life is the birthright of everyone. I'll tell them, "You need to heal by first forgiving yourself. You don't need to tell me what it is, but there is something you haven't shared. You need to deal with it." Because when I say these kinds of things, when I address the issue beyond the crime, men and women alike will cry, and in an almost whisper say, "How did you know?" My response surprises them. "I know because I can see the rocks that you're carrying. I can feel the pain of you carrying that heavy load. I see that you're carrying a backpack of heavy rocks, and you've got to let them go."

Just recently I had a woman in my court who had been a repeat offender. She was coming back because she was doing well, and her probation agent wanted her to get off early. She stood in front of me, and she looked good. She sounded good, much better than the first few times I had seen her.

"You're the one who told me I was hiding something," she said to me. "I thought I was doing so well. But I wasn't. I was addicted to meth. And then you looked at me this last time and you said, 'You still haven't figured out what keeps bringing you back. You need to dig much deeper. It's there.'" She paused and stared at me before she continued, then said, "I didn't know it at the time, but I did dig deeper into my problems, and I figured it out with my therapist. Now I'm here. And I'm clean. I'm working on myself. I'm finally happy. Thank you."

I'm not a therapist, but I do feel that it's my responsibility, that it's *every* judge's responsibility, to find out *What brought this person here? What is their background? What can turn this around for the better?* It's our responsibility to wake them up and ask, "What is happening?" "What is going on with you?" "What would you like me to know?" "How can I help?"

When I say this, I mean it. I am interested in hearing how we can rehabilitate the defendant if it's possible, even if it's an extreme case. For example, David Lee Arnold had been convicted of indecent exposure seventeen times when he came before me in court. He had exposed himself in all sorts of places—in coffee shops and many other public areas. He had a compulsion that he couldn't control. The prosecutor finally said, "This guy has got to go to prison. He's been in and out of the system, and he hasn't stopped doing this. We've got to protect the community."

But something didn't sit right with me. He liked to show his privates, yes, and of course that was unacceptable. I wouldn't have wanted any of my kids to have to endure something like that. But Arnold was not a pedophile. He had been happily married to a wife who had stood by him for over twenty years. Also, and this is a very important piece to the puzzle, Arnold *owned* what he did. I have dealt with many defendants who excuse what they did, who refuse to admit what they did, or who cannot admit to wrongdoing—case in point, Larry Nassar. (We will get to him later.) Arnold wasn't doing that.

"Yes, I have a problem," he said. "Yes, I'm willing to do anything." That's the kind of defendant I will go out on the line for. Because when you see somebody like that, basically on their knees begging, saying, "I just need someone to hear me," then you know what? I'm going to listen. I'm going to ask, "What would you like me to know, and what can we do to help you?"

The attorney representing said there was an experimental drug called Lupron Depot, which could possibly be used to reduce sexual urges. Lupron Depot, which lowers testosterone levels, is typically used to treat prostate cancer. Could we explore this option?

The prosecutor didn't like this idea. They told me I couldn't do this. But I don't believe in throwaway people. If there was even a remote possibility for rehabilitation, I wanted to try it. On the flip side, if it didn't work, then he had a prison sentence. In fact, I could have imposed a long prison sentence, which could have cost him up to the rest of his life and cost the taxpayer thousands of dollars every year. It is a balancing act I take seriously. So we had an evidentiary hearing about this drug. Again, this takes time, and it takes listening. The evidentiary hearing took half a day out of my docket. It took a lot of discussion. I didn't just order him to go on medication without diving into it.

At the time, a lot of articles in the paper questioned this treatment. After seventeen indecent exposures, was it ethical to not send him to prison, to let him out after a year? Was it ethical to give him this medication? The answer here was simple: this is a human being. There's a treatment available. We are not providing probation without the treatment. If we don't give him the treatment, or at least try it, then we throw him away for life. The punishment for this particular crime is one day to life. That means he would have died in prison without us ever taking a chance on healing him. He was open and willing. It was available. It was prescribed by a doctor, and it was overseen by a doctor. I prescribed nothing. I was simply ordering him to follow his treating doctors' recommendations, including taking all medications as prescribed, including the Lupron Depot.

Part of Arnold's sentencing was a year of jail time. His doctor ordered a prescription for him to take the Lupron Depot while he was in jail. After his year long sentence, I ordered five years' probation.

The Lupron Depot worked. It controlled his compulsion. Arnold recently just got off probation without one single violation.

* * *

A senior at a local high school who I will not name because I granted her a way to earn a nonpublic record (although the media reported on it so it was not as nonpublic as I would have liked) became the focus of attention when she poured gasoline in her bedroom, hallway, and bathroom, and lit it with a match while her parents were asleep.

Her family was from Albania and her parents had arranged a marriage for her. At seventeen, she was trying on wedding dresses while her friends were buying dresses for the school prom. At seventeen, her friends were getting taught to stand up for themselves while she was taught to be a wife.

As the wedding got closer, she became more and more distraught. She begged her parents not to marry her off. But there was a dowry, there was their cultural pride, and there was money involved. An agreement. They were not going to back down. They were going to bring her to Albania to marry a strange man. She tried, but no one would listen to her. She didn't see a way out of being sold off, so she lit her house on fire. She wanted to die rather than get sent to Albania to marry a man she didn't know and be traded like property.

Thankfully her father called 911 once he smelled smoke, and the fire was put out. No one was injured.

When she came in front of me in the courtroom, I asked her, "What would you like me to know?" She broke down. She was full of despair. She told me her story—that she didn't want to get married. She wanted to go to prom. She wanted to attend college. She wanted to have a life. She wanted to live her life as an American. She didn't want to kill her parents, she told me. She loved her parents, she said. But she did this out of desperation. Desperation to be heard.

Clearly, this was not your average arson case. This girl didn't just decide one day she hated her parents and was going to burn the house down. I didn't blame her. I didn't shame her. I listened and believed her. And I openly blamed her parents. During the sentencing, I admonished her parents. What they did by attempting to sell their child for a dowry is child abuse. It was unfortunate that they weren't in front of me because, if they were, I would have put *them* on probation. I understand that was cultural, but in America, we don't sell our children for a dowry. Not at any age.

I allowed her to earn a nonpublic record through successful probation, after which she would be twenty years old and , I hoped, fully engaged and happy in college and on her own. I can still see her grateful eyes as I sentenced her, and I can still feel her relief setting in when she heard my orders. I ordered surrender of her passport as part of her sentencing. This was to protect her from her parents or from anyone else kidnapping her. I also sent my order to Immigration and Naturalization Service, or INS, and instructed INS not to reissue a new passport. I was relieved to receive an immediate acknowledgment and agreement by INS. We couldn't take the chance of her parents trying to claim a lost passport or to renew her passport and then forcing her on a plane to marry her off before we found out. She was ordered to attend counseling and follow all recommendations of her treatment plan because she obviously had been traumatized. I allowed her parents to attend her therapy, if requested by the therapist for family treatment and healing. I can tell you I have had very few defendants with that much gratitude in their eyes during sentencing.

Not surprising at all, about a year and a half into her probation, I received a request for her to go back to Albania for a cousin's wedding. I denied it. There was no way I was letting her go out of the country. She was still in danger. She successfully completed probation without any issues; she earned a nonpublic criminal record, which was wiped clean; and fortunately, I learned her parents, after hearing everything during the sentencing, decided to attend counseling with her and their tattered relationship was mended.

The high school senior and Arnold were successful cases because I listened to their stories. I dug deep. I became creative. I let them know I believed them, I believed in them, and they mattered. I let them know that their criminal behavior did not define them and that they were worthy of following a lawful path and doing magnificent things in the world. This is a concept that should be utilized by all judges. Sadly, it's not. I had already been teaching for many years, but at this point, I was a law professor at Western Michigan Thomas M. Cooley Law School and at Michigan State University College of Law. I've taught a range of classes from civil and criminal trial practice to criminal procedure, criminal law, defending battered women, legislative process, elder law, animal law, military law, child abuse and neglect, and family law and family law trial practice, and in all those classes, I always impress the importance of best practices, which includes listening and treating all people with respect. It means treating each client like they are the only client. I emphasize that as judges, we should use our power to make positive changes in people's lives one case at a time. This is the way I know how to change things.

Several years ago, I had a young man in front of me who was under twenty-one. He was there for all the usual reasons: drugs, gangs, poverty. His grandmother was there in the courtroom, too—this feeble, wonderful old woman who sat with the rosary, praying for her grandson, as stoic as could be. I sentenced this young man to two years under the Holmes Youthful Trainee Act, known as HYTA. The HYTA program allows defendants to keep criminal convictions off their public records. Judges can order HYTA for most crimes (not all) and over the objection of the prosecutor for people seventeen and under twenty-one. Recently, the Michigan legislature expanded HYTA so that it can be granted to ages twenty-one and up to age twenty-four *with* the prosecutor's approval. I believe in HYTA because it is an excellent opportunity to provide young adults with educational and other therapeutic programs in addition to a fresh start. It is important to recognize that science now knows that brains are not fully developed until the age of twenty-five, something I've intuitively known as a mother and has guided me on the bench when sentencing young people.

Let me tell you a little bit more about HYTA because it's a program I not only really believe in, but I also allow qualifying offenders to participate often over objection, and I allow it not once but sometimes on multiple case files. I also allow them to earn HYTA on probation or while incarcerated. Some judges don't give it when they can, others take it away very easily, and others only allow it once. And this is why I like HYTA: In 1959, David Holmes was elected to the Michigan House of Representatives. He was a well-respected black representative out of Detroit. In 1974, he was elected to the Michigan State Senate, and when I was hired by Senator Kelly, I had the privilege of getting to know Senator Holmes and worked with him on the senate floor. He was a good man, the kind of thoughtful man who understood his constituency and knew that all children not only needed but deserved second chances—sometimes multiple second chances. They needed help. He had a simple theory about these kids who ended up in court: "Young and dumb." His words, not mine. He would say, "When you're young, you are young and dumb. You need an opportunity to learn from your mistakes and go forward and get past them."

Obviously, in the 1950s and '60s in Detroit there were a lot of other factors that were getting black kids arrested. There were race riots. There was severe poverty. There was injustice with police officers. There was discrimination. Senator Holmes knew this. He knew that the kids in his district needed a fresh start, and that's why he created and fought for this program. Through his many years of training and understanding of both the system and his community, he found a way to help these children and future generations.

When a defendant is sentenced under the HYTA statute, if the defendant can't complete probation on the outside, the defendant can go to a special facility at the Thumb Correctional Facility, which is just outside of Flint; the HYTA participants are kept completely separate from the adult inmates. I've visited it because I wanted to make sure that the young offenders were in a place where I would want my own child if they were in that kind of situation. It's set up very much like a community college with trade schools like the building trades and chef training, educational programs, and substance abuse and mental health programs and other rehabilitative programs.

Some of the kids who come before me have been through terrible situations. Some of these kids don't have a place to live. They've been abused mentally and physically. They've been trafficked. They're homeless. They're part of a violent gang. When I'm sentencing someone, I look at all the factors. I try to imagine them as my own children. And I look at these children as if they were my own because so many people don't have a mommy and daddy who provided for them, as I always explain to my law students. They didn't have a mommy and daddy like you did. They weren't told they were valuable enough to go to school, to be educated, to do anything other than wear a jail suit. I try to reprogram these kids. I always tell them, "I'm sorry. You didn't deserve to be treated that way. I wish I could take you home with me." And they'll start crying because nobody ever wanted to take them home and no one told them they were loved or that they mattered. No one told them they deserved a bright future. It just breaks my heart. I know that hurt people, hurt other people. Talking to both the victim and the young offender, allowing them to hear each other, allows them all to heal. I know it helps the victims to know more about the defendant, and they often agree with HYTA. I go home from work after days when I see young people like this and I hug my kids. My children get me through a lot, just by being there—something they likely don't even know about me. Every judge should be doing this, by the way. This should be a common-sense practice. Despite what judges might say about being busy, we each have the responsibility, the time, and the ability to listen for as long as it takes, one case at a time, and to make meaningful decisions.

So back to this kid in front of me with his grandmother in the courtroom. It was clear that he needed to be away from the gangs. Away from drugs. Away from the cycle of violence. HYTA was going to be a good fresh start for him. He had one thing to ask me. His grandmother who was sitting in the courtroom was dying of cancer. She had raised him. After two years, when he got out, she wouldn't be here. He wanted to hug his grandma. Just one last hug before she died. This sweet grandmother, with her rosaries and tears, watched.

And I said, "Yes, you may." They hugged and they kissed goodbye. It was very touching, despite being in a full courtroom and surrounded by deputies. And their whole family mouthed thank-you through their tears of joy at this hugging scene.

But the sheriff wasn't happy about it. He reported me to the chief judge and to the State Court Administrative Office (SCAO), saying it was a safety issue. But this wasn't a safety issue—it was a *human* issue. This was a kid who needed a hug from his grandma. He was not going to put a knife in someone's back. How can we be inhumane and expect people to come out being rehabilitated? We can't. This kid wasn't ever going to see his grandmother again, and I know what that feels like to lose a grandmother, someone who was like a mother to you. It leaves a hole in your heart forever. That hug was the last thing that kid received before being sent away, and he ended up doing exceptionally well. One of the reasons he did well was because he *knew* somebody cared. In that moment, he got his wish, and he respected that. I think that's part of rehabilitation.

And one additional point. As you know by now, I'm military trained. I know all about safety. I've attended military terrorism training. I've attended safety and security training. I also know about courthouse and jail security precautions. I also know that a hug can stop a bullet. A hug can stop an outbreak of dissidence. Allowing a hug tells people they matter, and, despite what they did, that I truly care—the court cares. I had been reminded many times by the sheriff that he runs the jail and that I run the courtroom. Shortly after this hearing, that male sheriff stood with the male chief judge and the male SCAO regional administrator to tell this female judge what I could and could not do in my courtroom. Not one of those men, who are all retired now, asked me what caused me to allow the hug. "I've heard you, and I'll do as I please in my courtroom." I said firmly and with a smile. I figure when the people who elected me tell me they are unhappy with me, they can vote me out. So far, I remain the largest vote-getter.

As a judge, I believe that it's my responsibility to take the time to say to the people standing in front of me, "Where do you see yourself in five years?" And it stuns many of them because they haven't thought past the next meal. They haven't just been hungry for food but also for affection, for education, for finding meaning in their lives. They haven't thought about the *next day*. I often use a question that my father posed to me, which is, "Do you want to *own* the bus, or do you want to *drive* the bus?" And they always say, "I want to own it." I give a reassuring smile and say, "Okay, then. Let's figure out a way that you can do that. Let's figure out a way you can be in charge of your life." Often with tears, they say, "Yes, Your Honor." But they say it almost in a whisper. I know that is because they don't believe in themselves. I also know that they haven't had anyone believe in them. I tell them I'm military, and if one of my soldiers spoke with uncertainty like that, I'd order them to do twenty push-ups. I ask them to answer with meaning, with feeling, loud and proud or to give me twenty push-ups. Their demeanor changes. They laugh and repeat it. They repeat until I know positivity rings in their gut. Then I say, "Deal?" They acknowledge: "Deal." I ask them to come back and show me the great things they have accomplished. And they do.

Recently, I had a young man convicted of felonious assault (assault with a dangerous weapon) who I had placed on probation. He was brought before me on two probation violations—he didn't show up regularly for treatment nor for substance abuse testing. His probation agent, following their procedures, recommended probation revocation and a prison term. But here's the thing—he tried. He tried under COVID-19 conditions, and he hadn't accomplished a lot, but he tried. He had taken a few tiny steps forward. I learned after asking "what would you like me to know" that he was trying to comply with my orders despite living in a tent in the backyard of his father's home. He was only allowed into his parent's house in the morning for food and grooming issues. When I ordered that he be continued on probation with services that included finding him proper housing and employment, he cried. When I explained that while his father may have his reasons, I didn't believe he deserved to be living in the backyard like a dog—I told him I thought he was valuable and mattered and that I was certain he could succeed. I asked him about his future aspirations and applauded his goals. I invited him back to one day show me his accomplishments. All he could do was continue to wipe his dripping eyes with his sleeve and tell me how grateful he was. He knows I saw him, I heard him, I believed in him, and I have every reason to believe I will soon sign his successful discharge from probation orders.

I always have externs and volunteers in my courtroom. And we talk about the matters I've just heard while we are on break. When these law students and prelaw students see what happens in my courtroom, they always ask, "How can you be so nice?" But I don't see it that way. It's not about being nice. I'm not always nice! Especially to defendants who have inflicted cruel punishment on their victims. Especially not to defendants who refuse to take ownership of their crime and admit to wrongdoing. It's not about being nice. It's about being *fair.* It's about not treating people like animals, even if they're criminals. I really try to impress this on my students because if I'm teaching them how to be a good lawyer or a good judge, then it's not just about the facts. It's about the person too. It's about listening and making individual decisions and understanding the ripple effects of crime and of healing. It's about treating people humanely and with compassion because they haven't had that in their life, because they can sit in jail or prison and get angrier or they can sit incarcerated knowing that someone cared and believed in them. Because, the truth is, when they are released from probation, jail, or prison, they do not have a scarlet letter on their forehead. They silently reintegrate into our community where our family and friends live. If they are angry because they feel they weren't heard and that they weren't treated fairly, the inner turmoil they carry bursts once they are returned to the outside and they commit other crimes, like shooting up parties or malls. If they feel they have been treated fairly, they vow to pay their debt and to do better, and we are all safer for it.

I love being a professor and teaching students the wisdom I have learned. It keeps me fresh with younger people and their opinions, but it also keeps me fresh on the legalities. Teaching means everything to me. And before you ask, yes, I can do all of this. I can help to change people's lives. Give everyone a fair shot. I can teach a new generation of students how to listen to people. Yet, no matter what I do, I'll still get a lot of flak for it from others, including my parents. Yes, still to this day. When I'm at home, my parents are saying, "You're a judge now. Why are you still teaching? You don't have to teach." It's the same kind of questions I've gotten my whole life. The kinds of questions that made me feel like I was being judged, blamed, and shamed. "Why are you joining the military?" "Why are you going to law school?" "Why aren't you focusing on your kids?" "Why are you starting a law firm when you could work for a real law firm?" "Why are you becoming a judge now?"

Society dictates that women fit into a certain role. You're a judge now, and that should be enough. You're in the military and that should be enough. You're a mother and that should be enough. Except it *wasn't* enough for me. *I* get to say what's enough.

From the time that Johanna learned to talk she would beg me for a sibling. Of course, she had David and Jennifer, my older kids, but it was a different relationship. David and Jennifer were much older than her. This isn't to say that Jennifer and David weren't amazing with Johanna. My two oldest have been the greatest big sister and brother that anyone could ask for.

Jennifer was seventeen when Johanna was born. She left for college at the end of August and attended her first year at Western Michigan University in Kalamazoo. Johanna was born in November. After meeting her for the first time, Jennifer couldn't stay away. A year later, she transferred to Michigan State University in East Lansing, where she joined a sorority. They allowed families to eat at the sorority for dinner. So that's what Johanna and I would do just about every other week: drive over to the sorority house near campus and have dinner with her big sister. Oh, Jennifer loved it. Her sorority sisters fawned over Johanna. It was adorable. Her sorority was also very involved in the community. Once a year, MSU's Greek community would close down some streets and sponsor a Halloween trick-or-treating event. Jennifer's house invited trick-or-treaters to come over for games and other fun things for kids. Johanna was over the moon to share this special event with her sister. And so was Jennifer. Despite their age differences, Johanna and Jennifer truly bonded.

But David fell in love with her too. He had gone to college for a few years but then decided to change his path and get into real estate like his dad and join the military like me. He came home to live with me while he made this adjustment and really pitched in with helping Johanna. He is the best big brother. He would babysit her when I had to work late or when I taught late. David put together the toys and the swing set. He was wonderful with that kind of thing. One day he was babysitting Johanna while I left to teach class and he had to change her diaper. He had accidentally ripped the diaper tape off and decided that gray duct tape would be the best option. I literally came home and the first thing I saw when I walked through the door was Johanna toddling over to me with duct tape wrapped around her diaper.

"Seriously, David?" I said, cracking up. "You couldn't get another diaper?"

"I didn't want to waste a diaper, Mom!"

They've bonded in so many ways with Johanna. They really did so much to be with her and to help me out. Once, around Mother's Day, they wanted to pick her up from day care. "Sure," I said, a little suspicious. "What are you doing with her?"

"Oh, nothing," they told me. "We just want to spend a little one-on-one time with her." Well, they went over to a photo studio and they took pictures. They gave those pictures to me for Mother's Day. It was the most thoughtful thing. They know that, to me, the best and most valuable art is family pictures. My kids coordinated their outfits and everything. It was an incredible surprise for me. I was so very proud of them.

Jennifer and David are such amazing kids, so present and so loving with Johanna, I wanted her to have that opportunity as well. To be the older sister to a sibling. To feel that bond with someone closer to her age.

This was a drastic change for me. When Johanna was born, I had my tubes tied. I thought I was done. I knew I couldn't afford another child. And I also knew I wanted to focus on my career. But everything changed when Johanna started asking for a sibling. I didn't like that I was raising her like an only child. I had three siblings. Jennifer and David had each other. I wanted this little girl to have someone to *at the very least* gang up against me with.

So, when Johanna started saying to me, "Mommy, I want a sibling. I want a sibling," I wanted to give her that gift. She never let up about it. Year after year. "When do I get to be a big sister? I don't like being alone, so you need to have more kids!"

Was I too old at fifty-one to have more children? Was having three children *enough*? That was something only I could decide.

chapter fourteen

The Rules for Stretching a Heart

Johanna was about eight years old when I decided that I would start looking into IVF. Yes, I knew that her siblings would be several years younger than her, but she still wasn't letting up on me. She still was desperate for siblings closer to her age than Jennifer and David were. Her deepest longing was to be a wonderful big sister like Jennifer was to her. I wanted to give her a sibling so badly. I felt it deep in my soul, in my womb, and in my heart.

But there was something else. Maybe it was selfish. Maybe all parents feel this way. I started thinking about her as a teenager. As a college student. At her tender age of eight, I started seeing her grown up and living a life without me. I was so young when I had David and Jennifer. When they left the house to go to college, I felt not just their loss but also the loss of being a parent. I lost the activities, the phone calls, the contact with their friends and the other parents. My children always had friends over. My friends would stop in. My father would appear on a whim to see the children. Sometimes I'd cook for three, sometimes for several. I often had a crowded table. My house went from a hub of exciting, chaotic energy every single day to being alone. I would come home to a quiet house, and it killed me. No one tells you how empty you'll feel when your children start their own lives. And I wanted them to have their own lives. I didn't want to control them. I wanted them to pursue their passions and their dreams. Yet I felt lonely. That empty nester feeling eventually dissipated when I had Johanna. And then it was just us. We settled into a new normal. But the longing for more children didn't. I was aching for more.

And something philosophically shifted, and something sparked inside. It had to do with being a new mother again, and that's when I knew I wanted more children.

I tentatively started sharing my thought process with people close to me. The reaction was stark. No one, and I mean *no one*, was supportive about this. Everyone said I was crazy. One friend said I better not. My family told me I should date. Other friends told me to get a dog. Many people told me to wait for grandchildren. A dog is not a child. And grandchildren must be returned. I'm selfish that way. I want my *own* kids with me all the time. Even my sister told me she wouldn't babysit if I did this. People really harangued me. My family's concerns? I was too old, and I was too busy.

At this point, I was fifty-one years old. I know my age is an issue for people and that they have a hard time wrapping their minds around it. But when I look in the mirror, I think, *What's happened to you?* Because my brain sees me as nineteen. Despite what the mirror says, I haven't ever really felt my age.

"Okay, fine, so you don't feel your age," people said. "Why would you want to be a single mother by choice?" This was a big problem for everyone around me. I already knew how hard it was to raise a child as a single mother because I had Johanna. Why would I want to do this alone again? Because I was still in a relationship with Jake, he and I spoke about it. He was still in Johanna's life but not regularly. I knew he was cheating on me with other women. People would sometimes even tell me that they saw him out with someone else. But he would always come back to me with the same story. He loved me. They didn't mean anything. Or he'd pull one of his manipulative moves and tell me that I was just imagining it all. Another memory lapse. I shrugged it off. I wasn't planning on forever with him.

Nevertheless, Jake and I spoke about us possibly having another child. Would Jake be a good father? No! He was not present, he was noncommittal, and our relationship was both turbulent and sporadic. But in my mind, I figured the devil you know is better than the devil you don't. And I liked the idea that Johanna and this new child would have the same parents.

Jake, it turned out, was completely for it at first. Yes, Johanna needed a sibling. We should do this for her. But then, gradually, his attitude changed. I can't explain exactly what it was, but it shifted. He slowly started backing off. He just wasn't interested in talking about it. And I could feel it in my gut, something wasn't right. I pressed the issue. I started going to the doctor to investigate my options. Jake agreed to go with me. And that's where I learned Jake had gotten a vasectomy at the same time we began talking about another child. He let me keep dreaming with him. Keep discussing and planning.

It was a definitive moment. This blatant, hurtful deceit gave me the determination to finally say to myself, and mean it, *I'm ready to turn the page and proceed without him.* Decision made; I followed my gut. Which was ultimately the right choice.

With or without Jake, this was still what *I* wanted. I didn't want to give up on wanting more children for anyone. For anything. If I wanted to do this, I was going to have to speak to my doctor to investigate if I was a candidate for IVF. And I was going to have to do it alone. I needed to see if I had eggs. If I had hormones. If I was too old! There were so many questions. My family loves babies. Despite my father always saying that every baby is a blessing, I didn't want any pushback from them. I know my friends, my family, and my kids love me. I also know that they know me. They know that I don't operate like everyone else. Which is why I couldn't tell them.

Creating firm boundaries, like I had done in my head as a child, was the only way I was going to go forward with this decision. I didn't want to have any discussion about how I was too old. About how I should get a dog. About how hard it would be. About how expensive it would be. That I had a demanding job as a judge. About how I would be alone, and they wouldn't help—idle threats I knew, but hearing them hurt. I didn't need permission. And I knew that asking them, or talking to any of them about my decision, would have led to pain not permission. I needed to avoid the conflict, dissension, and anger. I would have subjected myself to a verbal stoning.

Look, that's also why I try to help people who don't have a voice. My whole life has been this journey to find support for just being myself. And I've had to fight for every idea I've had, for everything I wanted, for everything I've accomplished. Support shouldn't be such a hard thing to get, but for me, it has been. It simply hasn't been there. I was choosing—because we all have a choice—*not* to allow people to feel badly about something that was not their decision to make. I kept going forward. In my story, I see myself as the heroine who is plotting her own future.

I created my own little bubble and stopped talking about this decision to my family and friends. If I wanted to do this, if I wanted to see if this could even work, I couldn't wait. My clock was ticking. And the louder it ticked the stronger I got. I literally felt my inner power grow with my decision, and with it, a weakening of the hold Jake had over me. My body. My decision. My life.

* * *

I went into the doctor's office with a neutral mindset. If I wasn't a candidate for IVF, then it's not meant to be. If the IVF doesn't take after one time, then it wasn't meant to be. I really was looking for an answer. I'm a religious person though I don't practice as often as I should. Still, I was looking for answers from God. I would have been fine with either answer because I already had three wonderful, healthy, happy kids. I know that so many women have a hard time getting pregnant. I've had friends in that situation, and my heart broke for them. But after three healthy pregnancies, despite not being a young new mother, I doubted I had any fertility problems. I felt in my gut everything would be okay.

We sat down in my doctor's office so he could tell me the results. I folded my hands in my lap. I didn't know what to think. I was fifty-one years old. *Was* this a mistake? Was something wrong? The doctor has asked me to take the same blood test three times.

I entered the office and sat across from him. "Is something wrong?" I asked. I leaned in and waited.

"I retested you because I thought the lab kept making mistakes." He paused with a grin. "Rosemarie. You have the numbers of a twenty-three-year-old," he said, enthusiastically. "If you want to do this. We can absolutely do it."

In August of 2009, my doctor implanted me with twins. Some people go on vacation in August when they're fifty-one. I decided to get pregnant.

* * *

I waited to disclose anything until after the doctor confirmed I was pregnant, there were two viable babies, and the tests showed a healthy boy and a healthy girl. The first person I told was my mother. I sat down at the kitchen table with her. "Mom, I'm pregnant. With twins."

She was in shock. "I don't believe you," she said with a laugh.

"Yes, Mom. It's true."

"You're kidding," she said. "Really? You are kidding?"

We went back and forth this way a few times with her staring at me, trying to process it. Naturally, she had a lot of questions. *What was the donor's nationality?* Italian and German, a surgeon, musically inclined, and an athlete. (I tried to find a Maltese donor, but there weren't any choices.) *What was I going to tell my kids?* That they were going to have more siblings. *How was it possible?* IVF. *Wasn't I too old?* Not according to the doctor. Not according to my body. Not according to my inner gut.

She made sure to tell me I was crazy a few times. "Maybe I am crazy," I told her, "but you're going to have two new grandchildren." Ah, grandchildren. I got her to smile. More grandchildren. Now, *this* excited her.

"Well," she finally told me, "I need to get some baby yarn, and you're going to have to tell your father." I wasn't *scared* to tell my father. It wasn't like I was sixteen all over again, living under his roof and not making my bed or neglecting to water his roses. We were living together. We were both in charge. Things were very different. I was a well-rooted responsible adult. I was a judge!

Shortly after I learned I was pregnant, my father asked me to go on a trip with him to Argentina. I thought it would be the perfect time to tell him. After he retired, he became the owner of a winery and vineyards in

Argentina where he produced *Aquilina Wines*. He asked me to join him to look at the vineyards. He'd made an award-winning Malbec that he was very proud of and, apparently, it's very good. I wouldn't know because I don't drink wine. Wine is not my friend. It makes me faint.

It was November, and I was about three months pregnant, but I was popping out rather quickly because I was pregnant with twins. I even packed the maternity clothes for the trip, thinking that within a week I'm going to be out of my regular clothes. We were in Argentina, and I couldn't stand wearing the smaller clothes anymore. I was so uncomfortable. I decided to put a maternity shirt on, and we went to a restaurant for breakfast. I ordered steak and eggs. We were eating. Not saying much. Then he looked up at me. "So, when are you going to tell me that you're pregnant?"

"You already know," I said, laughing. "So, I don't have to tell you."

For my whole life, as I've said, my father has always said to me—whether he was happy or not about a pregnancy—that with every baby comes a blessing.

Was this the first thing he said to me? No! This is my father we're talking about. First, he told me I was insane. But he calmed down once I told him it was IVF and that my doctor was a friend of his who helped perfect the IVF process.

"You're too old," he said. I reminded him we have longevity in our family. People live into their nineties in our family, and I'm not worried about it. Then he claimed his doctor friend was guilty of malpractice.

"But it's not malpractice," I told him, "it's science." He took my numbers. He ran tests. I'm perfectly healthy to have a baby. My father came up with every excuse in the book about why this was wrong.

Then we spent the next half of our trip with him

suggesting names and trying to convince me to let him name the babies.

"Well see," I told him. "We'll see."

It's always going to be that tug of war with my father between controversy and acceptance. Always. I learned a long time ago to accept it.

* * *

I've been lucky in that I've always had easy pregnancies. The twins were no different. I continued to teach several classes. I'd finished teaching all my classes but one—and I did finish that after I delivered. I had only been a circuit court judge for two years at that point, and I never missed a beat until my scheduled C-section.

My only hiccup: Johanna was still sleeping with me. I knew I was going to have to move her out of the bed soon. She was old enough, sure, but besides that, I had her new sister and brother coming in soon. It was a week before my scheduled C-section when I pressed the conversation with her that she really needed to sleep in her own bed and think about transitioning to doing that every night. She slid into my bed while I took a shower. It was late, so Johanna was already sleeping in my bed when I slipped between my sheets. And suddenly I was feeling . . . wet. *Maybe I didn't towel myself off well enough,* I thought. But I kept getting more and more wet. I leaped out of bed the instant it occurred to me: My water broke. My water didn't break with my other children, so I had only heard about this experience, though I'd always had towels in my car to be prepared and always cautioned other women to do the same. Yet there I was, with water dripping down my legs, and I realized, this was it.

I jumped out of bed and woke up Johanna and told her to grab me beach towels. "Go get your grandmother and call your Aunt Helen," I said. "We're having the babies!"

The delivery went really well. A few hours later, Marissa and Michael were born three minutes apart. Michael waited. My sister and doctor teased that it was because he was hanging onto my rib as long as he could. They were absolutely perfect. Midmorning, after the babies were born, I woke up to my nephews, my sister, my children, and my parents in my room, excited to meet the new additions to the family. Sure, everyone had questioned my decision, but at the end of the day, as my father always says, every baby is a blessing. And they *are* a blessing. My older kids, Jennifer and David, get it. When people ask them, they say, "Yeah, that's just our mom. She's crazy like that." They don't say, "Mom, we understand why you did this." What they understood was that it was normal for *me*, not them.

Look, having twins as a single parent is not easy. I'm not going to tell you it's easy. When I was nursing them, I didn't get any sleep. I hardly remember it because you'd nurse one, and then you nurse the other, and then an hour later, you had to do it again. There are some vague memories of me watching reruns of *Bewitched*. If only I had the option to wrinkle my nose to get things done. Johanna was thrilled to have a brother and sister. She loved holding them. She loved feeding them. She loved helping me change their diapers. They were like her little dolls.

The thing about twins that I didn't anticipate was how they have each other. Twins are in their own world, best friends, connected by the soul. As they got a little older, around six or seven, and Johanna would tell them what to do—ask them to help mom, clean your room, set the table—they would gang up on Johanna as twins do! They wouldn't listen to her. They wouldn't listen to me. Two against one. And that's just the way it is, still to this day. But each year is getting better, and I have a new respect for moms of multiples.

* * *

I still sometimes saw Jake. Not often. I had the twins. I was a busy working mom. Busy with Johanna. Busy being a judge, and a teacher, and an author. A grandmother to Jennifer's new babies. Busy with my parents. My life was full. I was happy. I felt more and more in control and less and less in need of anything from Jake. We checked in with each other, but I stopped feeling the need to answer to him. I finally disengaged in a very real emotional way. Family is everything to me, so I surrounded myself with my family.

Jake hardly made an effort to see Johanna, and I never pushed him to see her or to do anything. Time passed quickly, and Johanna became a teenager. By the time she was around fourteen years old, she rarely mentioned her father except to say she didn't want to see him. But of course, she was curious about him. He was her father after all, and I've never tried to get between my kids and their fathers. I know that children need both parents in their lives. Around that time, Jake and I started talking about going on a vacation together. His idea. Let's go somewhere so we can be alone. Reconnect. Talk like the old days. I was apprehensive but agreeable to it. Old habits die hard.

I had just picked up Johanna from volleyball practice and we were running into a store to get knee pads for her. She sat in the seat next to me and decided to look up her dad on social media. She hadn't mentioned anything about him to me, but that wasn't unusual. Again, she's a kid. She's curious about this man, her father, who had shown such little interest in her. I don't blame her whatsoever for wanting to understand who he was and trying to get glimpses of his life.

Johanna gasped. "Oh my God, Mom. Look at this," she said, and handed the phone to me.

It was a picture of Jake. And his new wife.

That's correct. He got married. Without telling me. Just a few weeks after we were planning this "trip" together.

Incensed, I called him immediately. "So," I said, "when were you going to tell me you got married?"

Did he say, "I'm so sorry I didn't tell you. I'm so sorry you're hurt. I know you must be shocked"? Reader, do I have to explain this to you at this point? Of course, I don't. His response was something along the lines of this: "Yeah, so what, I got married? She needed my health insurance for her child. You and I weren't going anywhere. You knew all about this—you're just crazy. More of your memory lapses." No mention of the trip we were planning. No mention that we had been talking every few days whether I'd seen him or not without one word of this person, this new wife, his new life. Nope. Nothing one might expect. Jake just screamed at me for stalking him on the internet.

"The internet is a public place," I sternly replied. "Plus, it wasn't me who found it. It was your daughter."

I learned so much more about him after that. I knew there had been more than several affairs over the years. Of course, there were. But Johanna's discovery prompted me to do a little digging, and I found out that he was seeing other women in other states and in other countries. He was a master manipulator. He, I learned, had at least two other women he was involved with who still didn't know about his marriage. And he didn't want them to know about each other or his wife. When I told him he needed to make sure his mess didn't affect our child, he accused me of threatening him and screamed at me that if his wife knew anything, she'd divorce him. "Not my problem," I said. I had no intention of getting involved in any way; only of protecting Johanna should he bring her into his disastrous life. And I told him I refused to take on any blame or shame. That was his alone.

All this new information confirmed what an absolute devil he was, but it also felt like a relief! Because now I was truly, absolutely done. I blocked his phone number so he couldn't call me. I refused to take any emails. No contact whatsoever. It didn't mean he had to cut off Johanna. But that's what he did.

I finally started talking to Jennifer about it. She was in her early thirties at that point. Jennifer is an old soul. She's an amazing daughter. An amazing mother. She has her own children, and career, and she shares her life with a wonderful husband. She's such a great big sister to Johanna, and she hated seeing Johanna go through this. She hated seeing me go through it, too, but she really hated it for Johanna. She wanted Johanna to have a relationship with her father. She didn't want Jake to cut off Johanna because of all of this. His wife still didn't know he was a cheater, that he was still cheating, and that he had another child. He deleted everything about him that could be found on social media. He sent threatening emails to me that I'd regret it if I did anything to expose him to his wife or family or girlfriends. I told Jennifer he felt threatened that I would expose his secret by taking him to court for child support. I told her I'd made an attempt to talk to him for Johanna's sake—to hope they could continue even a scant relationship—but I refused to talk with him again because he was irrational, demeaning, threatening, and just shouting at me.

Jennifer, to my surprise, contacted him. She and Jake met for coffee twice, without me knowing. At their first meeting, Jake told Jennifer he wanted to be part of Johanna's life. Then, they met a second time to discuss how to make that happen. During this second meeting, he twisted everything he said in the previous meeting and treated her like she recalled everything incorrectly and was having memory lapses. Boy did that sound familiar! The second meeting, if you can even call it that, lasted about ten minutes because when Jennifer realized he was lying and trying to manipulate her, she stormed out saying, "Are you f—ing kidding me? I'm done. I'm not listening to your bullshit. Johanna deserves better. You are a coward. Call me when you want to have a real conversation." She immediately called me from the parking lot of Starbucks and told me the whole story. She said that it was clear that bringing Jake into Johanna's life would only hurt her. She asked me how I could have been with him, how I could have stayed with him, how I could have tolerated that behavior for even one day. Knowing me, she didn't understand it. One thing people don't understand about abusive relationships is that even strong women like me can be in them. Jennifer did what I should have done.

After that, everything with Jake was over, for me, for Johanna, forever. A few years later, Jake passed away. A heart attack. Because of the second wife and because I knew his multiple girlfriends would attend the funeral, Johanna and I chose not to attend. There really was no place for us there. I like to picture him with his first wife, happy and in heaven. But a part of me wonders.

There are a few more gory details because there are always a few more details with a man like Jake, someone who was so deceptive and duplicitous and manipulative. But for me, romantically, it was completely and totally over. For Johanna, it's entirely more complicated. And I don't want to tell her story here. She has her own feelings and emotions around this, and that is her story to tell. One thing I can say about healing is that you have to find it. My intuitive, insightful, caring Jennifer bought Johanna the gift of a reading by a reputable psychic medium. After a year of waiting, Johanna went to have the reading. Jake appeared. The psychic could not have known about him. She told Johanna that her father wanted her to know that he made the wrong choices, he loved her and me, and he was very sorry. This brought some peace to Johanna. It brought some peace to me.

The only place Jake exists now is in my fiction books, *Triple Cross Killer* and *Feel No Evil,* and most recently, *All Rise,* where he appears as the evil villain. It's very satisfying to me. You know why? Because then I know he gets his in the end. There will always be a part of him in every evil character I write. It's my way of recapturing my control and my voice. But even beyond my fiction, I feel my successes trump the evil he imposed upon me.

There are times I think, *Geez, I wasted too many years with the wrong man.* But then I think, *Well, look at how much I accomplished.* Maybe someday I'll meet the right mate, but I'm okay if I don't. I have my kids. I have my career. I'm content with who I am. If the one thing God doesn't give me is the perfect relationship, I'm okay with that. I have so many other things that people never achieve in their lives, but I've done it. I'll continue to achieve until the day I die. In fact, I have so many things that I still want to accomplish that I constantly bargain with God to let me live to be a healthy 120-year-old before He takes me home.

I know I don't need a man to complete me or to make me happy. As women, we've been sold a bag of goods that marriage is about finding someone who completes you. That you can't do anything without a partner. Which is total horseshit. First and foremost, *you need yourself.* You have to be happy on your own. A partner doesn't complete you. You work in tandem with a romantic partner. And I want to find the person I work in tandem with, not someone who completes me. *I* complete me.

That's how I was raised, thinking that I had to be with a man. That was the thinking of the '50s. Right? And it's just so wrong. It's flawed. It's defective. It's science fiction. I want to return it and get a refund—with interest.

* * *

You can't avoid it. Once you have five children, you have a different perspective on life. There have been many cases over the years that have affected me as a mom, as a woman. Horrific cases where women are abused and raped, cut and burned. Cases where children are abused. Cases where friends murder friends. I could go on, but you hear these cases in the news every day all over the world. The thing is, I see and hear evidence of the horrific things people do to each other, up close and personal.

You don't have to be a parent for this particular case to pull your heart strings. The case revolved around the death of an infant. The mother, who had been a single mom, had to go to work. She opted to leave the baby with the baby's father instead of her own mother because she was trying to do the right thing and give the father some quality time with his daughter. She was a great mom who was doing all the right things.

The father had a few roommates, and they would get high together. They would get high on marijuana. They would get high on cocaine. They would get high on meth. The mother was unaware of all of this when she dropped the infant off. At one point, the baby was crying and didn't stop. Babies get colicky. They need changing, food, and attention. They need to be held. And so, one of the roommates testified, with tears in his eyes, about how he tried to calm the baby down and play with the baby and feed and change the baby and did what he could. But it wasn't his baby, so he felt he couldn't completely take over. When the infant began to cry again, the father took the baby and slammed her against the couch multiple times, and in the moment, there was nothing he could do to stop him. Now the baby had severe trauma. The roommate tried to help the baby but didn't know how. The father called the mother at work and complained about the baby being ill and uncontrollable. The mother was hysterical, begging him to call 911. But the father refused to make the call, telling her she needed to handle it. The mother was about fifteen to twenty minutes away, and meanwhile, her baby was screaming in pain. Of course, she called 911 immediately, and the roommate continued to try to help, but ultimately, the baby died. The father cared more about his illegal drugs and his own needs then that of his helpless infant.

That case haunted me. And again, you don't have to be a mom for this case to rip your heart out. It's heartbreaking. There have been many horrific cases I've heard, but this one I can't easily forget. Maybe because I saw the mother suffering in the courtroom and saw a piece of myself in her. She could have been me; she could have been any one of us.

I had seen many cases up to that point where innocent children are voiceless victims. It's our job as upstanding people in our community to protect them, to listen to them, to believe them, to give them voice, and let the legal process, fairly and impartially, determine what did or did not happen based on the evidence. Which leads us to one of the most public cases I've ever had before me. A case where no one—not one person—protected hundreds of girls from a monster named Larry Nassar for over thirty years.

chapter fifteen

How to Bring Healing

I realize that many might see the Larry Nassar case as the most monumental event in my career.

But this wasn't my first high-profile case or my first case that appeared in the national news. The murder of a child, Ricky Holland, by his adoptive parents and the alleged murder of Sally Sue Mercer, a doctor's wife, were assigned to me when I just took the bench as a district court judge, and both preliminary exams were two of the longest, most publicized cases in our county. As a circuit court judge, I drew the Detroit bankruptcy case, which was covered everywhere from *The New York Times* to ABC News to news outlets in China and all around the globe. I was also chosen by blind draw as a one-judge grand jury on a case that came out of the Michigan Legislature, and, although I can't talk about the case specifics, it was a high-profile case that had media coverage far beyond Michigan. At sentencing, Brian Farmer, a convicted serial rapist, threatened my life and that of the female prosecutor Debra Rousseau (now Martinez), and the story went viral. I could go on, but the point is that there have been multiple highly publicized cases that went far beyond our county and state throughout my judicial career.

No matter what the case, I try to be as free from

information from outside sources as possible. I follow the national news, but I try to steer clear of local news about cases that might get assigned to me so that I can receive as much information as possible when I'm in the robe. My introduction to this case was no different from any other.

I also had no personal connections. I don't watch gymnastics. I'd never heard of Larry Nassar. Despite the fact we lived in the same area, I'd never met him or seen him or his family in our community. I did not know that Nassar was a faculty member at Michigan State University and that he was the USA Gymnastics' team physician during four Olympic Games. I hadn't read, nor was I aware of, the first newspaper article that came out in 2016 about Rachael Denhollander, the first woman to file a police complaint against him. I didn't know that former gymnasts had accused Nassar of sexual abuse years ago when they were children and that nothing had been done. Until the case was bound over to me from district court after the preliminary examination on February 21, 2017, I had absolutely no knowledge or information surrounding the case. I looked at it with a neutral eye like I do in all my cases. I read the facts and listened to the facts during pretrial meetings with counsel.

What I learned was that Nassar was being charged with up to twenty-nice counts—fifteen that were first-degree criminal sexual conduct. Nassar's defense: he penetrated the gymnasts with his fingers because he was practicing something called "pelvic floor physical therapy." Experts on both sides of the case were to speak at trial. And based on everything I heard and read, it appeared to be a cross between a medical malpractice case and a criminal case. Initially, it was clear to me that to protect everyone—especially the minors involved—the file and related documents needed to be sealed. Counsel agreed.

As I've said, when I'm in the robe, the case in front of me is my focus. And every case is equally important because real people are involved. Giving everyone their time to be heard—the lawyers, the witnesses, the alleged victims, the defendants—that's my focus. I block out everything else around me. So while I continued to stay away from the news accounts as much as possible, my staff alerted me to newspaper headlines and news reports. By March of 2017, it was also clear that details and elements of the case had reached far beyond Michigan. The case picked up speed like a train plowing through everything in its way. Articles began appearing in local news, as well as in the newspapers and on media platforms across the country.

The victims were speaking to the press. The case had started with twenty-three women, and soon enough, more and more women came forward almost daily. Soon there were more women than counts charged against him! It was notable. Among them were women like Olympic gold medalists McKayla Maroney and Gabby Douglas. While I might not be glued to the Olympics, I knew those names.

Now that the media spotlight was on the case, my main concern was to give *both* sides a fair trial with an impartial jury. Finding a fair and impartial jury is always part of equal justice and is my job as a judge. How could we find a pool of jurors when the case was being tried in the media and public opinion was forming?

In an early pretrial meeting with the attorneys, I raised the issue of a gag order. A gag order would temporarily stop victims from speaking publicly about the case.

It was met with extreme unhappiness.

Nevertheless, I plodded forward. As a judge, my aim

is justice, not making people happy. After reflection, I told prosecutors and defense counsel that I intended to put a gag order in place on all the victims and witnesses. That included the many, many women who had come forward.

"The Constitution is here for a reason—to protect all people," I said. "It protects victims, and it protects defendants."

The women accused me of stopping them from speaking about their assault. Their attorneys told me they were upset and they hated me. The victims argued that it was their constitutional right to speak and I was shutting them down. Look, I have spent decades of my life defending all sorts of people and listening to and trying to help those who have been abused, threatened, and demeaned. I had been in an abusive relationship, parts of which I've only recently come to terms with, other parts I may never come to terms with. I only recently found the courage to break free. What the women were saying about me was contrary to what I believed. It was contrary to how I've always acted. But I also knew they didn't understand the legal process. Eventually, I knew they would come to understand that there had to be a fair trial. Stopping them from speaking, meaning the gag order, was the greatest protection I could give to the process of justice.

I've always figured that if I've upset both sides, I've done the right thing. Silencing these women was the last thing on my mind. I was simply trying to get a fair and impartial jury for both sides: the victims and Nassar. A fair trial is a right granted to all in our country. If I allowed those who accused Nassar to share their stories across the nation before the trial the trial even began, there was little hope that a fair and impartial jury would be found. Nassar's defense team was militant on this point and rightfully so.

The prosecution objected, but I held firm on this decision. "How will we find a jury otherwise? What are we going to have, a penguin jury on some kind of snow drift?" I asked them. "Because that's what we're going to be left with."

By March 29, 2017, the gag order was in place. And, as a result, and by no surprise, plaintiff attorneys soon challenged it. Former Olympic gymnast Jamie Dantzscher said in an affidavit, "In my view, this Order shoves all of us abused by Dr. Nassar and others back into the darkness of silence."

Unbeknownst to the victims, that would all change.

Despite the gag order, the case was still receiving a lot of media attention. How were we going to pick a fair and impartial jury who was immune to the daily media blasts and comments? I knew we had to be meticulous with questioning. I knew we needed more jury candidates than I'd ever ordered before. I spoke to our jury clerk, Gloria McGruder. Together, we decided to order 800 jurors in groups of 200. Each person filled out a special questionnaire that I developed with the attorneys. There were a lot of logistics: transport, seating, security, and locations. We had to make sure potential jurors *hadn't been* and *couldn't be* influenced by what they saw in the media.

Another thing came up. Nassar's attorneys wanted to move the trial. This wasn't an option nor was it necessary. Not only did we have proper precautions in place, but I'm a big believer that what happens in our county should *stay* in our county. Further, there was no escaping the Nassar case in our county. The headlines were present in the next county over and in the next state. So there was no need to move the trial. Between the gag order and the lengthy juror questionnaire, I was determined we would find a "clean jury" right here in Lansing.

Even with the number of alleged charges, Counsel

felt that once a jury was picked, the trial could be finished in about three weeks. In my naivety, I believed them. So, we scheduled four weeks for the trial on my busy trial docket. Once the trial was over, we planned to swiftly move on to the next case.

I know this might sound cold, but I have dealt with other horrific cases. Cases where female victims testify to being beaten, cut, and burned repeatedly with lit cigarettes. Where their husbands have thrown them down the stairs. I recently had a case where a woman couldn't speak without hysterically crying. We had to take breaks every fifteen minutes so she could gain her composure. It took two days to hear this woman's testimony.

Yet, as a judge, I have to see through the emotion and the horror of the situation, allow myself to be strategic in planning, and get the case to trial.

At trial, I have to dampen any personal emotions or feelings I might have, keeping myself in check so that I can follow the law and the court rules while upholding the Constitution. I compartmentalized the Nassar case in my mind. The timeline fit in a box. The procedures were on point with safety, expediency, and justice. The emotional aspect, I knew from experience, would come later, at home, when I was alone.

Jury selection was scheduled to begin December 4, 2017, with a short holiday break, and then opening arguments would begin shortly after the New Year in January 2018. I thought we were ready to move forward until Nassar's lawyers requested a delay. Why delay? Because earlier that year, Nassar had pled guilty to federal child pornography charges. He possessed over 37,000 images of child pornography, found on an external hard drive. His lawyers wanted me to delay our case for the federal case.

I declined that delay. Why? Because there was no legal reason to delay the case. Delay was a lawyer strategy.

Nassar's lawyers didn't want our case to influence his federal sentencing. I'm telling you about these details for a reason. I want you to understand how careful and fair I was in *every single decision* I made surrounding this case. No decision was made in malice or bias. It was made on logistics of the case.

In the meantime, my staff and I attempted to focus on the jury selection. I had an army of people working for me, including extra staff from the courthouse and extern law students. We started with 800 jurors and had narrowed down our selections. We were ready.

A few days before Thanksgiving, just a little over a month before the trial was supposed to start, the attorneys asked to meet with me. I figured it was to finalize jury selection details. But they collectively surprised me.

"Judge, would you accept a plea?" Assistant Attorney General Angela Povilaitis asked.

A plea? Really? After all that, he wanted to plead guilty?

This was the plea deal: Nassar would plead to seven counts of first degree criminal sexual assault and the pending charges of child pornography found on his cell phone would not be issued. I could sentence Nassar on the minimum between twenty-five to forty years with all counts running together. If I wanted to sentence him more than that, I had to allow him to withdraw his plea. And as provided in the law, I would determine how many years "life" was on the tail end.

Remember, he was initially charged with twenty-nine counts—fifteen that were first-degree criminal sexual conduct. Now he was pleading guilty to only *seven* counts as part of the plea agreement. And the assistant attorney general told me that other victims would be allowed to testify as part of the plea and that she'd done that in one other case. I told her that I applauded that, but I explained that it had been my practice since I'd been elected judge to allow everyone to speak without limits. It wasn't an issue. It didn't need to be agreed to by anyone. It was my courtroom; it would happen. And then I agreed to accept a plea at the last minute, which I didn't have to do. Why did I agree? Because a trial is difficult on the victims and there are no guarantees. After the plea was on the record and to ensure everyone affected—every victim—had time to prepare, I publicly announced everyone who wanted to speak would be allowed without limitation at the time of the sentencing hearing.

And I truly meant everyone, every affected person, no limit, no matter how they were attached to the case. The defense objected to a few people who they claimed were not direct victims. One, for instance, was a doctor who referred patients to Nassar. My response? "It doesn't matter who. I always let everyone affected testify. If you don't like it, make a record and appeal me."

The counsel and defendant signed the plea agreement, but within it contained a limit of 125 victims who could testify. I ignored that limitation. That was not my agreement. That was their agreement. And I do not need permission from counsel or a plea agreement to follow the Crime Victims' Rights Act—something I've always followed and read broadly, allowing the term "victim" to mean everyone affected by the crime, not just the obvious victim.

Sorry, but no, no limit. I had said *all were allowed to testify,* and I meant it. I mean it in every case; no limit to number, no limit to time, no limit to number of days, and no limit to either side. It's what I've done since I donned the robe my first day on the bench, and it is what I will continue to do. If I'm not allowed to continue, I will leave the bench if that's what it takes and lobby for that right. In this case, I knew that the victims who accused me of initially silencing them because of the gag order would finally get their day in court to tell the public what Nassar had done to them. We would *not* be limiting any testimonies. And sadly, months after the sentencing, I learned that there had been people who wanted to testify in front of me but they had been redirected to the other courtroom. Upon learning that, I apologized to those people who clearly understood I would have heard them too.

When my staff heard there would be a plea, my court reporter, Jean Ann Hamlin, who is the keeper of all the words said in the courtroom, was the first to rush into my office, pen and paper in hand. “How many days will you give them?” she asked. “And, how much longer should we add because we all know you’re going to talk to each victim.” Jean Ann and I arrived at four days to start with. We left a few days following those four days open on my schedule, just in case.

That morning of Nassar’s plea, the courtroom wasn’t just full, it was standing room only. Nassar stood there in front of me, visibly shaken and nervous. He was a small man, thin and worn looking, almost feeble. He looked like just another person. There is no special look that announces a person is guilty of or capable of sexually assaulting children. And, in his weakened condition, he looked more bewildered than like the confident predator who manipulated and abused hundreds of women, thousands of times.

After the prosecutor read the seven counts charged, I asked Nassar to admit each individual charge and admit further that these “treatments” had no medical purpose. That he did it for his own sexual pleasure. He sighed and hesitated. Then he said yes. Why did he hesitate? Why did he sigh? Because the guilty plea was a legal tactic. He *still* refused to accept what he had done. At the very least, he believed that he could still *convince* others that his actions were medical, not sexual.

I'd like to sidebar for a minute and talk about how Nassar managed to abuse so many women for so long. Larry Nassar was a man who, I learned, was respected in his community. He ran for school board in 2016 as a legitimate candidate. The girls thought of him as their confidant. As their best friend. As the one person who they could turn to. He seemed like he couldn't hurt a fly. But that's what must be understood about sexual predators. You might think a predator looks like a monster, that they're big and strong and scary and drive around in a creepy white van. But most of the time, that's not the case. There is no defined look of a predator. They can be anyone.

Everyone adored Larry Nassar—he was physically nonthreatening, sweet, playful, adoring of the gymnasts—always taking special care of them, and giving them gifts from the Olympics. He was able to successfully create relationships within the gymnastics community. He then used that community trust to manipulate and exploit. This is where the concept of grooming comes in. Grooming is how a sexual predator draws a child and their parents in by gaining their trust. Remember, Nassar didn't just groom these girls; he systematically groomed *everyone* around him. He groomed the girls' families into thinking he was performing legitimate medical treatments. He groomed the medical community. He groomed police detectives. He groomed the entire community. He groomed the girls' parents into thinking that this "treatment" was legitimate. That's what predators do. Studies show that ninety-three percent of sexually abused children will be abused by someone they know and trust. *Ninety-three percent.*

Even after complaints were made, Nassar continued to do what he wanted. He was supposed to have a chaperone in the room when he examined the girls, following medical protocol. He was supposed to avoid skin-to-skin contact. He was supposed to wear gloves when he was performing his "treatment." Yet those rules weren't enforced. Why not? Why did so many red flags go unchecked?

We must be more cognizant as a society to understand that this is how this kind of abusive pattern works. That this man fooled everyone. And he's not alone. I see so many cases like this. They all have the common thread of systematic grooming and gaslighting. As a society, we need to better understand the process of grooming and gaslighting so that we can do better. And such understanding includes learning about related forms of emotional abuse and victim manipulation such as ghosting, benching, and love bombing.

I deemed the women in this case Sister-Survivors. Because that's what they are to me. The abuse they suffered is their story, not mine. But I believe I have an important role to play too: to keep the conversation for meaningful change going. This is my role as a judge as well. To teach the current generations and the new ones being born about grooming. About the right to say no. About informed consent. About medical professionals asking permission to touch someone and offering an explanation about what will happen and the reasons for it. About using proper body-part names. About teaching children that they have rights from the time they are born. About invoking those rights from the time they say their first word. About teaching children that they have the right to say no and demand answers—of everyone, anybody, even a doctor.

Law enforcement needs to learn about proper questioning so that no victim is shut down, shut up, or blamed. Victims need a safe space to speak. They need to know who to report their story to. Prosecutors need to charge every single wrong touch so that predators know there will be a consequence each time and so that victims will be fully heard, not shut up and not silenced. Children need to learn that they can say no, what informed consent is, and that anyone who touches them needs their permission. I could go on. We need to fix a broken justice system, medical system, educational system, and athletic system. I have made it my mission to change the world and leave behind a better, safer world for all our children.

* * *

One night, we were having dinner together as we always do. My mother, my father at the head of the table, and Marissa and Michael and Johanna. It was a few days before the victim impact statements were about to start. Johanna asked if she could come watch the women speak. It was the first time she asked me about my job.

Johanna was seventeen, a junior in high school, and was growing into such a remarkable woman. I was so proud of her. She was so smart, was amazingly creative, and had so much artistic and musical talent. But she was doing the natural thing that kids that age do: separating from me and asserting her independence. But more than that, Johanna was angry at me. I wasn't just her mom but also her dad. Jake had no part in raising her. I was the rule maker and enforcer. Yes, we lived with my parents, and though my father was strict with me, he was a softie with her. And you know what? That's the way it should be with a grandfather. But it meant all her teenage rebellion was aimed directly at me.

Plus, as a judge, and a former military officer, I admit I'm not the easiest parent. Nothing gets past me, and I make demands I learned other parents don't make. I'm the mom who says, "Will there be a parent home? What is your friend's phone number?" And I make the call and speak to an actual parent before I grant permission for her to go to a friend's house. Then I might drive by to see if there is a party or not. If there is a party, I threaten to show up with some police officers, or, more likely, I'm already knocking on the door while calling the parents.

Yes, I have called my daughter to tell her, "You are past curfew. If you are not home in half an hour, I am making a police report." And, yes, I have made those police reports, and I have allowed police in my house with the drug dogs. And yes, my daughter during those events hated me, hated my job, hated my rules, and didn't understand my fears. But now, she's older, more aware, more exposed to troubling events and circumstances. She understands. She knows I love her. She knows I'm not a perfect parent but that I love her and all her siblings. She knows that they are my life. She and I both understand we won't always agree and it's not the end of the world. It took us a while and some counseling separately and jointly to get to this place. Surprising to me was that the Nassar case helped us get on the same path, one we'd veered from.

I am a hard ass. I know this. I wasn't a judge when David and Jennifer were in high school. If I had been, maybe I would have acted this way with them too. Because look, if I'm going to do this to someone else's child, my children are not exempt. I don't think we're above the law. If you're not home, I will absolutely call or drive to the police because I'm going to worry that you've been kidnapped. If your friend refuses to tell me where you are, I will show up at their house and talk with the friend and her parents.

Children getting stolen and placed into human trafficking happens in every neighborhood, in every community. And I worry. I share my concerns with other parents. I try to spread awareness. I care. I think of the worst-case scenario—it's my job, it's my nature. Of the cases I've seen, nothing is out of the realm of possibility. My biggest concern is safety. I didn't want to act like my father who refused to meet anyone I dated, who harassed me by opening and shutting the garage door. No, I wanted her to have a great social life, but one with boundaries and safety. Johanna is a social butterfly, much more than David and Jennifer were. But I see too much as a judge—too many broken families and destroyed parents to not be affected by the damage I've witnessed. Protecting my children is everything to me. That is just who I am.

And Johanna thought that was too hard. So here we were at the time when I was no longer "Mom" but "Judge" and she was the aggrieved "Rapunzel."

So when Johanna asked if she could come to the courtroom during the Nassar sentencing, it felt like the right decision. She was old enough to hear these hard things and see her mom at work. But more than that, Lansing was her town. She knew many of these girls. People in her school were discussing this. I called the school and let them know that after her exams, she would be coming to watch impact statements. Johanna and her boyfriend (plus her best friend for one day) sat there in the courtroom to watch the impact statements. The room was too crowded for me to notice her reactions, and I was too focused on the case to see her, but I was glad she was there. I could feel her presence.

When sentencing began, we had identified eighty-eight women who wanted to speak. That number grew every day, one voice empowering another to come forward. There were 169 people in total who spoke. Of that number, 156 of those people were survivors. Suddenly, the four days I scheduled turned into seven days. That didn't matter to me. I was prepared to listen for weeks, months, as long as it took. Even more women were set to speak in another case against Nassar soon after this case was wrapped up in my court.

Judge George Economy, a judge on my bench, now

retired, stopped me outside the elevators a few days after the sentencing. "You know that you set the bar. No judge will ever be able to limit the number of victims or narrow the scope of the Crime Victim's Rights Act ever again."

I smiled. Because I was glad! I used the power of the robe for good. The community, the victims, and even judges saw the outcome. Judges from all over the world contacted me. Most judges told me, "I'm studying what you've done, and I'm going to change what I do in my courtroom." There were a few judges who said I didn't deserve to wear the robe. And to those few naysayers, I say delete is a good button.

As I have mentioned many times already, I always talk to the victims and the defendants who come into my courtroom. I know speaking to people works. During the Sister-Survivors' statements. I gave those women words of encouragement, empathy, and support. "Leave your pain here," I said, "and go out and do your magnificent things." They were heroes for speaking out. "The military has not yet come up with fiber as strong as you," I told Bailey Lorencen. And I meant it. They've made a difference for so many others who have suffered like them. Sexual assault survivors are used to not being believed. And so I wanted them to know how much the entire community supported them. And that their courage was appreciated; the community *wanted to* and *needed to* hear their words.

And through many of their statements, it was clear that Nassar wasn't even paying attention. I was outraged when he wouldn't acknowledge the humans he assaulted who were speaking to him, publicly showing their pain. Instead, he was doodling, laughing with his lawyers, or simply zoned out and not paying attention. The girls had to keep saying, "Larry! Look at me when I speak!"

At home, after that first night, Johanna looked

stunned. It was hard for her to watch her friends and community speak and share their experiences. But she came to my court again those last three days, exhibiting her bravery by listening and witnessing.

* * *

In Michigan, and anywhere, a judge speaks through her orders, and I thought about my words carefully when it was time to sentence him. Because of the national attention this case received, it took on a symbolic resonance that spoke to the pain of girls and women, boys and men, of all ages, cultures, and sexual preferences, who have suffered at the hands of predators all around our nation and the world.

Prepared statements and writing things down word for word aren't usually my thing. Admittedly, I probably should write more down—I might get into less trouble that way! But in this case, I did write part of what I wanted to say down because I wanted to share statistics about child sexual abuse so that people could understand the full weight of this case. Statistics provide a different and compelling way to understand the story, and the sheer numbers of sexual assault make it clear that no one is immune. Predators are everywhere, even in the medical community.

As it is well documented. Larry Nassar wrote a letter stating that he wasn't treated fairly and that he was a good doctor. The media has repeatedly asked me to release the letter, but as I stated that day, I wasn't going to do that. I didn't want to revictimize the survivors by allowing Nassar to gain control and instill fear and pain with the full contents of his letter. That's why, as I explained that day in the courtroom, I decided to read only segments of the letter out loud.

In some regards, his letter was important because it showed his mindset. There's a common thread among criminals, which is *I'm smarter, I'm in control, and I won't get caught.* Nassar was the same. Empathy, sympathy, remorse—that's what I hope to see in defendants. But what I saw, what I read, and what I felt from Nassar was far away from recognition of his predatory behavior. In that letter, he insisted that everyone "referred" girls to him. That this treatment helped these women. "I'm a good doctor," he wrote. But the most shocking and offensive segment of his letter was this: "What I did in the state cases were medical, not sexual . . . The media convinced them everything I did was wrong and bad . . . they feel I broke their trust. Hell hath no fury like a woman scorned."

After I read that line, the courtroom gasped loudly, horrified. This was a man who had pled guilty! Who got the deal of a lifetime! Who wasn't even charged for all his crimes *because* of the plea deal? Who had just listened over seven days to 156 women say that he abused them as children! That he had abused them hundreds of times. That he broke their trust. That he was dangerous. Cold and calculating. He listened to an additional thirteen other people who admonished him for breaking his promises and their trust. But apparently, after all that, Larry Nassar still didn't believe he was guilty. He was still trying to groom people. Still trying to manipulate. He never owned what he did. He never once said a meaningful "I'm sorry." He never admitted to damaging all those lives. Instead, he said that he was taking a guilty plea to "help the community." He still wanted to be the center of attention. His tears were never about what he did, it was clear they were for what *he* lost.

I was outraged. Outraged because of the lies, the hypocrisy, and the manipulation. I was outraged for the community, for the parents, and most of all, for the Sister-Survivors who stood in my court and put themselves on the line talking about their abuse in the public eye. So I tossed the letter to the side. It was garbage. Every single insincere word of it. The letter-toss wasn't planned, and I didn't even recall doing it until I saw the meme. The letter toss was my gut throwing out his vile attempt at continued manipulation.

"Would you like to withdraw your plea?" I asked him. Of course, he said no.

Look, I knew that this was the first time many people had been exposed to this kind of horrific case. I wanted people to know that I took this *very* seriously. I wanted Nassar to know I took this very seriously. I wanted these Sister-Survivors to know they had been believed and heard and they mattered. Our community is connected, and people were greatly affected by this. I wanted people to know that I didn't just arbitrarily say what I said as a judge but I also spoke up as a human being. I was outraged on behalf of the public and concerned on behalf of the safety of all our children.

The plea agreement limited my ability to sentence him with what he might have otherwise received. The Michigan State University president apologized to the victims and created a $10 million counseling fund. It was a start.

All of this made me take a hard look at how I approach cases from the bench. What are we doing for sexual assault victims? Is it enough?

A recent case that came before me involved a retired Michigan State University professor, Robert Pittman. Allegations were made against him by an employee, Vance Kincaid. The events happened over twenty years ago, but they were clear. Pittman continually behaved in sexually inappropriate ways to Kincaid. Most egregiously, on the day of his retirement, when Kincaid went to shake his hand, Pittman grabbed him, kissed him, and shoved his hand down his pants.

It was like pulling teeth to get Pittman to admit that

he forced himself on Kincaid, that it wasn't consensual. Look, Pittman was Kincaid's supervisor at the time. "Having that authority over him is forcing him to comply with a sexual act," I told him. It felt urgent to make sure he understood, to make sure we all understand.

Something has shifted. We need to listen to the victims of sexual assault, whether the cases were from events that took place last week or twenty years ago, whether it was a young girl or a middle-aged man. We need to believe children. We need to learn and understand how grooming works, how predators operate. It's what the #MeToo movement is all about. When this kind of abuse is exposed, it means that something is very broken in our society. We need to address these problems before we can start to heal. First, we need to listen. We need to be able to ask defendants and victims this integral question: What would you like me to know?

What's changed in the courtroom since Nassar? Some defendants are scared to come to my courtroom. And if I see that they're nervous, I make sure to tell them that they are going to get my full attention, that I'm going to be fair to them and give them all the time they need. And mostly, defendants and victims come to my courtroom expecting to be heard. They often come with prepared statements. They'll pull a note out of their pocket, and they'll unfold it and say, "I have a statement. Can I read it?" I say, "Of course. You may proceed."

Recently, I had a twelve-year-old girl in my courtroom. She had a remarkably good relationship with her mom and dad. For twelve years, she had gone to her parents' bed, slept with them, and watched TV with them. One day, she crawled into her parents' bed, and it was no different than any other day. At least not to her. Mom was at the grocery store. Dad was tickling her because he always tickled her. And then something changed. Her father raped her. When it was over, she told her mother. Her mother called the police. Divorced the father.

Now, fast forward it to my courtroom where I'm listening to a letter the little girl prepared. She was too upset to attend the sentencing. Her advocate read the letter. She wrote that when her father left the home, he also took her dog, her best friend. She had been let down and broken in so many ways. She and her mother asked for nothing from him. No restitution. She didn't want to see him ever again and knew he would never answer the question "Why did you do this to me?"

I was moved for many reasons, but one of them was she was clearly inspired by the Nassar survivors, and she wrote a thoughtful, heartfelt letter. Watching the Sister-Survivors have the courage to share their stories gave her the courage to let me know how much she was hurt and hurting.

When it came time for the father to talk, he said, "Well, I've written a letter too."

"You may proceed," I directed him.

And I listened.

His letter didn't say, "I'm sorry." It didn't say, "Please forgive me." The letter said, "I want you to learn from my mistakes." His letter was garbage. It was his final attempt at control. But the little girl's letter was powerful, and it informed my actions.

"Where's the dog?" I asked him.

"The dog?" he asked, confused. "I gave the dog to a friend."

Why did he take the dog? To quiet her. To maintain the upper hand, control her, even from prison. Groomers like to keep control of their victims. This was his way of maintaining a hold over her.

"The dog was not yours to give," I told him. "And this controlling behavior will not happen in my courtroom."

In restitution, I ordered the dog. While she hadn't

asked for the dog to be returned, I knew she wanted it back. It was a way to return her voice and the control he'd stolen from her and to let her know she'd been believed and that she mattered.

The father didn't like this, of course. His defense attorney came back to me, not thrilled. "Judge, I've never had a dog ordered in restitution."

"Well, now you have," I said. "If you don't like it, file an appeal."

An hour later the court clerk called me. "Judge, there's no line for a dog."

"Create one," I said.

This little girl needed to be heard. And I did hear her.

And so the girl got her dog.

I also ordered a transcript of the sentencing hearing so that the little girl, when she was older and ready, could read it with the help of her mother and/or therapist. She would know she mattered and that she was heard. This is something I always do when victims don't have the strength to personally appear.

I am not required to do these things, but I choose to use the power of the robe in many ways. I choose to interpret the law with common sense and invoke a common-sense legal process. I choose to use the gavel for law and order, and I choose to also use it like a wand for healing. It's what I know works.

I sincerely hope that one of the lasting impacts of the Nassar case will be inspiring people to speak their truth, to show their pain, and in doing so, to find support, to find hope, and to know they matter.

* * *

Aside from my work on the bench, what really surprised me though was that people were eager to hear from me. After all, I saw myself as just the judge. I figured, like every case I've had, including high-profile cases, after a few days there would be a new focus. But everywhere I went, people wanted a moment of my time. It started to dawn on me that my role in the Nassar case meant something special to people. And something profound shifted inside me.

It's been over three years since the case was decided, and in that time, thousands upon thousands of people have reached out to me. I've received letters, emails, and calls from all around the country and the world, even places I've never heard of. Here are some of the messages I've received:

"When you talked to the girls, you were talking to me, and I didn't commit suicide that day. I've started to heal."

"I continue to hear your words. I play them over and over and over again when I get depressed, and it makes me go on."

"Because of your words, I decided to go to counseling."

People see me as a resource when they have nowhere else to turn. Recently, a woman reached out. She had been raped and had chosen to raise the baby that resulted with all the love in her heart. Now, her predator had just been released from prison and was trying to attain custody. Though I did not know her at all, and her case was outside of my jurisdiction, she saw me as a person who could help. And she was right. I did everything in my power to educate her about how to protect herself and her baby, and we now speak often. Because I care.

I'll tell you something. I try to write back to everyone who contacts me with an issue and respond with hope, a positive message, and in some cases, what their next step might be. I advise them that I'm not and can't be their counselor or their lawyer, but I believe them and believe in them. To the thousands who have sent me thank-you cards, messages, and letters, I am humbled. I know that not everyone has someone in their lives who can lend an ear and listen to their trauma and believe them, believe in them, and offer support like they truly deserve. I gave him 40 years on the minimum and 175 years on the maximum because if he won his appeal on the federal sentencing, he could possibly walk out of prison an old man, but a free man. 40 years for what this man did was a cakewalk. Divide 40 years by seven counts of first degree criminal sexual conduct. That's 5.71 years per victim on the pled-to counts (and remember each count only counted for one assault when we know there were many more). That doesn't seem fair, does it? Of course not. Because that's nothing. But victims need peace and they needed to see this man put behind bars. So that's what I did. And that is what justice called for.

A few minutes after I sentenced him, I told him what I knew to be true, what everyone knew to be true. That he didn't deserve to get out of prison. (Following my sentencing, he faced additional charges in another case in a neighboring county. Technically, that judge gave him an even harsher sentence because, although she sentenced him 40 to 125 years, there were only three counts. Looking at the math, that's 13.33 years per count. That sentence runs at the same time mine does. Larry Nassar was never, ever getting out of prison.

"I just signed your death warrant," I said to him. "Your decision to assault was precise, calculated, manipulative, devious, and despicable. I don't have to add words because your survivors have said all of that. I don't want to repeat it." I have received both praise and criticism for that line. That line wasn't planned. I said it for the comfort of the Sister-Survivors who needed to know they were finally safe and could begin to heal without fear of their predator. It is something I've learned from the hundreds, likely thousands, of victims I've spoken with over my career—they simply want assurances that they are free of the fear that their predator will appear in front of them.

If I were a man, it wouldn't matter what came out of my mouth. I would not have been criticized because I have seen and heard much worse from male judges in Michigan and around the country. Those men are not called out, not punished, not threatened. I'm a woman, but I'm a judge. And so I spoke out to honor the girls and all the victims. To let them know with certainty they are safe and that he can never harm them again. And, to put all this to rest, because I knew once he pled without apparent remorse just how problematic and systemic his abuse on his prey was. I have absolutely no regrets.

* * *

We sat down as a family for dinner after the last day of the victim impact statements: me, my mother, Johanna, Michael, Marissa, and my father. Eating and talking like we always do. Sometimes fighting and bickering like we always do. My father put his fork down and turned to me. Paused for a minute. Nodded his head.

"I'm proud of you," he said.

I paused. This was the first time my father told me he was proud of me. Ever. It took sixty years for him to use those words.

My reaction was . . . complicated. Did it feel good? I'm not sure it felt like anything, quite frankly.

After all I've done . . . *this* was the thing that spurred him to tell me he was proud of me? There have been so many other things that I've done that could have garnered these words. Making honor roll in high school every year, doing very well in college, going to law school, getting stellar officer reviews, receiving awards and promotions in the military, becoming the first female JAG officer in the Michigan Army National Guard, being one of the only women on the senate floor when I first started, or finishing law school after having two children (only one term behind my original class during a time when only a small percentage of women were even going to law school).

My father was finally proud of me for something that I do every day. Standing up for the victims. Giving marginalized people a chance to speak. This is what I always do. This is what I will continue to do.

For years I've heard my father praise my siblings, and then my nieces and nephews, for things that I accomplished with no assistance. With nothing but questions and criticism. No one told me how great I was for any of my accomplishments, and so over the years I've had my moments. "Hey! How about me?" I would say. Not that I'm not proud of my nieces and nephews and siblings, because I am! And I adore them! But it still gets to me. Because you're always a kid at heart.

I don't want to completely fault my parents. For one, you're always the hardest on the oldest. I was probably hard on David without realizing it as my kids were growing up. With the oldest, you always expect more. I was their oldest child and my grandparents' oldest grandchild. As a parent, I know that when you're in the midst of parenting, and when you have four kids relatively close together, and when you're trying to make ends meet, you're not necessarily in the habit and you don't have time to always check in on the emotional well-being of your kids. Growing up, I understood that. I understood that my parents loved me, but I also understood that they had my siblings to take care of.

So when my father said that to me, was it nice? Sure, it was nice. It was fine. But I've finally resolved that relationship with myself. I don't need anyone to be proud of me. I'm proud of myself. I'm proud of my reflection and the light in my eyes in the mirror. I don't have to prove anything to anyone. I am my best champion, and I can push my own damn golden button without permission, explanation, or shame.

* * *

Something else happened that night. Something remarkable. It happened softly and quickly, so smoothly that anyone else watching would have missed it. Except I didn't miss it.

"So, Mom, why didn't they come forward? Mom, I don't understand."

This was Johanna asking me this.

For a brief second, I thought about saying something. Oh my God, Johanna called me Mom! Did I hear it right? I'm Mom again! I don't know the moment it switched for her, but I didn't need to know. I didn't need to ask her any questions. Because I saw the switch. I felt the switch. I heard the switch. And I didn't need to say anything.

I always have the floor. This time it was my time to keep my thoughts to myself. To just let it be.

Since that moment, I have never been "Judge" again. Never. Not once. Even when she's angry at me, she's at least tried to talk to me with respect and calm. And even if she's upset, she still calls me Mom. And we do still have our tough moments. Those come with being a parent. They are necessary for growth. Johanna and I have learned to grow positively from our shared difficulties. I obviously can't speak for Johanna, but I believe after that day, she was able to really see me as a person who cares about people, who has a real moral center. She saw me for who I really was deep into my soul. That's the thing about our kids. They don't necessarily see us as people. And that's normal. I know that. Because we're not. We're their parents. It can take a long time to get to that point, but when they do, it's beautiful. Johanna was able to understand and internalize what I've said, what I've tried to explain: I don't just want a seat at the table, I want to be the chandelier that shines brightly, that makes a difference, that shares the light. I think that in my courtroom she felt that light and understands that we are all a part of something bigger and everyone has the opportunity and responsibility to make a difference, even if by one act.

Of all the wicked and terrible things that the Nassar trial revealed, I saw so much strength, growth, and beauty too. And for me, on a personal front, strengthening my relationship with my beautiful daughter meant the world to me.

chapter sixteen

How to Change the Conversation

I've often been criticized for taking my sweet time in the courtroom. Everyone is in a hurry to move on to the next case. Everyone except me. The sheriff sometimes gets annoyed. The defense attorney sometimes gets annoyed. The prosecutor even gets annoyed. But this is how I do things.

I believe we must give voice to those caught in the crippling ripples that come with every case—and that includes the victim *and* the defendant. I want to hear what they both have to say. This has been my practice since I donned the robe in 2004.

What I care about is the case in front of me. That is where my attention is focused until it concludes. There are no time limits in my courtroom, which only hurt people who deserve a chance to share their words. My philosophy is that I borrow the courtroom: really, it's the people's courtroom, and the people have a right to have their day no matter how long it takes.

So, victims—anyone affected by the case—and defendants have a chance to say what they want and need to say in my courtroom, and at the conclusion of a case, I *always* speak during sentencing. Come into my courtroom any time and you will hear me speaking to defendants and victims, encouraging them, lifting them up. But looking back at all that has transpired since the monumental seven days of the Nassar sentencing, I know in my heart that the words I shared on the bench that final day were essential in a very public way. A shout out into the darkness that is sexual assault. One that echoed far and rippled wide. My words were a hand up to each individual girl. They had not been heard for nearly thirty years, and the Sister-Survivors deserved to be heard and to hear my voice championing their bravery. My words were a message to the community. A declaration that we can do better.

Shortly after the Nassar case was over, despite acknowledging that he was guilty more than once, he filed an appeal claiming I was biased during sentencing. His lawyers argued that my language was too harsh during sentencing. To this I say: I took an oath as an attorney, and as a judge, that I would be the voice to those without a voice. I also vowed to be fair and impartial, at all times, including at sentencing. And that I would uphold the Constitution. That I would be the voice for the community. During the Nassar plea and then the sentencing, there was no bias. I was fair and impartial. I upheld the law and imposed the sentence he and his attorneys agreed to based on his continued acknowledgment, under oath, that he was in fact guilty. I followed the four factors in *People v. Snow*, 386 Mich 586 (1972) and *People v. Adams* 430 Mich 679 (1988). These four factors are reformation of the offender, protection of society, the disciplining of the wrongdoer, and the deterrence of others from committing like offenses. As a judge, I am also able to consider the severity and nature of the crime, the circumstances surrounding the criminal behavior, the defendant's attitude toward his or her criminal behavior, the defendant's social and personal history and subsequent offenses. I must also make sure that the punishment is proportional to the crime(s) committed. I was up for election as I wrote the Audible version of this memoir. I didn't have an opponent. With gratitude, I won another six-year term and felt the overwhelming support of the community for what I do as their judge.

Whatever happens in the appeal case, he will still spend the rest of his life in prison because of the two other sentences he's serving. This appeal is really about control. This is about him and his embarrassment. One of his lawyers even argued that his family members were afraid to come to the court during his sentencing because of the animosity that I spread. That it was somehow *my* fault. It was *my* fault they were embarrassed to support him at court. Please.

If I hadn't spoken, if I hadn't continued to be outraged on behalf of the public in the Nassar case, I can assure you the fallout would have been greater. The stress in the courtroom would have led to dangerous outbursts. Yet people still, after all this time, aren't used to hearing women be angry. They are not used to our rage. It makes them uncomfortable. But I am here to tell you our rage is not going anywhere.

And indeed, things have begun to change. After the sentencing, everyone wanted to investigate further into the wrongdoings within the gymnastics community and into the Olympic organization as a whole—gymnasts were not the only athletes assaulted. What was uncovered was sobering. *The New York Times* found that between the beginning of the FBI investigation and the *Indy Star's* first article, Nassar sexually abused forty women and girls. Unfathomable.

We all learned more troubling details about the broken system the girls were in. When they were training for long periods of time at the USA Gymnastics National Team Training Center at Karolyi Ranch, no other adults were present when they went in to do their treatments with Nassar. They were forbidden to call their parents. These young women were treated like machines. What went on at the Karolyi Ranch was only the tip of the iceberg. It was part of a world where adults were complicit and where the girls were unable to speak about any negative things happening to them. They were told to toughen up and stop complaining. They were forced to compete while injured, and they needed Larry Nassar to help them feel better. They were caught in a trap.

Michigan State University was also to blame. The NCAA opened a formal investigation into how the university handled the case. The president of the university resigned. The resignation of the university's athletic director followed two days later. The head of the United States Olympic Committee demanded that the entire board step down, and they complied. USA Gymnastics stopped working with the Karolyis. The new Michigan State University president apologized to the victims and created a $10 million counseling fund. It was a start.

The Karolyis have continued to dispute the allegations against them, but in light of the reporting that's been done on the case, particularly in the *Athlete A* and *At the Heart of Gold* documentaries, I believe the girls.

There have been further troubling developments. During the sentencing I stated, "There has to be a massive investigation as to why there was inaction, why there was silence. Justice requires more than what I can do on this bench." And I don't take credit for the obvious need for investigation, but what has transpired is unconscionable. Massive systematic failures by the FBI have been uncovered in the Department of Justice's report.

On a note of further closure, USA Gymnastics agreed to pay the Sister-Survivors $380 million dollars. There is no amount of money that makes any victim truly whole, but the ability to close outstanding matters, regardless of what they are, helps victims to rebuild their lives.

In Larry Nassar's shadow and sixty miles away, over 1,047 victims have filed civil law suits, including many prominent football players and other athletes from basketball, wrestling, track and field, swimming, hockey, and tennis have emerged against the University of Michigan and the late Dr. Robert E. Anderson who was on staff. (There are over 2,000 victims of Dr. Anderson, who have been identified, but not all will come forward publicly.) There have been similar incidents the University of Southern California and Ohio State University, with more cases on the verge of being made public.

Everyone deserves their day in court. Everyone is presumed innocent until proven guilty beyond a reasonable doubt, until they plead guilty, or until the charges are dismissed. But to get to a final result, we must take the proper actions that include taking all accusations seriously, reporting them to the proper authority where a full investigation can be done, and letting the legal system work. Mob mentalities do not work, but neither does silence.

I stand against silence. I believe in our system of justice, but we must partner together and do better. As I said during sentencing, and it applies to all crimes and misbehavior, "Inaction is an action; silence is indifference. Justice requires action and a voice."

* * *

People have criticized me for doing public events with the survivors of this case. And each time I was asked to do something, I was very clear that this was their story, not mine. It was their time to speak. Yet people wanted to hear from me. And the survivors wanted me to be present. They wanted my support. They urged me to attend various events, which continues today. I am regularly asked to join their voices at events; to help change laws; to help educate; to help change the justice system, which often feels like an injustice system; and, along with them, to keep the conversation going for change.

I am asked to speak around the world about empowerment, how to recognize predatory behavior, how to fight against and rise above the naysayers and bullies around us, and any number of topics that affect us in our daily lives and that are often difficult to discuss. I am honored that people of all professions and walks of life, professional organizations, and parents trust me enough to want to hear from me and that they are comfortable enough to ask me questions.

And even today, despite everyone moving forward, years after the sentencing, when one of the Sister-Survivors has a bad day, needs to hear positive affirmations, or one of their parents is upset, they reach out to me for a comforting word or an understanding ear or a referral for assistance, or for multiple reasons. They do not want to talk about the case that is closed; they are moving forward. But they reach out to me as a person in power, who they trust, who listens without judgment or question, who they feel cares about their healing. Sadly, they tell me this is unique.

Let me address this. What I said in any public events with victims, in the courtroom, or on my own was already discussed on the record in the courtroom. I have not added any additional information to any conversations I've had with the media or outside of the case. And trust me, I could have. In the journalist Abigail Pesta's book, *The Girls*, she interviewed twenty-five Nassar victims about their horrific experiences with him. She details how he groomed them, how he assaulted them, and how his behavior was institutionally accepted. Erin Lee Carr and Sarah Gibson detail the abuse in the documentary *At the*

Heart of Gold, interviewing journalists, survivors, and experts. I thought it was appropriate to be interviewed in each of these projects because I wanted to support work that would continue the dialogue for understanding and meaningful change. My goal is to be a voice, to change the culture around sexual abuse, to change the language, and to put safety before money and medals. To be the voice of change in broken systems—including the legal, medical, and sports worlds—with cultures that don't always listen, believe, or take timely action. Nothing I say or do will change what Nassar did to those women. I couldn't possibly even scratch the surface of what happened to them or sway anyone to have a different reaction about the horrors they have endured for more than thirty years. That story belongs to the Sister-Survivors. My story is one of keeping the conversation going for meaningful change, accountability, and extinction of what caused the silencing by Nassar, and others like him who have preyed on innocent, unsuspecting victims and led to the need for the #MeToo Movement. My story is also one of speaking out in hope of continuing to fix a broken justice system. I am hopeful I can contribute positively to giving voice, empowerment, education and add to the protection of future generations, my children, and all our children.

This kind of case makes you take stock in your life. There's been such a profound effect from this case on me, the community I represent, and more importantly, on victims around the world who have chosen to finally emerge, use their voice, and have entrusted me and others with their stories—crimes against them that they felt silenced about for years. This has deeply affected me. I can't help but reflect on my life and how I got here. How did I become a voice?

Because my voice was taken from me as a child when I was taken from my grandparents' house without explanation. Because my grandparents always uplifted me, encouraging me to speak, to sing, to laugh, to feel, to know I mattered no matter what. Because my brother always wanted to hear more from me—more stories, more attention, more time. Because my parents, even though they were strict and even though we had our problems, always encouraged me to rise above animosity and to push past any fear I had. They always taught me to rise up against poverty and prejudice. To reach for and live the American dream. Because of the hard times I had with my family, and because of the pain I felt, I became invincible, and I created my own path for myself without apology.

Because I stood up for myself against my father, I knew I could stand up to anyone. Because every time he said to me, "Why do you think you can be a lawyer?" or "Why do you think you can pass the bar?" or "Why do you think you can be a judge?" I pushed myself further. Because when my father and my husband tried to convince me not to join the military because I was a woman and a mom and that's not—according to them—what women or mothers do, I became the first female JAG officer in the Michigan Army National Guard. Because when I saw a place for myself in society, a place where I could personally make a difference, I ran for judge. As a judge, when I saw that defendants weren't getting what they needed to complete a sobriety program as part of their probation, I fought to get them what they needed and set up a specialty court foundation that, after over a decade, continues to support those in need.

Because I was married to a man who didn't believe in me, I proved to him that I could be not just a mother, not just a wife, not just a woman around the house serving *his* needs, but a successful lawyer. Because when I got pregnant, I never put aside my dreams of becoming a lawyer. Because when I got pregnant again, I kept on going, graduated from law school, and passed the bar. Because when I was faced with sexism at my workplace, I plowed forward and wouldn't let it stop me. Because when I was in the most abusive relationship of my life, letting a man treat me like garbage for years on end, I finally told him that I had enough and never looked back.

Because I had that bathroom mirror. Really, that bathroom mirror got me through some of the hardest times. I'd look at the light in my eyes and say to myself, *Rose, you can do this. Failing is not an option.* And when I did fail, I'd say to myself, *Rose, you matter, you will reinvent yourself, and you will succeed.* Being my own best friend in that mirror allowed me to develop an internal strategy so that failure turned into success. And that has just been true with everything I've gone through. I don't know where I'd be if there were no mirrors in the world! Because there have been so many times that the strength that I got was from the light in my eyes. It was me inside, saying, *You're here, you're present, and you can do better.*

Has my life been easy? No. Has anything been handed to me? No. Never. But I wouldn't have it any other way because it made me who I am today. And I'm a fighter. The platform that I've been given as a lawyer and as a judge isn't just a voice for my family but a responsibility I bear for the voiceless in our world.

Part of telling my story is about letting go. When you tell your story, a huge burden lifts from you. A burden that sometimes you didn't even know you had. These stories must be released. You can't walk around carrying pain. No one can. You must listen to yourself. Listen to your story, and share it with others who you trust and feel safe with. Even if it's just one person. They need to know the real you and who you are. That's the only way to start. It's something I've always done on the bench, but it's something I've impressed on my kids, and I've tried to do it for myself. I'm telling my story because for most of my life, no one has really asked me the question I ask everyone else: "What would you like me to know?" This is what I want you to know about me. I hope you can look inside yourself too. And maybe one day, you'll be ready to tell your story as well. It's yours to decide.

afterword

Writing this memoir has given me the benefit of reviewing my life. I have set new personal and professional goals. I am dating again, open to a relationship that is mutually positive and lasting, but I find that I question myself with each step to ensure I do not reenact past mistakes. It is a curious, challenging, and wonderful experience. My twins were in a bus accident, suffered physical and emotional trauma, were not listened to, and I was not called for several hours. Their physical wounds have healed, but the emotional trauma is a daily struggle, and despite all my training and experience, they teach me new things every day. My father has advanced Parkinson's and my mother a heart condition, and I continue to be grateful we all live together so that I can be their advocate when it is needed most. My siblings are helping me in this difficult journey, and I am keenly aware, now more than ever, that the elder population is underserved, discounted, and not heard. A battle we all need to fight and one I will pursue.

There is no surprise that I continue to fight many battles, personal and public. However, amid the battles, I am always surprised and encouraged by the kindness of people I have met and the awards and recognition I have received for my work. These include most recently my novel *All Rise* receiving the SABA 2020 Book Awards "Audience Choice" and "Top 13 Best Author Fiction" and being inducted into the Michigan Military and

Veteran Hall of Honor, placing me alongside former US president Gerald R. Ford, former governor William G. Milliken, and former state senator John "Joe" Schwarz, MD.

I have fully grasped that my destiny is to fight battles that others ignore, to be the voice for others until they are heard, and to fight upstream for meaningful change even when I stand alone. I speak out with confidence that once an important issue is raised, others will join me, and for that reason, I never feel alone. As you know, I do not worry about the consequence to me. I have found that, at this point in my life, being the troublemaking voice is not only expected but welcomed by those who know me. This is evident now more than ever. I rarely hear comments about how I disappointed or offended someone. Instead I hear, "How is it that you are always the one who speaks up?"

I am grateful not only for my successes but also for my failures because both are teachable moments. I am always receptive to learning and sharing the lessons life has shown me.

The issue in my life that I didn't talk about, and I am currently fighting, is judicial bullying. I share it with you now because bullying must be addressed at every level and no one is immune to it—not even me. It is an important issue that I have been working on changing since I was elected. It is an issue no one wants to believe in, discuss, or acknowledge. It is an issue silently and stoically faced by many judges. It is another issue where the culture of acceptance and silence must be changed. Below I give you a brief view of it. I will be speaking out about it in the future in detail.

Within days of my election to circuit court, red flags and a pattern began emerging that I could not ignore. I quickly began questioning if I had done something wrong, or offensive, and in frustration, turned to a few female judges who I trusted and discussed my concerns with them. They willingly shared their experiences: they, too, were enduring bullying. There is no comfort in learning that other female judges were bullied and that my feelings of being bullied were valid.

Being the target of a judicial bully who was given the title and authority of *chief judge* was difficult to admit, but easy to see once I researched the issue and discussed specific instances with my female judicial colleagues. But I needed to be certain of all the issues, and I needed clarity to develop a plan of action. Like many lawyers, I began with research. I discovered that one in four employees is affected by bullying. I learned that bullying is not always overt—it can be rather subtle, slow, and insidious mistreatment that is often not recognized by others.

One article I found provided a framework and information that I was able to share, and reference, when discussing the issue of bullying with those who I thought would help. ERC's HR Insights Blog published"20 Subtle Sign of Bullying at Work" on November 5, 2013, which defined bullying as "repeated, health-harming mistreatment of one or more persons (the targets) by one or more perpetrators that takes one or more of the following forms: verbal abuse, offensive conduct/ behaviors (including nonverbal) which are threatening, humiliating, or intimidating; or work interference—sabotage—which prevents work from getting done." This article was a foreshadowing of what was to come, both subtly and overtly.

I partnered with other female, bullied judges, a few from my bench and a few from neighboring jurisdictions. We educated. We complained. We documented. We demanded change. You might think that other judges, the State Bar of Michigan, the State Court Administrative Office, or the Michigan Supreme Court would've helped, investigated, intervened, or tried to do something, but that simply was never the case. We were not protected then, and we are not protected now. However, speaking out against judicial bullying is beginning to receive traction.

You might be questioning what happened when the initial bully chief judge I worked with was no longer in charge. The answer is simple. Power often creates bullies. And bullies who are not admonished or retrained impart the message to others that bullying behavior is normal, which results in that bad behavior becoming expected and normalized. Judicial bullying continues today. Not dealing with this issue has given each chief judge in circuit court who I have worked with (and those prior to my being elected) permission to continue the pattern of bullying.

Judicial bullying didn't begin with our courthouse. It began decades before I was born. Remember, females and diversity had no place in higher positions, certainly not in the law, certainly not in judicial office. Thankfully that is changing—more women and minorities are serving on the bench than in past years, but we have a long way to go.

While I can withstand the bullying, I should not have to. I'm strong. I'm vocal. I'm not easily intimidated. I'm a judge who loves my job, my community, and my country. The bullying culture must end. I could step down like others have chosen to do because being bullied takes the joy out of working, but for now, I have chosen to stay and fight.

I have seen bullied judges retire with the same PTSD symptoms that I have seen in soldiers who have returned from war. I would be happy accepting any number of jobs I have been offered, but when I leave office, I want to leave on my own terms, not because I am bullied out. I enjoy being a circuit judge, but my job does not define me, nor do the bullies. Under the robe, I am a whole person. I have a full life with many options, and I enjoy doing many diverse things. I do a lot of self-care. I don't like to give up on important battles.

What can be done to solve this problem? The solution to bullying is simple: Create policies that are strictly adhered to and that everyone is trained in. Treat all victims with respect. Train people to recognize and document what they see and hear so that subtle patterns can be found and properly addressed. Investigate all reports, provide detailed explanations, and implement realistic solutions.

More importantly, why am I raising the issue of bullying? Because no one is immune to bullying. Because judges can be bullied. And because I am not the only judge who has experienced and reported judicial bullying. We must look at this issue on a global scale and eradicate it in every workplace, schoolyard, and home. Victims of bullies must be believed, heard, and protected. The reality is that no one should have to tolerate being bullied—not any child whether at home or in school or in sports, not any employee, not any elected official, not even a judge. The effect and stress of being bullied on a regular basis without recourse is unacceptable. Bullies exist everywhere, and we need to call bullies out for their unacceptable behavior, not be silenced by it.

I am not a quiet woman. I speak out. I will not stop talking. I will be heard. I will not be a silent coconspirator to bad behavior of any kind from anyone. I would rather stand tall, speak loudly, and fight for safety and change than accept the status quo and unacceptable mantra of *That's the way it has always been done*.

Thankfully, I am now joined by other bullied judges in this fight for change. This bullying didn't just happen to a few of my colleagues and me. Bullying has happened and continues to happen in neighboring counties. Many excellent judges have simply retired because there was no recourse. It happens not just across our state, but across the United States. It happens to female judges, but it also happens to male judges. And it's difficult to acknowledge that, despite rising to the top of our profession and having a powerful job, what happens behind the bench and in rooms that aren't open to the public is that some judges are beaten down, demeaned, and bullied.

Very recently we created a working group that includes a supreme court justice and the head of the SCAO. This is our current attempt at resolving this issue—all other attempts have failed, and there have been many over the years. We are asking for meaningful solutions, including retraining, continued training, and accountability.

You may be asking, "How did things get so bad and stay that way for decades?" Easily. When bullies are allowed to stay in power, they give silent permission for the next one in power to become a bully. The inaction of addressing bullying allows it to flourish. And bullying and bad behavior left unaddressed grows like a plant given super fertilizer: it escalates quickly and in alarming ways. It is learned behavior.

And, more importantly, what happens behind the bench should never affect what happens to those who appear before the bench. That is my biggest fear. Not the consequence to me but to the public who entrusts every judge with the job of listening, following the law, and imposing fair and impartial justice. Can this truly happen when we judges carry the bruises of bullying underneath our black robes? This worries me, and I hope it worries you.

Other projects I am working on include multiple writing endeavors: writing a family cookbook, another nonfiction book about empowerment, and the next novels in my fictional series *Triple Cross Killer* (thriller), and *All Rise* (cozy mystery). I am creating a foundation to help victims of crime based on a need and pattern that I have observed hearing cases and viewing evidence while on the bench. I took part in a documentary that will be released in spring/summer 2022 and hope to participate in many others. I am exploring a new podcast series, and over the lockdown due to COVID, Shari Botwin, LCSW, and I hosted a series of podcasts called *Warrior Women Speak,* which I enjoyed and was well received. I am represented by Creative Artists Agency who advises me, and I am thankful for their direction and input on projects, and we are working toward many more creative endeavors. I am a motivational speaker fortunate enough to address groups around the world about many important issues including, but not limited to, how to listen and help those without a voice; how to improve our legal, medical, and educational systems; keeping your power; how to empower yourself and others; best legal practices using Zoom; and other related and diverse subjects. I enjoy speaking because it gives me the ability to share what I have learned, to learn from others, and to keep the conversation moving forward for meaningful change. The best part about speaking to groups is the interaction I have with them and their heartfelt questions that are meaningful to both the audience and to me. I have been invited as a guest on several episodes of Dr. Phil and am grateful to both he and his wife, Robin, his amazing staff, and loyal viewers for continuing to unapologetically and openly explore important issues that affect us with the goal of awareness and change. I have been invited to speak at bookstores and book clubs both locally and around the globe and have found a kinship with those who appreciate my fictional character friends. Overall, I am enjoying my life, and no bully or naysayer will steal that joy from me.

I continue to strive for my goal of leaving behind a safer, better world for my children and yours and our communities. I am considering many other ventures—some to help my profession, others to change the world, personal ones for self-care, and a few simply because they make me happy.

Thank you, dear reader, for spending your valuable time with me. You are appreciated! And for all of you who keep asking me what's next: just watch me!

Made in United States
North Haven, CT
09 June 2023